WHAT YOUR COLLEAGUES ARE SAYING . . .

A must-have for new teachers! This book could be called *Everything I Should Have Learned in College About Teaching Math*. Universities should use this in tandem with Van de Walle: easy to read and well organized to understand how to teach math versus what to teach. It includes countless tips, and the notes throughout about access, agency, and equity are invaluable.

Colleen Pollitt
Math support teacher
Adjunct professor,
Towson University

From the Introduction through Chapter 6, this easy-to-read book summarized what all elementary math teachers should know and do. The ideas and suggestions are doable in all of our classrooms. This book will be on my desk as a reference to read as well as share with the teachers I coach. Thank you for reminding this Year 30 teacher of many procedures, practices, and routines that I need to reinstate after the horrendous 2020–2021 School Year!

Laura Vizdos Tomas
Math coach,
School District of Palm Beach County
Cofounder of LearningThroughMath.com

As a former teacher, and currently as a K–8 principal, I find this book to be an invaluable resource! The book is structured in such a systematic way that it allows the reader to start on page 1 or strategically turn to a chapter that will lend guidance to a specific question or need. The book is a must-read due to its practical application that is grounded in research. As a principal, this book also serves as a tool to assist me in giving valuable feedback to teachers.

Scott Gaudet
Principal,
Greene-Hills School

As a teacher who just completed her second-year teaching, I can attest that new teachers would benefit greatly from this book. This is an easy-to-use answer guide to many questions regarding mathematics teaching principles including building community and engaging students in math talk. It is an invaluable resource for new teachers and anyone who is looking for extra guidance in mathematics instruction.

Lauren Cope
First-grade teacher,
Lincoln Public Schools

What an absolute treasure of a resource this book is! This book should be in every elementary teacher's class as well as on every building leader's and coach's bookshelf! This resource takes the abstract and loftiness out of what we know about best practices in math education and makes it accessible and actionable! I can already envision this book being number one in my toolbox for coaching conversations! Thank you!

Elise Paone Archibald
K–5 instructional math coach,
Consolidated School District of New Britain, Connecticut

Answers to Your Biggest Questions About Teaching Elementary Math: Five to Thrive is a delightful game-changing instructional playbook for new teachers and those of us who want to be effective at cultivating a love for math in the students we serve. This will be the companion of teachers of math for years to come. Read this book, and gain tools to thrive.

Sharon C. Thomas
Assistant principal,
East Baton Rouge Parish School System

Developing a formula for success in mathematics teaching and learning can take decades of experience and study, especially for elementary educators. Yet the authors have encapsulated it in this easy-to-read book through an honest and practical approach. A must-have resource for every mathematics educator!

Tara Fulton
Mathematics coordinator,
Crane School District

A practical how-to resource for cognitively engaging educators in crafting a math community with students at the center! Through examples and non-examples, activities, and specific and intentional guiding questions, no stone was left unturned in how to structure, engage, and move students forward in a math community!

Kellie Joy
Elementary school principal,
Lincoln Public Schools

The authors offer fresh and pragmatic insights into teachers' biggest questions related to building community, classroom structure and management, engagement, discourse, and assessment in elementary mathematics. This is a must-read resource for teachers and math coaches committed to the effective teaching of mathematics and the pursuit of deep learning!

Sorsha-Maria T. Mulroe, NBCT
Math support teacher,
Running Brook Elementary

Answers to Your Biggest Questions About Teaching Elementary Math: Five to Thrive addresses the "how-to"s of establishing a culturally responsive, student-centered, rigorous, inclusive mathematics classroom. From how not to "hijack a lesson" to how to support students when they are stuck, it provides thorough rationales for the research-based practices it promotes. This book can be a reference guide for new teachers and those transitioning away from the traditional methods of teaching mathematics.

Karen Riley Jeffers
Numeracy coach,
Prince George's County Public Schools

Answers to Your Biggest Questions About Teaching Elementary Math: Five to Thrive is a must-read for new and experienced math teachers alike! Learn how to develop a strong mathematics community—a community that includes *everyone*, from the ground up. This will be a nice book to keep on hand and refer back to throughout the year.

Lukas Hefty
Elementary mathematics specialist,
Pinellas County Schools, Florida
National Milken Educator, FL '16
FCTM Region V director
PCTM president

Working to ensure all students have access to high-quality math instruction at the elementary level raises a number of questions for educators. In clear, easy-to-read, and practical terms, the authors effectively outline essential components and strategies to guide educators in fostering a student-centered approach to mathematics instruction that gives all students the agency to be successful "doers" of mathematics. This must-have book provides illuminating examples of best practices, sound tips and resources, and authentic samples of student work to showcase key methods and ideas that are grounded in research and, most importantly, classroom tested.

Ann Marie Spinelli
Education consultant and instructor of mathematics education,
Central Connecticut State University

Answers to Your Biggest Questions About Teaching Elementary Math: Five to Thrive is a must-read question-and-answer guide for mathematics educators and leaders. The authors paint a vivid picture of student-centered instruction and share how to implement mathematics instructional shifts to prepare students for a future in which they can reason, think critically, and become doers of mathematics.

Mona Toncheff
NCSM president

ANSWERS *to Your*

BIGGEST QUESTIONS *About*

TEACHING ELEMENTARY MATH

FIVE to THRIVE

ANSWERS *to Your* BIGGEST QUESTIONS *About*

TEACHING ELEMENTARY MATH

John J. SanGiovanni

Susie Katt

Latrenda D. Knighten

Georgina Rivera

CORWIN

For information:

Corwin
A SAGE Company
2455 Teller Road
Thousand Oaks, California 91320
(800) 233–9936
www.corwin.com

SAGE Publications Ltd.
1 Oliver's Yard
55 City Road
London, EC1Y 1SP
United Kingdom

SAGE Publications India Pvt. Ltd.
B 1/I 1 Mohan Cooperative
Industrial Area
Mathura Road, New Delhi 110 044
India

SAGE Publications
Asia-Pacific Pte. Ltd.
18 Cross Street #10–10/11/12
China Square Central
Singapore 048423

President: Mike Soules
Associate Vice President and Editorial
   Director: Monica Eckman
Publisher: Erin Null
Content Development Editor:
   Jessica Vidal
Senior Editorial Assistant:
   Caroline Timmings
Production Editor: Tori Mirsadjadi
Copy Editor: QuADS Prepress Pvt. Ltd.
Typesetter: Integra
Proofreader: Barbara Coster
Indexer: Integra
Cover Designer: Gail Buschman
Marketing Manager:
   Margaret O'Connor

Library of Congress Control Number: 2021943661

This book is printed on acid-free paper.

21 22 23 24 25 10 9 8 7 6 5 4 3 2 1

CONTENTS

Acknowledgments   xi

About the Authors   xiii

Introduction   1

1   HOW DO I BUILD A POSITIVE MATH COMMUNITY?   **10**

How Do I Get to Know My Students Mathematically?   12

How Do I Nurture Students' Math Identity?   15

How Do I Establish and Maintain a Math Community?   19

How Do I Make Mathematics Culturally Relevant for My Students?   22

How Do My Words and Actions Focus on Students' Strengths?   27

How Do I Make the Growth Mindset a Reality?   30

What Are Math Practices?   33

What Should I Have on My Classroom Walls?   38

How Do I Make a Good Anchor Chart?   42

How Do I Engage Families? How Do I Share Information With Them?   45

2   HOW DO I STRUCTURE, ORGANIZE, AND MANAGE MY MATH CLASS?   **48**

How Do I Plan to Make Mathematics Student Centered?   50

What Is Whole-Group Collaborative Math Instruction?   53

How Do I Use Small-Group Instruction?   56

How Do I Begin the Math Class?   59

What Are Instructional Routines? How Do I Use Them?   63

How Do I Facilitate a Math Lesson?   66

How Do I Plan for Diverse Learners?   70

How Do I Close a Lesson?   75

What Do I Need to Consider About Math Homework?   78

3   HOW DO I ENGAGE MY STUDENTS IN MATHEMATICS?   **82**

What Does It Mean to "Know the Math"?   84

What Should I Plan to Avoid?   88

How Do I Select High-Quality Tasks?   91

What Do I Need to Know About Manipulatives? 95

Which Manipulatives Should I Use? 99

What Other Visual Tools Help Students Learn? 103

How Do I Use Literature in the Math Classroom? 106

How Do I Teach Problem Solving? 109

How Do I Support Student Thinking and Reasoning? 113

What Do I Do When Students Get Stuck? 116

How Do I Select and Use Games and Centers? 119

What Should Practice Look Like? 123

Why and How Should I Incorporate Estimation? 127

How Do I Help Students Learn Basic Facts? 130

Why Teach Different Strategies for Computation? 134

How Do I Help Students Develop Fluency With Operations? 138

4 HOW DO I HELP MY STUDENTS TALK ABOUT MATHEMATICS?

144

How Do I Plan for Mathematical Discourse? 146

How Do I Plan the Questions I Will Ask? 149

How Do I Debrief the Learning? 153

How Do I Use Representations to Support Understanding and Discussion? 156

How Do I Develop Math Language and Vocabulary? 160

How Do I Use Math Journals? 163

5 HOW DO I KNOW WHAT MY STUDENTS KNOW AND MOVE THEM FORWARD?

166

How Do I Find Out What Students Know? 168

What Should I Look for as Students Work? 171

What Math Behaviors Do I Look For? 174

How Do I Assess Student Thinking? 177

How Do I Help Students Self-Assess? 181

How Do I Give Feedback? 185

How Does Assessment Inform My Next Steps? 188

How Do I Celebrate My Students' Progress? 191

6 WHERE DO I GO FROM HERE?

196

What Activities Can I Pursue to Learn and Grow? 197

What Resources Should I Use to Learn and Grow? 200

References 206

Index 208

ACKNOWLEDGMENTS

As a team, we would like to acknowledge and thank the many math teachers, leaders, researchers, and partners who have helped shape our understanding of what teaching high-quality mathematics can and should be. We are thankful to the teachers who have welcomed us into their classrooms, trusted us with their questions, and partnered with us for our mutual growth. We thank all of those who give back to our professional organizations, creating opportunities for continued learning and connecting. We thank the Corwin team for their hard work, partnership, problem solving, creativity, and vision for how to help teachers. In the past year of the COVID-19 pandemic, each of us was continuously reminded of how hard educators work for their students. We are inspired by them. We look forward to a new normal that rekindles the best practices of the past, builds on the successes of distance learning (and there were many!), and looks to do even more for our youngest mathematicians.

John would like to especially thank his wife, Kristen, who always listens, supports, and encourages him during a project. He thanks those special math people, especially Kay Sammons and Skip Fennell, for their mentorship and friendship. He thanks his current math team and the other math coaches he has had the privilege to work with over the years. He thanks this author team for their hard work, brilliance, humor, patience, and tolerance of his "humor." John also gives a special thank you to the team's editor and publisher, Erin Null, for her support, thoughtful questions, patience, humor, friendship, and willingness to answer her phone.

Susie would like to send a sincere thank you to her husband, Jason, for being supportive of the work she is so passionate about. She thanks her kids, Tenley and Huxton, for their flexibility and patience. Susie is thankful for her dad's encouraging words and constant reminders of the value of hard work and taking risks. She sends a special thank you to the friends, colleagues, and students who have pushed her to grow and learn, both personally and professionally. And she wants to thank John, Gina, and Latrenda as she is most appreciative of their wisdom and collaboration.

Georgina would like to thank God, who is always faithful and provided the opportunity to work with John, Susie, Latrenda, and Erin, an amazing author and publishing team! She thanks her husband, who listens and shows care as she advocates and follows her passions. She is thankful to all her math mentors, colleagues, and friends who have guided her along the way, with a special thank you to her long-time mentor Ann Marie Spinelli, who is as brilliant as she is kind. A special thank you to her parents, godmother, aunt, and grandmother, who prayed, believed, and sacrificed. Finally, thank you to the students, whom she continues to learn from each and every day.

Latrenda would like to thank her mom and four sisters for their constant support, patience, and encouragement. She is thankful to her math "family"—the many mentors, friends, and colleagues who provide support and guidance in so many ways. She would also like to thank her extended family—the many educators, parents, and students who nurtured, supported, and guided her when needed and also served as mentors, collaborators, and cheerleaders. Finally, she extends a huge thank you to John, Gina, and Susie for their support and collaboration.

PUBLISHER'S ACKNOWLEDGMENTS

Corwin gratefully acknowledges the contributions of the following reviewers:

Emily S. Fenner
Elementary teacher and instructional coach, Fauquier County Public Schools
Warrenton, VA

Emily Dwivedi
Supervisor of elementary mathematics, Baltimore County Public Schools
Catonsville, MD

Dr. Kristine Allen
Senior faculty evaluator, Teachers College WGU
Manchester, NH

Helene Alalouf
3–12 Instructional coach
New York, NY

ABOUT THE AUTHORS

John J. SanGiovanni is a math supervisor in Howard County, Maryland, where he leads math curriculum development, digital learning, assessment, and professional learning. John coordinates the mathematics leadership graduate program at McDaniel College. He is an author and national consultant. John is active in professional organizations, recently serving on the board of directors for the National Council of Teachers of Mathematics (NCTM) and the National Council of Supervisors of Mathematics (NCSM).

Susie Katt is the K–2 math coordinator in Lincoln, Nebraska, where she leads professional learning, assessment, and math curriculum development. She is an author and a national math curriculum consultant. Susie is active in the NCTM as she has served as the chair of the editorial panel for the journal *Teaching Children Mathematics*, and as a member of program committees for annual meetings and regional conferences.

Georgina Rivera is a passionate math educator, coach, author, and presenter focused on equity, collective teacher efficacy, culturally relevant pedagogy, and teacher leadership. She currently serves as a school administrator for Bristol Public Schools. Prior to this position, she was the district's math coach and elementary STEM (science, technology, engineering, and math) supervisor; she began her career as a middle school math teacher. Georgina serves on various local and national boards focused on math education and leadership. She is beginning her new role as NCSM vice president in September 2021.

Latrenda Knighten is the elementary math curriculum content trainer in Baton Rouge, Louisiana. She has been an educator for more than 30 years, and is an active member of many professional organizations. She currently serves as the NCSM Southern Region 2 team leader for Louisiana and secretary for the Benjamin Banneker Association, Inc. Latrenda is also a past member of the NCTM Board of Directors.

From time to time, we (the authors) think about our first few years of teaching elementary school. Usually, it brings back warm memories and funny moments. It also always reminds us of how much we didn't know about teaching mathematics. In fact, we've often joked about the idea that our students "deserve their money back," though we're not quite sure how that would work in a public school setting. We know that we learned as much, if not more, than our students—especially that first year. We remember having many questions but not having access to someone who knew the answers.

We now know that there were all sorts of questions that we didn't even know we had, let alone where we could look for answers. We have come to realize that our own math learning as students didn't always serve our understanding as adults and potentially also underserved our math instruction. In fact, each of us remembers the lesson in which we learned why square numbers are called square numbers (the rectangular area makes a square), thanks to an observation by one of our students! We also remember pausing in that moment to wonder to ourselves if that is how cubed numbers got their name.

We also know that we thought about numbers in ways that weren't taught to us in school. Instead, we "discovered" them through our experiences outside school by counting change or finding batting averages of our favorite baseball players. We learned to break apart numbers to multiply 25 by 12, thinking it the same as $25 \times 10 + 25 \times 2$. We used inverse relationships to subtract, counting up to solve $400 - 177$. We compared fractions through their relationship to a whole rather than find common denominators ($\frac{3}{4}$ is greater than $\frac{2}{34}$ because $\frac{2}{34}$ is very close to 0). But we didn't, at first, think to ask why we didn't teach our "discovered" strategies to our students in class. After all, those strategies weren't in the book.

We didn't think to ask ourselves, "Why was mathematics taught to us in certain ways? Could there be other ways to do it? Why was mathematics needed? Why were we learning it?" We didn't think to ask, "What happened to our classmates who didn't do well in mathematics? Why didn't they do well?" And although we taught mathematics every day, we didn't, at first, see the bigger picture. In many ways, this book represents what we wish we had then—a book that answers the questions we didn't know we had, one that could have helped us see the big picture right when we needed it.

WHY IS TEACHING MATHEMATICS DIFFERENT TODAY?

There are no longer telephone operators working at a switchboard or elevator operators in hotels and businesses. You would be hard-pressed to find someone who works on typewriters or delivers milk to homes. Take a moment to think about a job that was around when you were a student that isn't any longer. Maybe you think of a Blockbuster employee (or the movie rental business in general), someone in the "pager industry," printers of maps and atlases, or someone who sold ads for a phonebook. Now think about the jobs today that didn't exist when you were in kindergarten. Maybe you think of web page developers, drone technicians, or social media advertising designers.

> I WAS AFRAID TO TEACH MATH MY FIRST TWO YEARS. I WASN'T VERY GOOD AT MATH AS A STUDENT, AND I WASN'T SURE HOW TO TEACH IT WELL. I WISH I LEARNED MATH THE WAY WE TEACH IT TODAY.
>
> —FOURTH-GRADE TEACHER

Think about current elementary students. What jobs exist today that will no longer exist when they are adults? You might think of cashiers, bank tellers, letter carriers, and maybe even travel agents. You can go online to find fascinating projections from economists and futurists about this. And you might be surprised to find that truck drivers, taxi drivers, delivery services, and even fast-food workers could be extinct in their adult future due to autonomous vehicles, self-serve kiosks, and machine-prepared foods. Keep in mind it's not just service industries but loan officers, real estate agents, and even college professors who will likely see a decline in numbers if not extinction altogether due to self-serve apps and distance learning courses.

We teach mathematics differently today because our students' futures depend on understanding, thinking, and reasoning. Answers to low-level questions that can be answered by Siri or a Google search don't have the same value or purpose as they did 20 or 30 years ago. This is not to say that students shouldn't learn basic skills and procedures. They should! But more important, they should be taught to understand them so that they can retain them, develop them into more complex ideas, transfer them to different situations, and apply them to solve new problems.

But teaching mathematics differently is more than just a projection of the skills and services students will need in their future. It is also largely based on decades of research and understanding. To put it simply, we know more today than we did years ago about how students learn, how brains develop, and which teaching strategies work best and which do not. And new learning has other implications. Most notably, some of the questions we answer in this book will likely be answered differently 20 years from now, though we suspect that many of the answers will remain somewhat intact because the underlying themes of student-centered instruction, thinking, reasoning, representing, and language development are unlikely to go away.

Mathematics is about making sense of the world around us, for making predictions, solving problems, and drawing conclusions. It is about innovation, creativity, and finding beauty. Understanding mathematics deeply is at the core of doing these things, and it is why mathematics is taught differently today than how many of us learned it in the past.

WHAT EXACTLY IS DIFFERENT ABOUT TEACHING AND LEARNING MATHEMATICS TODAY?

You have likely seen a social media post about "new math" or have read, maybe even said, "That's not how I learned it!" You may look at your curriculum guides and think, "That's not how I would do it," or ask yourself, "How does *that* work?" This is all because math instruction is approached differently today than it has been in the past. Make no mistake, the mathematics you learned is still true. Four plus four still equals eight and one-half is still equivalent to two-fourths. It's just that today math instruction

- is a balanced pursuit of conceptual understanding, procedural fluency, and application of math content;
- incorporates a collection of strategies for students to make sense of and use the mathematics they learn;
- is focused on thinking and reasoning;
- encourages students to collaboratively solve problems; and
- asks students to communicate their thinking and reasoning.

Today's approach to math instruction sparks questions, and occasionally pushback, because it differs from what many adults experienced in the past.

Mathematics was about	Math instruction today is about
Speed and recall of facts and steps	Efficiency and flexible but deep thinking
Working individually	Working collaboratively
Acquiring and using a procedure someone shows you (teacher or textbook)	Developing one's own understanding while also learning about how to use common procedures
Calculations	Concepts, procedures, and applications of concepts and procedures combined
Learning basic skills	Thinking deeply about mathematical concepts and relationships
Using one specific procedure	Selecting from a set of strategies or developing one's own strategy for solving a problem
Finding an exact answer	Finding an answer and explaining your thinking
Separating those who can do mathematics from those who cannot do it well	Providing access and opportunity for each and every student to learn mathematics
"Naked number" computation problems	Learning mathematics in authentic, relevant contexts

Something you may notice right away is that teaching and learning mathematics today are not centered solely on procedure and recall. We want students to be able to do traditional things like calculate and convert between measurements, but it is more important for them to develop skills in problem solving, communication, modeling, and determining reasonableness. For example, measurement in primary grades was once taught in a way that told students to line up the end of a ruler with the object being measured to "ensure" a correct answer. Today, the goal is for students to understand how a ruler measures the difference between two points and that a 6-inch crayon is still 6 inches if you measure it from the 3- to 9-inch marks, from the 5- to 11-inch marks, or by starting with the 0 mark on the ruler. Today, we also want students to think about when a ruler is useful and when a yardstick would be a better option. We want them to have references for about how long an inch is, how tall a door might be, and a sense of when 24 inches is reasonable (e.g., the width of a chair) and when it isn't (e.g., the length of a pencil).

> I ALWAYS THOUGHT MATH WAS ABOUT WHO COULD BE THE FASTEST. IT MADE ME ANXIOUS BECAUSE THERE WERE A FEW KIDS IN MY CLASS THAT I COULD NEVER BEAT TO THE ANSWER. I'VE TRIED TO MAKE SURE MY MATH CLASS WASN'T LIKE THAT FOR MY STUDENTS.
>
> —SECOND-GRADE TEACHER

The differences in math instruction today extend beyond content and teaching practice. Notions about what it is to do mathematics, who mathematics is for, and why mathematics matters are also changing, even if slowly in some circles. Math instruction today must nurture productive dispositions about the subject. It must discard the myths from the past about learning mathematics and counter them with facts. Saying "I'm just not good at mathematics" must be as socially taboo as saying "I'm illiterate."

Myths about mathematics	Facts about mathematics
Mathematics isn't for everyone.	Everyone is capable of learning mathematics.
Learn it for the test, and move on.	Understanding isn't forgotten.
"I'm not good at mathematics" is acceptable for some students.	"I can do mathematics" coupled with a growth mindset is necessary for all students.
Mathematics isn't used every day like reading.	Mathematics is everywhere and a part of everyday life.
Some students, especially boys, are better at mathematics than other students, like girls.	No one group is better at mathematics than another; everyone is able to do high-quality mathematics!
Some people are just better at mathematics.	Some people have more and better opportunities to learn and play with mathematics.
I don't have a math brain.	Everyone can think and reason about mathematical ideas and concepts.
If you are good at mathematics, it should be easy.	Engaging in productive struggle is an important component in learning mathematics.
Mathematics is a collection of tips, tricks, and shortcuts.	Mathematics should make sense, and students should understand how it works. This includes common efficiencies or shortcuts.
Being fast with mathematics is evidence of doing it well.	Doing mathematics with understanding, depth, and thoroughness is doing it well.

You may be thinking, "But I loved mathematics when I was a student!" If you did, that is fantastic! Maybe you were good at mathematics because you had lots of support at home or because you are naturally drawn to games, puzzles, building blocks, and similar things. You may have enjoyed the competition and speed or the opportunity to think linearly. All of this is wonderful, but what about those who didn't have the same support, interests, or passions?

You may be thinking that while you didn't love mathematics, you still turned out ok. If so, look back at those myths just above. Think about adults you work with or your friends. What do they say about mathematics? How do they use it? Think about the classmates you had or the students you knew in schools across town or throughout your state. Did the approaches to math instruction used in the past serve each of them well?

You may also be thinking, "But not everyone wants to be an engineer." You're right, but the fact is everyone should have the option to be an engineer and have access to the learning it takes to become one if they choose to do so. Unfortunately, for many, that door is shut before they even leave elementary school. And yes, many will choose not to be engineers, but jobs that rely on low-level skills are being replaced with computers and automation. Failing to provide teaching that promotes understanding, thinking, and reasoning—the things machines don't do well (yet)— fuels inequitable outcomes. Approaches to math instruction today aim squarely at repairing that inequity.

Teaching mathematics well is not solely about job opportunities. Skills like reasoning, critical thinking, and collaboration are life skills. They are necessary to being a productive, informed citizen. There is no reason why those skills shouldn't be part of learning mathematics in the same way they are a part of language arts or social studies classes.

WHAT IS EQUITY IN MATHEMATICS?

Mathematics is a ticket to life! Equity is about access and opportunity. Equity is about each and every student having access to high-quality, on-grade-level curriculum and instruction. This means that students aren't relegated to fixed small groups that focus solely on skills from previous grades, keeping them perpetually behind. Instead, students are able to access on-grade-level instruction through supports and scaffolds, as needed, and there is instructional time outside of first instruction so that certain skills and concepts are retaught or given additional practice.

Equity is about high expectations for each and every student. It is the belief that all students bring knowledge into the math class, that mathematics is for every student, that every student can learn to do mathematics, and that every student deserves an opportunity to learn it meaningfully. This also means that high-quality teaching practices are for every student. To put it simply, we don't reserve the "good stuff" for some students who are deemed worthy. The good stuff is for each and every student. This doesn't mean that every student gets the same thing but, instead, each student gets the support and resources they need as individuals to succeed (NCTM, 2014).

It is especially important to understand that equity isn't a "stand-alone" topic in teaching and learning mathematics. It permeates everything you do. For example, in this book we answer questions about introducing and using manipulatives (see Manipulatives, p. 95). Manipulative use is an issue of equity, as you must consider that each and every student must have access to and choice about the manipulatives they use as they learn and do mathematics. Opportunities for learning a variety of strategies to add, subtract, multiply, and divide (see Fluency Strategies for Operations, p. 138) are for every student to use, not just a select few for whom they are deemed appropriate.

So as you read the answers in this book, we want you to look at each through a lens of equity. Ask yourself,

- How does this position all students as being capable of learning mathematics?
- How does this create equitable learning experiences for all students?
- How does this affect my thinking about math instruction so that I ensure it meets the needs of every learner in my classroom?
- What do I need to intentionally do to ensure that all students receive the highest-quality math instruction?

Equitable mathematics is *for* students and *by* students. It is about helping form students' math identities so that they see purpose and value in investing their time and energy learning and doing mathematics. Their math identity is framed in capability and confidence. Equitable mathematics creates student agency as students see themselves and act as doers of mathematics. That is, they do not passively acquire someone else's strategy or reasoning by listening to a lecture or merely repeating someone else's method. Instead, they have the opportunity to develop and apply their own strategies, reasoning, and understanding. Math instruction is not *delivered* to students. It is done with them and by them.

HOW DOES THIS BOOK HELP?

This book is a collection of our years of experience and learning. We have worked as teachers, team leaders, math coaches, administrators, curriculum specialists, and professional developers. We have been (and still are) active in our math professional organizations and have endlessly pursued our own learning. The questions this book poses are those that come to us most often from the teachers we work with, as well as those we didn't even know to ask early in our teaching careers. The answers to these questions are equal parts experience, practice, and learning from research. These questions are organized into five categories framed by overarching questions:

1. How do I build a positive math community?
2. How do I structure, organize, and manage my math class?
3. How do I engage my students in mathematics?
4. How do I help my students talk about mathematics?
5. How do I know what my students know and move them forward?

These questions frame the five areas of effort we feel will help you most thrive in your elementary math instruction—community, classroom structure and management, engagement, discourse, and assessment—the "Five to Thrive." Woven throughout, you'll find sidebar notes on fostering identity and agency, on access and equity, and on teaching in flexible settings, and sidebars with related great resources for deeper learning.

We are grateful for the ideas and contributions of the many leaders, researchers, and teachers in math education who have influenced our understanding of what it means to teach mathematics well. Robert Q. Berry III, Rochelle Gutierrez, and Julia Aguirre have influenced our pursuit of equity in math teaching and learning. You'll see ideas about the growth mindset from scholars like Carol Dweck and Jo Boaler. You will see how the giants of math teaching, like Marilyn Burns, John Van de Walle, Peg Smith, Bob Reys, Barb Reys, Francis (Skip) Fennell, Karen Karp, Marian Small, Cathy Seeley, Cathy Fosnot, and many, many more, have shaped our understanding of math content and pedagogy. You'll recognize that Gloria Ladson-Billings has helped us understand what culturally relevant mathematics should look like in our classrooms.

We have relied on truly exceptional works that support teaching of math content. Many of them are noted in the Great Resources sidebars and the suggested resource list at the end of the book. For example, the different editions of *Teaching Student-Centered Mathematics* (by Van de Walle et al., 2019) have been our "math bibles" for over a decade. These are the books that helped us deeply understand the math content we teach, along with a good pedagogical foundation.

And, of course, we have seen some excellent teaching in action, influenced by these research-based resources but really crafted by teachers as they worked day by day with children to understand what was working best for them in learning mathematics. We have yet to come across a briefer and more digestible, broad yet comprehensive book that helps busy professionals focus on the most critical nuts and bolts of the *pedagogy* around student-centered math teaching. We set out to create an easy-to-read book that offers reliable, practical guidance so that more teachers can benefit from the experience of those who have figured out a lot. We have not found this guidance in any one place. There are many wonderful books that break down, in detail, single facets of teaching elementary mathematics, such as those that deal with number talks, routines, centers, small groups, or discourse. This book doesn't offer that kind of finite detail about singular aspects of math content or instructional practice. Instead, it gives you a sound place to begin.

> I LEARNED SO MANY THINGS ABOUT TEACHING MATH MY FIRST FEW YEARS. MY BEST ADVICE IS TO JUST TRY NEW THINGS. IT WON'T ALWAYS WORK BUT YOU CAN PLAY WITH APPROACHES AND MAKE THEM YOUR OWN.
>
> —THIRD-GRADE TEACHER

WHO IS THIS BOOK FOR?

To be perfectly clear, the questions presented in this book are not solely from new teachers. They are the questions of those who are new to teaching mathematics, teachers who have changed grades, and veteran teachers who haven't had opportunities, or the time, to get new ideas or have *their* questions answered. It is for special education teachers, multilingual teachers, and para-educators who co-teach or support math classes.

Others have these questions as well. This tool can help administrators better understand best practices for teaching mathematics. They might use it to guide their observations and classroom visits or as a resource to share with teachers who are seeking to grow their practice. It might offer ideas about instructional strategies to feature in their school improvement plans or professional learning communities. It can also be used as a reference tool for giving feedback to math teachers.

Math coaches and district curriculum specialists can use this tool to calibrate practices across a team, school, or district. It should serve them well as they look to support teachers by providing specific guidance on how to implement effective math teaching practices in their respective classrooms. The structure of this tool will be useful for one-on-one conversations, grade-level meetings, and large professional development groups that revolve around professional growth. The questions and answers can be considered individually or bundled together from a "big idea" perspective (e.g., engagement or assessment), providing flexibility.

HOW SHOULD YOU USE THIS BOOK?

We wrote this as a practical tool for "just-in-time" learning and support. We hope it becomes your guide to growing and learning as a teacher or as someone who helps teachers. It can be read from cover to cover, but that's probably not the most practical approach. Instead, we suggest keeping it on your desk or at your workstation. Refer to it as day-to-day events spark your questions. Take a look at it after you get feedback from an observation or after a discussion with colleagues during lunch. We think the ideas in this book will help you. We encourage you to continue to pursue your growth and learning and when you're ready use the ideas and resources at the end of this book to dive deeper into your journey. We know it won't always be easy and there will certainly be bumps in the road. But we also know that you *can* do it!

chapter ONE

HOW DO I BUILD A POSITIVE MATH COMMUNITY?

We have learned that teaching mathematics is not about teaching content but about teaching kids. Imagine a math classroom that students can't wait to get to. It is a space where each and every student feels safe, supported, respected, and appreciated for their contributions. It is a classroom community that nurtures student curiosity and engages them in thinking and reasoning. It is a community that sews together the unique strengths of its individuals into a cohesive, productive group. It is a place where learning is about exploration, growing through mistakes, supporting each other through struggle. So what would that classroom look like? How can you make it *your* classroom community?

This community starts with you. First, you must know who you are as a math person and a math teacher. Knowing your identity helps you think deeply about what you do and say as a math teacher. It helps you identify your strengths and how you can build on them. You then need to know who each and every student is as an individual. You have to learn about their interests, passions, preferences, and fears. You have to see their strengths so that you can leverage them and build on them too.

With you as a model, this community embraces a growth mindset, valuing each individual and knowing the value of making mistakes not only in words but also in actions. The collective group determines common values and creates norms or agreements for interactions. The community is grounded in trust between you and your students and among the students themselves.

You ensure that this classroom community is also rich with evidence of teaching and learning. You use math vocabulary word walls, concept anchor charts, manipulatives, and a board filled with ideas captured from students. Any visitor who walked into the room could see that "math lives here"—not just by what is on the walls but in the way students engage with one another as they solve problems, share ideas, represent their thinking, and persevere through setbacks.

The bond that holds this community together comes from the relevancy of the mathematics you teach. Here, students want to learn mathematics because they see themselves in it. And this community extends beyond the classroom walls as it engages families as partners in the work.

This chapter helps you create and maintain your classroom community by providing answers to questions such as the following:

☐ **How do I get to know my students mathematically?**

☐ **How do I nurture students' math identity?**

☐ **How do I establish and maintain a math community?**

☐ **How do I make mathematics culturally relevant for my students?**

☐ **How do my words and actions focus on students' strengths?**

☐ **How do I make the growth mindset a reality?**

☐ **What are math practices?**

☐ **What should I have on my classroom walls?**

☐ **How do I make a good anchor chart?**

☐ **How do I engage families? How do I share information with them?**

As you read about these, we encourage you to think about the following:

☐ **What does this mean to me?**

☐ **What else do I need to know about this?**

☐ **What will I do next?**

How Do I Get to Know My Students Mathematically?

It is common to do "get to know you activities" at the beginning of the year to gain information about your students. Do you do the same type of activities to get to know who your students are as mathematicians? Getting to know who your students are mathematically will give you a better understanding of their strengths, what they might perceive as their challenges, and how they view themselves as mathematicians. Consider different activities for your students that not only will help you gain a richer perspective on who they are as math learners but will contribute to their own understanding as well.

USE INTERESTING PROBLEMS

It isn't a good idea to welcome students to your class at the beginning of the year with a math pretest. This may send an unintentional message that you mostly value content and right answers. Rather, offer interesting tasks. Give your students math problems to solve that will invite them to be fully engaged in thinking and doing math. Your job will be to observe them while they work. The goal isn't to see who comes up with the correct solution but rather to gather information about your students' preferences for working, how they interact with others in collaborative groups, the ways they reason and what they do when they get stuck, and so on.

CONDUCT A MATH BELIEFS INVENTORY

A math inventory can provide insight into your students' beliefs about how they best learn mathematics. An inventory doesn't have to be overly sophisticated but should be designed to gather information about your students that you might not uncover otherwise. Ask students to respond to the statements using a rating scale such as *always, sometimes*, or *never*. Younger students might use a "thumbs-up" icon for *always*, a "sideways thumb" for *sometimes*, and a "thumbs down" for *never*.

Math inventory questions for K–2 students	Math inventory questions for 3–5 students
I am good at mathematics.	I believe I have the ability to do well in mathematics.
I feel happy when doing math.	I feel joy when I solve math problems.
I like puzzles and blocks.	I like math puzzles and games that involve strategy.
I like to work alone.	I like to work alone.
I ask for help when I get stuck.	I like to work with others to solve math problems.
I like to work in groups.	When I get stuck, I try different strategies.
I keep trying when things are hard in mathematics.	I have a growth mindset about mathematics.

You might find it helpful to ask your students to complete the same inventory at different times of the year. By doing so, you will become aware of changes in your students over time.

USE JOURNAL PROMPTS

A journal is a tool for students to record their thoughts and feelings (see Math Journals, p. 163). While journals are often used in teaching literacy, they are a great way to learn more about who your students are in relation to mathematics. Younger students may draw pictures or communicate their thoughts and reflections through a few words or simple sentences in their journals. Older students may write a few sentences to convey what they are feeling or share their mathematical thinking. Students' journal reflections should never be graded or shared with the entire class. Instead, think of them as a communication tool between you and your students that provides you with more detailed information about who your students are as mathematicians. If you ever want to share a journal response with the class, ask the student's permission first and give them the chance to share their mathematical reflections.

> I STARTED USING JOURNALS AROUND WINTER BREAK. I'M GLAD I DID BECAUSE I LEARNED SO MUCH ABOUT MY STUDENTS AS MATHEMATICIANS THROUGH THEIR DRAWINGS AND WRITING.
>
> —SECOND-GRADE TEACHER

Writing in a math journal shouldn't become a daily activity. Rather, purposefully choose prompts that you can ask students to respond to. Here are some prompts you might use to get your students started writing:

- My favorite thing about today's lesson was . . .
- The thing I'm most proud of myself for learning this week in mathematics is . . .
- I think learning mathematics is like learning a new hobby because . . .
- I wish I was better at _____ in mathematics because . . .
- Mathematics is really fun when . . .
- One thing that was difficult for me in mathematics was . . .
- I learn mathematics best when . . .
- If I would win an award for my learning in mathematics today, it would say . . .

OBSERVE YOUR STUDENTS IN PLAY

A great way to learn about your students is when they play math games, solve puzzles, or engage in open math activities. This might happen during the first few weeks of school or throughout the year if a lesson is completed a bit early or during indoor recess. As you observe your students, you will see their ability to find patterns, develop strategies, use estimation and number sense, and engage in mathematical practices. You can also gain insight into their creativity and curiosity about mathematical ideas. Games provide a safe space for students to try out new ideas while giving you a chance to see what they know about mathematics. Here are some games or manipulatives where you can observe students' mathematical abilities:

K–2 games	Grades 3–5 games
• Dice games • Board games • Pattern block and tangram puzzles • Card games • Chalk walk math	• 24 Game • Product game • Coordinate plane battleship • Dice games • Card games

Great Resources

Petersen, J. (2013). *Math games for number and operations and algebraic thinking: Math games to support independent practice in math workshops and more, grades K–5.* Math Solutions; Childs, L., & Choate, L. (1999). *Nimble with numbers.* Didax Educational Resources; *Fundamentals.* Origo Education; Britt, B. A. (2015). *Mastering basic math skills games.* NCTM.

CONTINUE TO GET TO KNOW YOUR STUDENTS THROUGHOUT THE YEAR

Your students' math skills and relationship with mathematics will evolve and develop over time; therefore, it is important to continue to implement activities throughout the school year that add to your understanding of who your students are as learners of mathematics. These activities should not become daily occurrences or so routine that they lose their novelty. Rather, think about how you might "sprinkle" these activities within your instruction so they complement what students are learning. As students learn the content, they will also gain a richer perspective of who they are as mathematicians. This mixture is a recipe for student success.

Don't miss opportunities to observe, listen, and learn more about your students. The better you get to know your students as learners of mathematics, the better you will become at being their math teacher. Having insights into your students' strengths, perceived challenges, and feelings regarding mathematics will provide you with valuable information that you can use as you plan and implement your lessons.

Notes

How Do I Nurture Students' Math Identity?

In school, many of us saw ourselves as either math people or not. *Mathematical identity* is how one sees oneself as a doer or learner of mathematics (Aguirre et al., 2013; Anderson, 2007; Boaler, 2002; Grootenboer & Zevenbergen, 2007). Understanding your own math identity is important because it affects how you approach teaching mathematics and how you view your students. Your students have math identities too, which has a major impact on how well they perform in mathematics and how they view themselves in relation to their peers in the class. Student experiences and interactions at school, in the community, and at home shape their identities. As a teacher, you must nurture your students' math identities so that they can grow and learn as mathematicians.

Agency and Identity

Identity influences motivation. Motivation drives action. And action creates outcomes. So then, attending to identity is a critical step to helping each and every learner succeed in mathematics.

HOW DO I BEGIN TO NURTURE MATH IDENTITY?

Start with your own identity by reflecting on your own math experiences and how you view yourself in math spaces. Know that your math identity has changed as you have. Think about who you are today.

> I NEVER THOUGHT I WAS A MATH PERSON, BUT THE MORE I LEARN AND DO MATH, I REALIZE I AM!
>
> —THIRD-GRADE TEACHER

Here are some questions you may ask yourself that may help you reflect and your students reflect, followed by other ways to nurture identity:

Question	Strongly disagree	Disagree	Agree	Strongly agree
I see myself as a math person.				
I enjoy learning mathematics.				
I feel confident when doing math.				
I am comfortable talking about mathematics with others.				
I see value in different ways of doing math.				
I feel like my ideas are valued in our math community.				
I see mathematicians who look like me and learn about their contributions.				
My family had a positive experience learning mathematics.				
I know what to do when I am struggling with a mathematical problem.				

LEARN EACH OF YOUR STUDENTS' MATH STORIES

No matter what grade level you teach, each of your students has a unique math story. They have had experiences that have helped shape who they are as learners. Having your students capture their own math stories is a way to gain deeper insights into who they are. A student's math story won't be written in one day. Think about how you might have students write their story over time, maybe adding to their story throughout the year.

Many elementary students will be challenged to sit down and write a long, detailed story about themselves all at once. Consider other fun, creative ways to help your students capture their stories over time. Perhaps they can create scrapbook pages that each tell a part of their math story. You can use brief and targeted journal prompts (see Math Journals, p. 163) that ask students to write about their math strengths or math "superpowers." Students can write about the good things that happened to them in mathematics or times when they enjoyed mathematics. Or they might draw pictures or show examples to illustrate their own perceptions of why it is important to learn mathematics.

Keep in mind that identities are shaped outside school too. These influences play an important role in how young mathematicians grow, develop, and perceive mathematics. Ask students to interview family members to see what they think about mathematics and how they use it. Ask them what they know about people who use mathematics in the world.

BUILD MEANINGFUL RELATIONSHIPS WITH YOUR STUDENTS

To help students build a positive math identity, you have to spend time getting to know your students and their families. You have to build and maintain meaningful relationships. That means "getting-to-know-you activities" are not just for the first day or week of school. You also have to encourage them, support them, and help build their identity (see Math Identity, p. 15) throughout the year. One of the most important skills you will need is listening, which helps build trust and understanding. Trust is built through sharing stories and getting to know your students.

For this you need to do the following:

1 Share your math story with students, and frame mathematics in a positive way. Refrain from saying that you were never good at mathematics. And if you say you didn't enjoy it, tell them why and how you're working to help them understand it so that they can enjoy it more than you did.

2 Interview your students to learn about their math history so that you know what things they enjoy and what situations make them uncomfortable, so you can avoid them.

3 Have everyone create identity boards, including yourself. By sharing interests, hobbies, and passions outside mathematics, you can incorporate them into your math instruction.

Georgina Rivera

Sources: Clothes Rack by iStock/LightFieldStudios, Reading a Book by iStock/Alina Rosanova, Bicycle by iStock/sompong_tom, Jewelry by iStock/Ayman-Alakhras, Flowers by iStock/Mumemories, Travel by iStock/thitivong, and Beach by iStock/Anastasia Deriy.

4   Give students opportunities to do math on their own first to see what they think about skills, concepts, and problems, so that you can build on it and (eventually) show them your way of doing the math.

5   Position students as thinkers, doers, and authors of ideas by making their thinking the focus of discussions. Do this before you share your thinking or potential explicit instruction.

6   Use student surveys to gather and use feedback from them about what is working and not working for them in the classroom.

7   Communicate and engage with families (see Engage Families, p. 45).

KNOW THAT REPRESENTATION MATTERS

For students to see themselves as doers of math, they must see people like them both doing math and being successful in STEM careers. Representation matters! Students learn through stories and visual representations, so showing only one group of people as doers of math diminishes their view of who can and cannot do math. This means that as you work with students, you should be intentional about

- including math literature by diverse authors;
- highlighting math contributions from people who represent diverse backgrounds;
- spotlighting how mathematics is used in diverse, authentic ways; and
- inviting community speakers to tell their math stories and showcase how they use mathematics.

Great Resources

Jones, S. M. (2019). *Women who count: Honoring African American women mathematicians.* American Mathematical Society.

MONITOR STUDENT PROGRESS

Student identities are dynamic. Identities change and grow over time with more and more experience. Posing journal prompts and surveying students at different points along the year will help you see how they are changing. In fact, you can give the same beliefs survey at the beginning, middle, and end of the year or at the end of each quarter. Use the information you gather from these activities to change instructional approaches. Give feedback about their reflections and help them see positives when challenges and setbacks occur. Students' math performance significantly shapes their identity as well. This means that you will have to frequently monitor their progress in a variety of ways beyond summative assessment (see Find Out What Students Know, p. 168) and celebrate their learning and their growth (see Celebrate Progress, p. 191).

Notes

How Do I Establish and Maintain a Math Community?

A mathematical community is important as it provides a space where your students will learn and grow together. No one mathematical community is exactly like another. The intentional actions you take in establishing a community will help your students realize they are valued, respected, and important members of your group. The time you invest in building and maintaining a healthy, supportive mathematical community will pay off for you and your students.

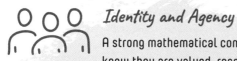

Identity and Agency

A strong mathematical community lets each student know they are valued, respected, and important.

FORMING A MATH COMMUNITY

A math community doesn't happen magically or form itself. You will want to be intentional in how you establish your classroom community and find ways to nurture it over time. Here are some tips for building and maintaining a math community in your classroom:

- Imagine the type of community you'd like to see in your math classroom. Think about how it might be equitable, safe, respectful, cooperative, and fun.
- Find activities to help students get to know one another and develop trust.
- Make revisions when necessary to the list of agreements.
- Revisit the common understandings the community establishes periodically, to keep the ideas in the forefront and shift from agreements to expectations.

COMMUNITY AGREEMENTS

Students may not be familiar with what common agreements might be in a math classroom. Elicit their ideas about what a particular agreement might look like and what it doesn't look like in their eyes, and put these on an anchor chart. You might do this as a whole-class activity or have small groups of students generate their own lists. Post these lists, and refer back to them often (see Anchor Charts, p. 42). Some examples of common understandings are shown here:

In our math community . . .	What it looks like	What it doesn't look like
We work together.	• Sharing the work • Allowing everyone to participate • Considering everyone's ideas • Believing everyone has the right to learn	• Allowing one person to do all of the work • Considering only one idea • Not inviting others to join in the work • Thinking some people can't learn
We respect others' ideas.	• Listening to others' ideas • Asking questions if something is unclear • Critiquing other people's work respectfully	• Laughing at others' ideas • Believing your way is the only way to solve a problem • Criticizing other people's work meanly
We learn from making mistakes.	• Recognizing that mistakes help us learn • Being okay with making a mistake • Examining mistakes to learn what happened	• Believing that making a mistake means one is not good at mathematics • Believing that mistakes will shut down understanding
We take risks.	• Being brave to share your thinking • Asking others questions about their ideas • Disagreeing with others' work when appropriate • Trying new ways of thinking	• Refusing to share • Offering an answer everyone knows is correct • Always agreeing with a classmate • Avoiding trying new strategies
We don't give up.	• Understanding it's okay to get stuck • Trying a different strategy • Asking someone for help	• Saying, "I don't get it!" • Letting someone else do all of the work • Trying only one strategy • Stopping the work on a problem
We know that mathematics makes sense.	• Working to understand math ideas • Using tools/ representations • Talking with others about the mathematics • Solving problems in ways that make sense • Asking questions	• Having someone else tell you how to solve a problem • Being worried only about the right answer • Resisting talking with others about the math ideas • Believing that there is only one way to get an answer

NURTURE THE COMMUNITY

Once you establish a math community, you can't ignore it. You and your students must support and nurture it throughout the school year. Find opportunities to revisit and reinforce your common agreements. For example, you might have your students draw illustrations of what the agreements look like. These may be in the form of a comic strip or a captioned picture. Post their illustrations next to the anchor chart you previously developed, or compile them into a book that you can revisit when you need to review the common agreements as a class.

You might feel the need to revise or update the list of common agreements you initially established, which will keep them fresh and relevant. Make sure to address what your students need so the learning community in your classroom continues to develop and grow stronger over time.

> # TEACHING MATH IS ABOUT BUILDING A COMMUNITY OF LEARNERS! MY WHOLE CLASS LOVES TO WORK TOGETHER. IT CAN GET LOUD SOMETIMES, BUT IT'S A GOOD LOUD.
>
> —FOURTH-GRADE TEACHER

CELEBRATE THE COMMUNITY

Make sure you recognize students' desired behaviors that contribute to a productive mathematical community. Be on the lookout for students who exhibit behaviors that are aligned with your common agreements, and recognize their efforts. This could be as simple as saying, "Franco, I noticed you took a risk today by sharing your thinking. Way to go!" You will also want to celebrate the group's efforts as a whole. Place a marble in a jar or a dot on a ten frame to recognize students' behaviors that are aligned with the common agreements. Do something fun to celebrate when the class meets a predetermined goal. This reinforces the desired behaviors and sends a message to the entire class that they are working together as a community of learners.

Notes

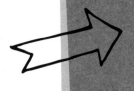

How Do I Make Mathematics Culturally Relevant for My Students?

"Culturally relevant pedagogy is an approach that empowers students intellectually, socially, emotionally and politically by using cultural referents to impart knowledge, skills and attitudes" (Ladson-Billings, 2009, p. 20). Culturally relevant pedagogy is an approach that honors students' knowledge and learning styles, and the culture they bring into the classroom. Instead of centering you as the teacher, this approach centers students, which makes them leaders of their learning and builds their agency. Students have mathematical brilliance, and when you connect what they already know to the standards, students thrive because their culture is welcomed into the math classroom and they are able to learn from the cultural perspective and experience they have lived.

> I KNOW MANY OF MY STUDENTS LIVE IN CLOSE-KNIT COMMUNITIES. WHEN I LOOKED AT MY CLASSROOM SET UP IN INDIVIDUAL ROWS, NOT ALLOWING FOR STUDENTS TO WORK TOGETHER, I NEEDED TO MAKE A CHANGE. THE SETUP OF MY CLASSROOM DID NOT MATCH THEIR STYLE OF LEARNING.
>
> —FIFTH-GRADE TEACHER

1. Believe that *all* students are brilliant and can learn mathematics at high levels.
2. Share your own culture and honor and learn about your students' cultures so you can incorporate them into your instruction.
3. Be aware of social justice issues in the school or community and show students how mathematics can be used to create positive change.

These three facets of culturally relevant instruction are critical, but they can't be willed into existence. In other words, it is how you enact them, and how your students experience them, that matters the most. Let's look at what actions are indicative of a classroom that makes math culturally relevant.

DEMONSTRATE BELIEF IN ACADEMIC EXCELLENCE FOR *ALL* STUDENTS

When designing culturally relevant lessons, you must first begin with your own mindset. We know that using deficit language, applying labels, and putting students into categories can influence the way you think about students' abilities and therefore affects the tasks you assign them. According to *The Opportunity Myth* (The New Teacher Project, 2018), only 44% of teachers believe that their students are capable of success on grade-level standards. As a result, only 26% of lessons in the study were grade appropriate, meaning that many students are getting below-grade-level instruction, putting them even further behind. To demonstrate your belief that all students are capable, you must do the following:

- Provide all students access to grade-level tasks and activities.
- Provide supports, or scaffolds, as needed to ensure they can actively engage.
- Set high expectations for all students.
- Use feedback (see Give Feedback, p. 185) to help build students' math identity.

KNOW YOUR STUDENTS' CULTURE

To teach mathematics in a culturally relevant way, you must start with getting to know your students and their culture (see Culturally Relevant, p. 22). This includes getting to know their ethnicity, their individual interests and hobbies, and the ways in which they learn best. It's equally important to get to know their families and the community in which you teach (see Engage Families, p. 45). To do this, visit places in your community where your students live, do home visits with your colleagues, and watch documentaries or read books about the cultures in your classroom. You need to be curious and want to genuinely get to know them. Taking the time to get to know your students' culture will go a long way in better understanding them as mathematicians, and it will build trust in your classroom community.

One simple way to get to know your students is to ask them about the math they do in their everyday life. Start by showing your students the mathematics in your life before asking them to do the same, so that you can see who they are and what they like to do. A collage of images and words works great.

Flexible Learning

You can do this with Google slides or something similar, in which students can add images, links to online resources, audio clips, and more.

COMMUNITY

Sources: Blue Pattern by iStock/horizon2531, Soccer Game by iStock/gorodenkoff, Marketplace by iStock/ioriyoshizuki, Portuguese Dancers by iStock/florin1961, Queen Maria Cake by iStock/IvanSpasic, and Gold Bracelet by iStock/phanasitti, respectively.

You can also learn more about students' lives and interests through journal entries (see Math Journals, p. 163) and parent surveys (see Engage Families, p. 45).

BRING SOCIAL JUSTICE ISSUES INTO YOUR MATH CLASSROOM

You might be wondering how to bring social justice issues into K–5 mathematics. When teachers are working on culturally relevant teaching, this is one area they avoid because they are afraid or wonder if the issues will be too political; but we must not shy away from what students are scared about. Elementary students will say things to you such as "That's not fair!" Your response should be "What is not fair about it? Can you show me some math to prove it?" Students are really engaged in mathematics when it involves topics they care about or things they desire to change in their school or community. Some examples of social justice tasks students might look to examine are the following:

- Recycling issues at school
- Homelessness in their town
- Food deserts (lack of fresh produce) in their community
- Healthy lunch selections
- Student schedules
- Closing of a local school
- Dress code policy
- Length of recess and specials

These are just a few issues that students can examine. They all include mathematics and are issues that may come up in their school or community. These are common issues. The key is to have students learn about the social justice issues they care about and become advocates by using mathematics to empower them to help create changes.

SELECT TASKS WITH RELEVANCE IN MIND

One of the most direct ways to infuse cultural relevance is through the mathematical tasks you use. You want to select and use tasks that represent and connect to the cultures of the students in your class. For example, finding volumes of rectangular prisms is generic and abstract. Instead, you can look for tasks that pose the same problem in a meaningful, related context. In the following example, pretend that you have a student named Idalina who loves fish. You can select a task related to fish tanks or modify an existing task using fish tanks. Then, to launch the task, you can have her share her background knowledge. Doing this shows how she and her passion are honored, respected, and included. You can also add her name to the task to make it connect more directly.

Original task	Modified task
A rectangular prism has a volume of 120 cubic feet. What are the dimensions of the prism? Explain your thinking.	Idalina's fish tank holds 120 cubic feet of water. What dimensions could Idalina's fish tank be? Explain your reasoning.

HAVE STUDENTS PERSONALIZE THE TASKS

Some contexts may be unfamiliar to students. Other contexts may be generic. You can modify tasks to improve familiarity and show student interests so that they see themselves in the math tasks. When using tasks to introduce contexts in the community that may be unfamiliar to students, replace the name with "you" or "a person in our school/ community" to connect it back to them. Next, take the time to clarify the context of the task to be sure students can visualize the context, provide an image or video, or show them the actual object if you can. The first example shows an original task that is modified for higher quality (see Tasks, p. 91). The second example shows how a task can be modified for higher quality and better relevancy.

Original task	Modified for better quality	Modified for relevancy
A movie starts at 2:00 p.m. and ends at 3:55 p.m. How long was the movie?	A movie is 1 hour and 55 minutes long. What are the possible start and end times for the movie? Use pictures, numbers, and words to show your thinking.	You want to watch _____ (fill in a movie you would like to see), which is 1 hour and 55 minutes long. What are some possible start and end times for the movie? Use pictures, numbers, or words to show your thinking.

USE OPEN TASKS

Use tasks that are open, and invite students to share data or information from their own lives that you can then mathematize, meaning put into a math context. For example, in a Number of the Day routine, you can use a student's favorite number, giving them a chance to first share why it's their favorite number before using it in the routine.

Today's Number Is _____'s Favorite Number

Break apart the number in three different ways.

Write a true equation that uses the number.

Tell how it compares with three different numbers.

USE INSTRUCTIONAL PRACTICES THAT SUPPORT CULTURALLY RELEVANT MATHEMATICS

Here are some additional practices you can try:

- Use instructional routines (see Instructional Routines, p. 63) to build community, provide structure, and honor the ideas of your students. Leverage them to hear students' thinking and perspectives, positioning students as leaders in the room.
- Use math language routines to support the development of math vocabulary and increase student discourse. Language routines enable all learners, including multilingual learners, to be heard in the math classroom (see Diverse Learners, p. 70).
- Look for possible answers beyond what the answer key gives. Be open to ideas and algorithms that may be unfamiliar or new to you but are familiar in your students' cultures.
- Allow students to work in ways that are familiar within their culture. In some cultures students work alone, while in others students work in community. Honor your students by giving them time to do both.

Notes

How Do My Words and Actions Focus on Students' Strengths?

Traditionally, we have often focused math teaching in a way that prioritizes attention to what students don't understand, what they don't know, or what they have yet to learn. This has been done with the best intentions as we want to always add to our students' understanding of mathematics. However, this deficit way of viewing student learning can also prevent us from realizing what our students are fully capable of. What if we used a different lens and thought of what they know and what strengths they bring? What if our actions tightly align with these strengths? How might that empower them and help them grow in confidence and competence? It is important to uncover and nurture the mathematical strengths of your students as they will then be more engaged and eager to learn mathematics (Kobett & Karp, 2020). It will also make for a more productive learning environment in your classroom. There are certain aspects of strengths-based instruction to be mindful of as you plan and implement lessons.

Great Resources

Kobett, B. M., & Karp, K. S. (2020). *Strengths-based teaching and learning in mathematics: Five teaching turnarounds for grades K–6.* Corwin.

BELIEVE THAT ALL STUDENTS CAN LEARN

All students are capable of learning, regardless of their current skills, the services they might receive, or what happens when they walk out of the school building each day. Instead of focusing on the aspect of a student's life that may make learning a bit more difficult for them, think about everything that will help a child be successful. There is an old saying, "If you think they can't, you are right." Frame this differently by saying, "If you think they can, you are right!" Design lessons with this idea in mind, leveraging what students are capable of and what prior knowledge they bring. Allow your students to apply their thinking, grapple with concepts, and engage deeply with mathematical ideas and concepts. Look for what your students know and can do, not what they are lacking. When you observe in this way, your tendency to spot students' strengths and build on them will increase.

AVOID DEFICIT LANGUAGE

We need to be mindful of how we talk about our students, as our statements can reveal our underlying beliefs about their capabilities. Instead of highlighting what is challenging for your students, state your comment in a positive way. By doing so, you will become more aware of what your students can do and be able to build on it.

Don't say this!	Say this instead!
Joey doesn't know his facts!	Joey knows his multiplication facts for tens and fives.
Raphael can't draw a representation to solve a problem.	Raphael uses manipulatives to help her make sense of problems.
Ben takes a long time to solve a simple problem.	Ben analyzes all parts of a problem before reaching a solution.
Annika doesn't participate when working with others.	Annika listens keenly to her peers as they talk and provides thoughtful contributions that move the group forward.

PROVIDE JUST-IN-TIME SUPPORT

As teachers, we want our students to be successful, so we often preplan supports we believe our students will need to reach the desired goal. Prior to a lesson, we make decisions about what representation we'll have our students draw for multiplying 94 by 36 or what process we'll have them follow for subtracting two 3-digit numbers. Resist this urge!! Try not to jump to conclusions about your students' abilities or skills before you begin the lesson. Rather, consider all the ways you can be prepared to offer support if it becomes necessary.

Scaffolds and supports can be helpful, but they shouldn't reduce the complexity of a problem. Instead, they should allow a student access to the problem. If you have a problem about a ferris wheel and are unsure if your students will know what one is, then have a picture of a ferris wheel ready to show your students if one is needed. If you believe comparing fractions might be tricky, then be prepared to pull out a few tools, such as a number line and fraction strips, that students could choose from to use if necessary. This differs from offering these ideas without knowing if your students will need them or not, and it does not remove their opportunity to think. As you plan, consider the strengths your students bring, and build from there. While you should be prepared to offer a scaffold when students need it, it is better to not prematurely prescribe the one support you believe your students will need to be successful. It is your job to offer suggestions and guidance by providing "just-in-time" support while your students are engaged in the learning.

Remember it is okay for your students to grapple with a problem. They might experience a bit of discomfort or uneasiness. These uncomfortable feelings are a good thing as students who struggle and overcome the struggle develop their own understanding of the math content. These students will also develop new skills and strategies for overcoming new challenges both inside and outside the math class (SanGiovanni et al., 2020). Be prepared though to not let a student's struggle become unproductive. If you feel that a student is getting to this point, then offer a suggestion or support to help them move forward.

HONOR STUDENT THINKING

Find every opportunity within your lessons to honor student thinking. When a student shares their knowledge that a guinea pig is a small mammal when solving a problem about these animals, tell them that information is helpful in understanding the context of the problem. Or when another student offers an unconventional way of solving a problem, tell the student they have thought about the problem in a way you hadn't thought of. Be careful not to use language that prohibits a student from applying their own reasoning to a problem or that does not value their way of thinking. "No, that isn't how you solve that problem" or "You need to approach the problem in this way" are statements that can quickly shut down a student's thinking and motivation to learn. Honor the contributions of all students by lifting up every student's thinking.

Use student work in conversations during the lesson (see Student-Centered Math, p. 50). By showcasing student work during discussions, you send a message to the students that their work is valued.

IF I HAD TO GIVE A NEW TEACHER SOME ADVICE, I WOULD TELL THEM TO FIND WAYS TO ENCOURAGE STUDENTS TO SHARE THEIR MATH THINKING OFTEN. IT'S AMAZING HOW THEY CAN SHARE WHAT THEY KNOW AND HOW WELL THEY LEARN FROM ONE ANOTHER!

—THIRD-GRADE TEACHER

Having them discuss their work reinforces that message. Invite all students to share their thinking and reasoning with the rest of the class. It is important to not have a few "go-to" students—those you are confident will arrive at the correct answer or who you always ask to come to the front of the room and share. Instead, make sure each and every one of your students has opportunities to do so over time. All students can contribute to the collective group's collective learning!

Notes

How Do I Make the Growth Mindset a Reality?

Growth mindset refers to the idea that intelligence is not fixed and that we can all grow as learners. In school, you may have heard that some people are math people and some are not. Research has proven this to be false. Having a growth mindset means embracing the idea that we are all capable of learning mathematics. As teachers, we have to position students as doers of math by helping them access the mathematics they already know and can do from their everyday life and building on it. We also have to help them see that engaging in productive struggle when some problems are not familiar yet is part of the learning process—just like in life, where we come across things that seem easier for us than for others and some things that seem more difficult. The key is to get students comfortable learning and growing from mistakes, seeing them as opportunities to connect their current thinking to a new idea or concept! If we focus on what students know, we can use asset-based language to help scaffold their understanding, ultimately giving *all* students the opportunity to learn fully and deeply.

START WITH YOURSELF

As teachers, we make mistakes on a daily basis. It is part of the job. What makes great educators great is the ability to use mistakes to both reflect and learn. While some teachers want their students to see them as perfect, others make their mistakes and struggles transparent to students. The truth is students need to see teachers not only making mistakes but also recognizing them, learning from them, and engaging in productive struggle when a task seems daunting, so they will also do the same. Here are some ways you can model a growth mindset:

> I USED TO THINK MISTAKES WERE BAD, AND NOW I KNOW MISTAKES ARE PART OF THE LEARNING PROCESS AND HELP ME TO GROW. I WORK TO HELP MY STUDENTS LEARN THAT TOO!
>
> —FIRST-GRADE TEACHER

- Create a classroom culture where having a growth mindset is expected.
- Use growth mindset language while teaching (see the chart in the next section).
- Make your own mistakes visible, and ask your students, "Who sees my mistake?" and "Who can help me revise my thinking?"
- Do and assign math tasks that you find cognitively demanding so you can share your own productive struggle with your students.
- Share with your students how you too reflect, learn, and grow as a math teacher. Tell them how you work with coaches, learn from your students, learn from families, read, and most important, reflect on your daily practice.

GROWTH MINDSET AND EQUITY

Having a growth mindset and learning from mistakes must be part of the classroom culture if we want students to view mathematics in a positive light. When approaching a growth mindset through an equity lens, it is imperative that *all* students understand that it does not mean telling your students to simply work harder, nor does it mean praising all effort. Here are some things to consider:

	• Telling students just to work harder without any support, which puts students who are already marginalized in stressful situations. • Praising effort when they are not truly learning—this sends students the wrong message. • Telling students to work hard but having them work in isolation or not tapping into their funds of knowledge.
	• Praising the effort when you see authentic learning happening. • Encouraging students to seek out their peers and work as a community to solve problems. • Providing students with specific feedback without giving them the answer when you see them working hard but getting stuck.

Adapted from REL Northwest "Growth Mindset in Math" Presentation: https://ies.ed.gov/ncee/edlabs/regions/northwest/pdf/math-attitudes-training/powerpoint-growth-mindset.pdf

TEACH AND USE GROWTH MINDSET PHRASES

Having a growth mindset entails helping students change their language from a deficit lens to a strengths-based lens when they engage in discourse and self-talk and while they productively struggle. Students may not be familiar with growth mindset phrases if they have never been introduced to them.

Instead of thinking or saying . . .	Try thinking or saying . . .
I am not good at this!	I am not good at this yet, but I can learn.
I am stuck!	What am I missing?
I make so many mistakes!	Mistakes help me to learn! What is this mistake teaching me to help me get closer to the answer?
I give up!	What strategies have I not tried yet? Who can I ask to help me continue on this problem?
This is too hard!	Where can I start? What do I know about this?
I got so many answers wrong!	Which ones did I get right? How can those help me with the ones I have not learned yet?
I am not a math person!	Everyone is a doer of math.

HIGHLIGHT GROWTH MINDSET SUCCESS

Another way to make a growth mindset a reality is by highlighting the success of students, staff members, and community members who embody a growth mindset. Highlight diverse mathematicians like Katherine Johnson (*Hidden Figures*,

Melfi, 2016), Maryam Mirzakhani, and John Urshel, who persevered and made contributions to the field of mathematics. Welcome community members or former students into your class to share their individual stories of how having a growth mindset helped them persevere and learn new things. When you do this, be sure to include stories from people who represent all the different identity groups so students both learn about the growth mindset and can see role models from all groups of people and hear their experiences (see Math Identity, p. 15). You can also invite former students, teachers, professors, and community partners to do math with your class to foster a sense of community while building their mindset.

ADDITIONAL STRATEGIES TO ENCOURAGE A GROWTH MINDSET

If you truly want to make the growth mindset a reality, you must ensure that you are posing interesting problems where students are engaged in productive struggle. Have students go back and fix their thinking when they have made mistakes so they can learn from them. Some activities that help foster a growth mindset include the following:

- Praise the process and the effort, not the person.
- Give specific feedback (see Give Feedback, p. 185) often, before assigning grades.
- Have students identify mistakes or unfinished thinking and revise.
- Teach your students how the brain learns.
- Mark only the correct answers, and have students go back to the questions that are unmarked to fix them.
- Use a routine like "My Favorite No: Learning From Mistakes" from the Teaching Channel (n.d.).
- Create a growth mindset phrases anchor chart with the students.
- Have an unsolved math problems wall that students can work at over time so they know math problems take time and more than one attempt to solve.

Notes

What Are Math Practices?

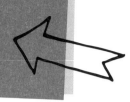

Mathematics comes alive through "mathematical practices," sometimes called "mathematical processes." They describe the behaviors and habits of mind of mathematically proficient people. They are the essence of what it means to do math. Practices help build students' agency—their belief that they can do math effectively (Aguirre et al., 2013). The practices described in this section are the Standards for Mathematical Practice that are part of the Common Core State Standards (National Governors Association Center for Best Practices & Council of Chief State School Officers, 2010). And though your state or district might not use these standards, know that every set of state standards has a very similar version of practices or processes.

WHAT DO THE PRACTICES LOOK LIKE?

Each practice can be characterized by a collection of student behaviors. Here are how they may look in different grades:

#1 Make sense of problems, and persevere when solving them.	
Students	**Examples**
• Describe a problem in their own words. • Select and use strategies. • Maintain composure and change strategies when necessary. • Ask if their answers make sense.	• A first-grader draws a picture of the problem. • A fourth-grade student listens to their peers' strategies when solving a problem and tries different strategies when they have difficulty in solving the problem. Students will often use a different method to check their answers.

#2 Reason abstractly and quantitatively.	
Students	**Examples**
• Represent problems with symbols (equations). • Consider the meaning of numbers in the problems and how they are related. • Use numbers flexibly.	• A second-grader records equations for a two-step problem. • A fourth-grader subtracts $8,000 - 4,988$ by adding up 12 to get 5,000 and then 3,000 more to find 3,012 as the difference.

#3 Construct viable arguments, and critique the reasoning of others.	
Students can	**Examples**
• Justify their strategies and solutions. • Listen to others. • Ask others about their thinking.	• A first-grader explains how they compared 36 and 63. • A fifth-grader asks a classmate how they knew $5 \div \frac{1}{3}$ would create a quotient of more than 5.

#4 Model with mathematics.

Students	Examples
• Use manipulatives to represent concepts and problems. • Work with drawings and diagrams. • Make connections between representations (e.g., drawings and equations).	• A third-grader shows that fractions are equivalent with Cuisenaire rods. • A kindergartener uses ten frames to show 6 + 3.

#5 Use appropriate tools strategically.

Students	Examples
• Know how to use tools. • Know when to use tools. • Select the best tool for a given task. • Represent data with graphs.	• A second-grader knows that a pencil is 4 inches whether measured from 0 to 4 inches or from 3 to 7 inches on a ruler. • A fifth-grader uses a calculator to add four different seven-digit numbers in a problem.

#6 Attend to precision.

Students	Examples
• Use math vocabulary. • Compute accurately. • Use units and labels appropriately. • Know when to estimate and when to use exact terms.	• A student uses "sum" instead of "answer." • A student correctly labels the unit on an answer instead of just answering with a number.

#7 Look for and make use of structure.

Student behaviors	Examples
• Use structures like place value. • Use patterns to show their thinking.	• A first-grade student uses the make-a-ten strategy to add 4 + 6 + 4. The student states that the first two numbers can be added to make a ten, so 4 + 6 + 4 = 10 + 4 = 14. • A fifth-grade student uses the characteristics of quadrilaterals to determine what a shape is.

#8 Look for and express regularity in repeated reasoning.

Students	Examples
• Notice and use patterns in problems and computations. • Look for shortcuts.	• A student applies patterns of make ten (9 + 7) to new problems (19 + 7, 39 + 7, etc.). • A fifth-grade student connects place value and their prior work with operations to understand algorithms to fluently multiply multidigit numbers and perform all operations with decimals to the hundredths.

WHAT IS IMPORTANT TO KNOW ABOUT MATH PRACTICES?

Every teacher must work to develop these behaviors in each and every one of their students. Math practices have a long-standing history in math education but have often faded into the background of math instruction. Here are some things to know so that this doesn't happen to your students:

- *You have math practices in your curriculum:* Regardless of how they're articulated, all states have some version of practice or process standards that attend to these behaviors. You will often find them woven throughout your instructional resources.
- *Practices don't happen in isolation:* To put it simply, practices cannot be taught independently or separately from the math content. Math behaviors are developed and reinforced by engaging students in learning and doing math. Also, the practices themselves are not isolated from one another. Multiple practices should be evident in a lesson.
- *They aren't taught just once:* Math practices are complex and develop over time. You can't expect students to show mastery of these behaviors through a single exposure. Moreover, you want to revisit them consistently throughout the year.
- *Know them well:* To teach these practices, you have to know what they are, what they look like during class, and what you have to do to develop them in your students.
- *Teach what they mean:* Students can't exhibit these behaviors if *they* don't know what they are or what they look like. Teach and model the behaviors. Consider having students create anchor charts (see Anchor Charts, p. 42) that capture the meaning of these practices.
- *Spotlight them, and reflect on them:* Take note of when students exhibit a practice so that they understand what it is and how to show it. Stop the discussion, and showcase examples of practices when students display them. You could even add these examples to the class anchor charts. Have students reflect on these practices from time to time during the closure of your lesson (see Close the Lesson, p. 75).

> I TOOK PICTURES OF MY STUDENTS WHEN THEY WERE ENGAGED IN THE PRACTICES AND PUT THEM ON A BULLETIN BOARD IN MY CLASSROOM. THEY WERE SO PROUD OF THEMSELVES WHEN THEY GOT TO BE ADDED TO THE MATH PRACTICES BOARD!
>
> —THIRD-GRADE TEACHER

- *Assess them:* You assess what students are learning relative to the content. Assess your students' development of these behaviors as well (see Math Behaviors, p. 174).

WHAT DO I DO TO DEVELOP AND ELICIT THESE BEHAVIORS?

You have to intentionally develop the behaviors in students. The following list highlights some of the actions you can take to do this. Keep in mind that many of the bulleted actions can be applied to other practices too.

Tip #1 Make sense of problems, and persevere in solving them.

- Select problem-based, high-quality tasks.
- Provide time for students to engage, process, and make sense.
- Circulate to monitor and ask questions.
- Teach students different strategies for solving problems and for getting "unstuck."

Tip #2 Reason abstractly and quantitatively.

- Explicitly connect symbols and equations to problems.
- Provide opportunities for developing flexible thinking about numbers.
- Discuss the meaning of numbers in the context of a problem.
- Practice determining reasonableness.

Tip #3 Construct viable arguments, and critique the reasoning of others.

- Establish and facilitate a safe environment for discussion.
- Ask students to justify their thinking through writing, representation, and discussion.
- Provide opportunities for students to listen to others.
- Avoid giving too much assistance as students solve problems or share their thinking.
- Model desired behaviors through think-alouds, and so on.

Tip #4 Model with mathematics.

- Allow time for using manipulatives, drawings, and other representations.
- Know how to use manipulatives (yourself), and make them available.

Tip #5 Use appropriate tools strategically.

- Make tools available (including calculators).
- Know how tools (e.g., rulers, addition charts, number lines, manipulatives, calculators) work, and use them during instruction.
- Talk about when a tool is needed and when it isn't.

Tip #6 Attend to precision.

- Take note of efficient strategies for computation during instruction.
- Teach and use precise math vocabulary (see Vocabulary, p. 160).
- Talk about when an estimate and when an exact solution is needed.

Tip #7 Look for and make use of structure.

- Provide time for applying and discussing patterns and properties.
- Highlight structure in mathematics (e.g., place value).
- Ask questions about the application of patterns.
- Highlight different approaches for solving problems.

Tip #8 Look for and express regularity in repeated reasoning.

- Provide tasks and problems with patterns.
- Record ideas so that patterns are more easily observed by students.
- Spotlight shortcuts only after students have understood the concepts and have had an opportunity to discover them on their own (e.g., adding zeros when multiplying by multiples of tens, hundreds).

Notes

What Should I Have on My Classroom Walls?

Classroom walls are a great opportunity to display shared knowledge, a place where students can reference back to math vocabulary and concepts and also celebrate their classmates. Many times, teachers feel the need to cover all of their bulletin boards and classroom walls with posters and premade materials so their classroom looks inviting on the first day of school. You can still honor that and prepare your math classroom by covering the boards with paper and adding a border, but resist the temptation to put up premade materials, knowing you are instead going to fill those boards with the mathematical brilliance of your students! The question then becomes "What should be on the walls, and how should students interact with that content?" Every classroom is different, and wall space is limited, but the following are some suggestions to consider.

DISPLAY YOUR STUDENTS' MATHEMATICAL BRILLIANCE

Posting student work is the first opportunity to showcase both student thinking and the models they create to solve problems. Designate a special "Our Mathematical Brilliance" place on the wall. When you come across exemplary pieces of work, post them along with the students' names to showcase their mathematical brilliance. Have a gallery walk to allow classmates to look at the posted work and discuss the various ways in which math problems were solved, and then students can refer to the work if they get stuck. Be sure that at some point all students have their work showcased by swapping. You can work this out during each of your units. It also is an opportunity for you to take photographs and share with families when their child's mathematical thinking is displayed along with the student's name. In addition, create a more student-centered classroom by asking students what they would like displayed and where.

CLASS-CREATED ANCHOR CHARTS

There are many premade anchor charts out there that you may be tempted to post in preparation for a math unit of study. Instead, we urge you to create anchor charts with your students as you go through the unit. These should reflect the most essential mathematical concepts and strategies that students would want to refer back to both during and after the unit. Also, because anchor charts are a way to capture student thinking and honor the ideas of the class, co-creating them helps students see them as valuable because they showcase their ideas. One action you can take ahead of time is to write the title and some keywords, working with students to fill in the rest. Note that this means from year to year the chart may look slightly different depending on the mathematical ideas your students bring into the class. This is okay!

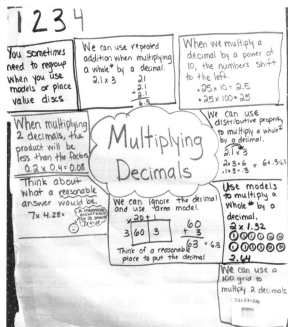

> ## I FIND WHEN MY STUDENTS HELP CO-CREATE THE ANCHOR CHARTS THEY GO BACK AND REFER TO THEM BECAUSE IT HAS *THEIR* IDEAS!
>
> —FOURTH-GRADE TEACHER

You want to create anchor charts for your current unit of study, but don't put them away once the unit is done—especially those related to major concepts. Find a place in the classroom where students can still refer to them. You can laminate them, attach them to a pants hanger, and hang them on a small clothing rack. Students can go back and grab them at any time because they saw them as their own. That is the power of student-made anchor charts!

OUR MATH VOCABULARY

Mathematics is a language. Much of the vocabulary in math class is not used outside that class time, so ensuring we revisit math vocabulary is critical. One way to do that is with a word wall. Here are the most frequently asked questions about vocabulary and word walls:

Question	Thoughts
How should I post math vocabulary?	• Post it in a place where students can refer to it during a lesson. • Display the words along with a visual or example and a student-friendly definition. (*Note:* If the definition is too confusing, it will not be helpful to students.)
When should I post the words?	• Post the word after you have introduced it several times and students have used it in class. • When words are posted too early or with premade definitions with no context, students see this as not helpful. Instead, have a strip of paper with the word ready, and when the class can clearly define it, write the class definition along with a visual.
How long should the words be on the wall?	• The words should stay posted for the whole unit. • After the unit, you can take the words down and file them in a folder with the topic name, allowing students to refer back to them. • If there are words you use all year, keep those words up for students to refer to.
How do I make my word wall interactive?	• Making your word wall interactive shows that you value the words on the wall and the definitions students have co-created with you. • Refer to it throughout the lesson and during transitions. Create fun opportunities for students: try turning down the light, shining a flashlight on one of the words, and having students write or draw a definition. You can also reverse the idea: you give a definition or a picture, and students flash the light on the correct word.

A WONDER WALL OF MATH PROBLEMS

Classroom walls are a great place to post interesting or perplexing math problems that students have to work on over time to solve. Many times in class, you may come across math ideas or problems that you want students to grapple with (see Problem Solving, p. 109). Posting them on a math wonder wall gives them time to work with their classmates and share ideas as they work on the problem. Math puzzles and problems are great interactive things to post on your walls, allowing students a place to go and think together.

HIGHLIGHT DIVERSE MATHEMATICIANS AND STORIES

Identity and Agency

Representation matters. When students see mathematicians who represent diverse backgrounds, it helps them see themselves as doers of math.

A great way to build student identity is by ensuring you are posting pictures of diverse mathematicians on your classroom wall. We want all students to see themselves as doers of math, so we must honor mathematicians from all backgrounds, along with their contributions. Another way to ensure representation is by the math literature you have out. Does the math literature represent the makeup of the class and also highlight representations of people who do not make up the class community? Finally, posting pictures of your students engaged in mathematics and the ideas they come up with is a brilliant way to cover your classroom walls and honor both their thinking and their mathematical ability. Representation matters, so ensure that your classroom walls reflect the students you serve (see Math Identity, p. 15).

WHAT SHOULD NOT BE ON YOUR WALLS?

Here are some things you want to avoid when setting up the wall of your math classroom:

- Posters that reinforce math tricks (CUBES, keywords, and rules that expire)
- Premade materials that do not reflect the mathematical ideas of your students
- Too many items—avoid information overload by keeping everything up all year
- Only your ideas—students should decide what needs to stay and what should go so you can collectively make room for new ideas
- Vocabulary words with no definitions or visuals to support students' understanding (see Vocabulary, p. 160)

As you prepare your classroom walls for the new school year, remember to leave open spaces to showcase the mathematical thinking of the students who are coming into your class. Resist the temptation to have the wall all filled up before they enter the room. Instead, see this as an opportunity to create a shared space with your students and to post the mathematical brilliance of the students you serve!

Notes

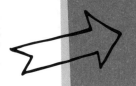

How Do I Make a Good Anchor Chart?

Flexible Learning

You can make virtual anchor charts with virtual whiteboards, Google draw, slides, or anything similar. After you make them, take a screenshot of the work, and use that as the poster to refer to.

Anchor charts are versatile tools for reinforcing instruction and bolstering the learning environment. These posters commemorate skills, concepts, and procedures. They help students remember the content and how to apply it. You can also use anchor charts to post community norms (see Community, p. 19) or reminders for how to get unstuck (see Stuck Students, p. 116). You can include certain tools, like hundreds charts, number bonds, and concept maps or graphic organizers, to help students retain and recall what they have learned.

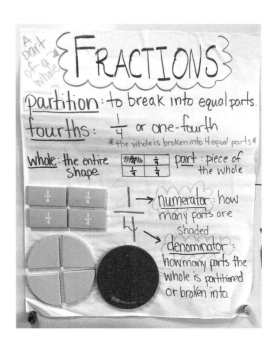

TYPES OF ANCHOR CHARTS

Concept and reference charts: Concept charts help students make sense of the concept by representing it in a variety of ways. This third-grade example shows different ways students can represent multiplication. Notice the labels and illustrations, and consider how these help students understand the concept. These charts are also useful for reinforcing vocabulary.	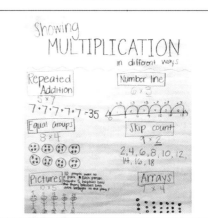
Process charts: These charts show a mathematical process or procedure, or they can capture the steps in an algorithm. Notice in this example that the algorithm is just one of the choices for the process the class has developed. First, students estimate the sum. Then, they choose one of the processes for finding the exact sum. The solve section of this poster shows use of a grid (1), base ten blocks (2), partial sums (3), and an algorithm (4). This class also created posters explaining each of these strategies.	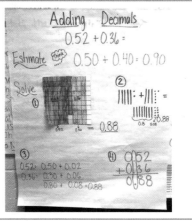

Community charts:

These charts display classroom norms, including how to work with a partner, how to share materials, or how to play games productively. These charts also remind students what they can do when they get stuck. Of course, other community charts might capture that day's schedule or small-group assignments.

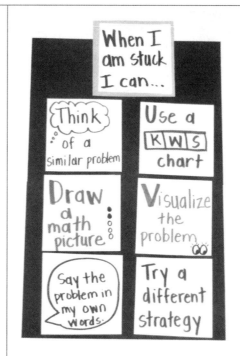

Source: SanGiovanni et al. (2020).

Interactive charts:

These charts complement instruction or thinking routines. They might replicate student versions of mind maps or other organizers, like place value charts (see Visual Tools, p. 103). You might laminate these so you can reuse them. The example here is a number web in which the teacher posts a different number in the center each day and students think about a variety of ways to represent it.

ANCHOR CHARTS: WHAT TO DO AND WHAT TO AVOID

Do	Avoid
Make your own anchor charts. Making your own charts is simply more meaningful than using a premade, purchased chart. Don't worry if you're not an artist! It's okay. Class-made anchor charts galvanize and honor the learning.	*Purchasing anchor charts.* Purchased anchor charts might be pretty, but there isn't a personal connection for your students. And they cost you money!

(continued)

(continued)

Do	Avoid
Give your students a voice. Ask students what needs to be included on the chart. Or have small groups make examples, and have the class come to an agreement about what should and shouldn't make the final version.	*Reusing the same posters every year.* Anchor charts commemorate the learning from recent days or weeks. They can (and should) capture memorable moments or big ideas. Your students need to see themselves and their learning in the chart.
Make a rough draft. It can be hard to create an attractive, clean, neat, and organized poster on your first try while students give ideas. Instead, collect their ideas, create a draft, and unveil the "final" version a day or two later.	*Trying to nail it on your first attempt!* The class poster will change as students give new ideas. Trying to make it perfect on the first try might frustrate you. It's okay to solicit their ideas, think about it further, and then share a "finished" version a little later.
Use the chart to capture what has been taught. Anchor charts must memorialize the teaching and learning in your classroom.	*Crafting or sequencing lessons to accommodate a premade anchor chart.* Standards and students should drive your instructional decisions.
Solicit student feedback. Anchor charts are for your students! Ask students for feedback about the images, diagrams, or notes on the chart. Ask them if they agree with the work and for suggestions to improve it.	*Framing the chart as your understanding.* Of course, you want to make sure the mathematics is accurate. But you also want the chart to capture student thinking.
Post them in a timely manner. Post them right after you make them. Keep them up as long as needed, but keep in mind that you have limited space and want to keep only the most critical charts.	*Worrying about how long a chart is up.* If a chart is useful or needed and your students are using it, keep it up! And remember that you can save a chart for use later in the year as a refresher or a tool for making connections to new content.
Use them! Anchor charts are good to refer to during a lesson or discussion. As students explain their thinking, connect their thoughts to the anchor chart to confirm their logic or push back on their thinking.	*Hanging them up and then overlooking them.* Sometimes, anchor charts are made and hung up in the room and never referenced again. They become an artifact of what was done but aren't used actively. Hang current topics at eye level and close to the board so you (and your students) remember to use them.
Take a picture. It's a great artifact of your teaching and student engagement. It's helpful for planning in the future. And you can send pictures of anchor charts home to communicate with parents to reflect on what has been taught.	*Throwing the ideas away.* You probably can't keep all of the charts. But you do want to capture the ideas and use them in the future.

> MAKING CHARTS WITH MY STUDENTS GAVE THEM OWNERSHIP . . . AND SAVED ME MONEY BECAUSE I DIDN'T HAVE TO BUY THEM!
>
> —FIRST-GRADE TEACHER

Notes

How Do I Engage Families? How Do I Share Information With Them?

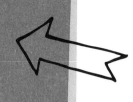

It is likely that you are not teaching mathematics the same way your students' parents or guardians learned mathematics. Seeing an emphasis on using multiple strategies, building conceptual knowledge, and engaging in mathematical practices, parents sometimes will say, "I don't understand the math my child is learning," and they may even get upset. To get ahead of this, you need to positively engage families to help them better understand your work and help you better understand your students. Be sure to talk to your teammates and your principal to ensure you know the school-wide expectations for communicating with parents. Here are some helpful communication tips:

Tip #1: Send home a math survey to families.

Surveys will give you insights into family views and feelings about mathematics. This is important because experiences at home shape student math identities. Surveys can also help you find out how families believe their children learn best. Questions you might use include the following:

1. Do you see yourself as a math person? Why or why not?
2. How do you use mathematics at home or at your job?
3. How does your child learn best?
4. What types of things do you and your child like to do together?
5. What things does your child do well?
6. How has your child traditionally felt about mathematics? How does your child see themselves mathematically?
7. What is their favorite topic in mathematics to learn about?
8. What has been their favorite math-related activity?
9. When they are home and stuck on a problem, what helps them to get unstuck?

Tip #2: Share the current topic of study.

You want families to have a chance to preview the content before you teach it. You might send them a short, one-page newsletter, a video modeling a concept or strategy, a game that helps practice the topic, or a list of questions and ideas to help their child as they do homework. The key is to keep the communication clear and simple. Try not to overwhelm families with too many representations or too much vocabulary. And remember, a visual model (see Visual Tools, p. 103) goes a long way to help families help their child at home.

> I KNOW EVERY PARENT WANTS TO HELP THEIR CHILD BE SUCCESSFUL. I FIND IT REALLY HELPS TO SHARE WHAT I'M TEACHING SO THAT THEY CAN HELP AT HOME.
>
> —KINDERGARTEN TEACHER

Great Resources

Kreisberg, H., & Beyranevand, M. L. (2021). *Partnering with parents in elementary school math: A guide for teachers and leaders.* Corwin. This is a great tool for learning how to engage parents and build partnerships.

Tip #3: Share students' progress.

Families want to know how their child is progressing throughout a unit. It is critical that you communicate frequently so families feel like a partner in their child's math education. Waiting until the report card to share progress can cause families to feel out of the loop, especially when their child is struggling. You can send home the following:

- Progress reports, a few times during a unit, that convey growth or mastery in the content students are working on
- Work samples with feedback and data on how they are doing
- Pictures of their child engaged in mathematics using family communication apps
- Phone calls or emails updating on strengths and areas of growth

Tip #4: Host school-wide family math events.

Getting your school community together to do math is an engaging way to get parents involved. Math events should focus on educating families on the math students are doing, showcasing their learning and suggesting where families can find resources to best help enrich their child's mathematical experience. You may consider hosting the following events:

- *Math and Muffins:* Morning is a great time to invite families in to talk to them about mathematics and play games to start off your day!
- *Math Game Night:* Invite families to come play math games, and share how the games connect with the content their child is learning. Have coworkers and students teach families games. Card and dice games are best because many families have those at home. When they leave, be sure to send home the supplies to play the games at home.
- *Math Olympiads:* Host math olympiads where students work together to solve math problems, and invite families to watch and also help.
- *STEM events:* Many schools have maker spaces or do STEM activities. This is a fun and engaging way to bring families in to learn about mathematics and coding. Families work together through STEM challenges, which helps bring them together to engage in productive struggle.
- *Math Story Time:* Use math literature, and host storytime events. You can read the story to the families and students and then engage in math activities that are related to the math content in the story (see Literature, p. 106).

Equity and Access

Translate games and other resources to home languages so multilingual families feel welcome and can play the games at home.

Tip #5: Teach families how to help.

Possibly, the most important way to engage families is to help them know how to support their child when they get stuck! Share ideas about where they can go for help—including online resources like Seesaw or Google Classroom videos; examples from notebooks, journals, or anchor charts; and questions prompts to get them unstuck (see Stuck Students, p. 116).

Tip #6: Communicate homework policies.

It is also critical that you are clear about the time students should spend working on math homework and what families should do if students have difficulty with it. Remind families that students should do much of their homework independently but that a little help is always okay. Be sure they know how to communicate with you if their child is really struggling, so you can best help the child the next day (see Homework, p. 78). Knowing you are there as a partner to help is important to develop strong family partnerships!

Tip #7: Know how to communicate with multilingual families.

When you have students who are multilingual or whose families do not speak English, you may feel overwhelmed as to how best to communicate. Ask if anyone in your building speaks that language or if the family has someone who can translate conversations for you. Having a translator can help make both you and the family feel connected and help the family feel engaged because they know what is going on (see Diverse Learners, p. 70). Investing in apps that translate, like Talking Points, allows you to text families by translating the information for you and them. You can also send home pictures and progress updates that way. When hosting math events or parent-teacher conferences, try to have a translator there if possible. The key is to keep communication clear and consistent so they too feel like part of your classroom community.

Notes

chapter TWO

HOW DO I STRUCTURE, ORGANIZE, AND MANAGE MY MATH CLASS?

- -

We have learned that how we shape the day-to-day operations of our math class contributes significantly to how effective our instruction is. Structure, management, and organization create familiarity, productivity, and efficiency. Familiarity helps students know what to expect during class and how to work within the routines and structures of your classroom. In a student-centered classroom, students find comfort when consistent and predictable structures are in place that provide them with a safe learning environment, where they can focus on math content and feel free to exchange ideas with peers.

Most important, we have learned that structure does not mean static. There needs to be flexibility for making intentional adjustments to the day-to-day operations. You can probably recall a classroom where students engaged in daily activities so seamlessly that their actions and the classroom itself appeared to be like a well-oiled machine. And you may have seen the same classroom on another day using different activities, rotations, groups, and transitions, but it ran just as smoothly. A closer examination would have revealed that clear, intentional structures and procedures were put in place to ensure that the students always knew what to do throughout the lesson, how to access and use resources, who to work with, when to come together as a whole class, and how to participate in each activity.

In a student-centered classroom, students engage in meaningful and purposeful activities structured to meet their needs and in which they know what is expected of them. You do this by using whole- and small-group structures to target specific needs as they change from day to day. You use games and center activities to help students practice and extend their learning of the skills and concepts that have been taught.

Your math classroom will be composed of learners with a wide variety of needs and interests. Clear and consistent structures allow flexibility to accommodate students' needs while promoting productivity and efficiency in your classroom. This chapter answers questions about how to structure, organize, and manage your math class by expanding on each of the following questions:

- [ ] **How do I plan to make mathematics student centered?**
- [ ] **What is whole-group collaborative math instruction?**
- [ ] **How do I use small-group instruction?**
- [ ] **How do I begin the math class?**
- [ ] **What are instructional routines? How do I use them?**
- [ ] **How do I facilitate a math lesson?**
- [ ] **How do I plan for diverse learners?**
- [ ] **How do I close a lesson?**
- [ ] **What do I need to consider about math homework?**

As you read about these, we encourage you to think about the following:

- [ ] **What does this mean to me?**
- [ ] **What else do I need to know about this?**
- [ ] **What will I do next?**

How Do I Plan to Make Mathematics Student Centered?

The goal of high-quality math instruction is to make it student centered. This means that students are the ones who are doing the thinking, talking, and sense making. Teachers make instructional decisions with students in mind. This is in contrast to a teacher-centered approach, such as when a teacher demonstrates how to solve a problem and asks the students to replicate the process. You might find yourself often defaulting to a teacher-centered approach as it is most likely what you experienced when you were a student. There is a misbelief that when you are talking, you are teaching (and working). A teacher-centered approach feels as though you have better control of the class and tends to feel less risky or unpredictable. To make sure you provide student-centered instruction for your students, allow yourself to be vulnerable. Think about how you can structure the lesson to provide your students with opportunities to engage with the mathematics, apply their own thinking, and construct their own meaning.

> AT FIRST, I THOUGHT TEACHING WAS TELLING AND SHOWING STUDENTS HOW TO DO THINGS. IT TOOK SOME PRACTICE TO GET TO A POINT WHERE IT WAS ABOUT THEM DOING AND TALKING.
>
> —FIFTH-GRADE TEACHER

There are certain aspects of instruction, or instructional tips, that drive student-centered opportunities in your classroom:

Tip #1 Activate their thinking and curiosity.

Launch into a task or problem by activating curiosity. You might first ask students what they notice about a problem or what they wonder about it. You might ask them what it reminds them of or how the context relates to their personal lives and interests. You can present an image that is related to the problem. A picture of kids playing soccer at recess may spark a conversation regarding the number of kids on each team, leading to a task about finding the number of players on a team or in a league. You might kick off a lesson by reading literature that sets the context for the math task, which also helps students activate their prior knowledge (see Literature, p. 106).

Tip #2 Let students try it first.

A student-centered approach invites students to engage with the problem first. In a teacher-centered classroom, the teacher would pose a problem and lead students through solving it, asking somewhat surface-level questions along the way. Or sometimes the teacher poses a problem and shows students how to do it. Instead, in a student-centered lesson, the teacher poses a problem, and students try to solve it in their own way before discussing strategies and solutions. After that discussion, you can explicitly teach how to do something or suggest a different, possibly more efficient strategy or approach. Having students do the math first enables them to grapple with the skills and concepts while giving you insight into their thinking, reasoning, and misconceptions. During the follow-up discussion, you can then build on those observations.

Tip #3 Don't do all the talking.

In a teacher-centered approach, you might find that your lessons somewhat resemble a presentation, where you are doing most of the talking, which means that you are most likely also doing most of the thinking. To create a more student-centered classroom, provide your students with opportunities to talk about the mathematics. Discussing their ideas contributes to their sense making. As you plan your lesson, determine moments throughout the lesson where students can talk about their observations, strategies, and obstacles (see Plan for Discourse, p. 146). Keep in mind that student-to-student discussion is just as important as student-to-teacher discussion.

> ONE THING I LEARNED THAT I'D SHARE WITH OTHERS IS TO MAKE SURE TO LET YOUR STUDENTS DO MOST OF THE TALKING. IT WILL PROBABLY FEEL CLUNKY IN THE BEGINNING, BUT STICK WITH IT AS IT IS TOTALLY WORTH IT!
>
> —FIRST-GRADE TEACHER

Tip #4 Don't suggest only one way to do math.

In a teacher-centered lesson, the teacher will generally model how to solve a problem. This insinuates that there is only one approach to doing the math or that only one approach is preferred. Often the "how-to" that is offered to students is the one way that the teacher prefers, understands the best, or was taught when they were in school; is dictated by the textbook; or is the most traditional approach. For example, if you are teaching double-digit addition, the traditional algorithm isn't the only way to find the sum (see Fluency Strategies for Operations, p. 138). There are other strategies that are just as good, if not better! The goal of your instruction is for students to make sense of the mathematics. It is critical that you make sure you honor student thinking and explore with your students different ways to solve a problem. You can do this by

- considering different ways to solve a problem as you plan,
- having students try the mathematics first before you teach it explicitly, and
- making connections between the problem, their strategies, and the method that you teach them.

Tip #5 Let students decide which manipulatives and representations to use.

It may be tempting to suggest which manipulative or representation your students should use. This removes the opportunity for students to determine which tool makes the most sense to them. When you present a task, you might provide a few

Identity and Agency

Students who have an opportunity to try mathematics first develop a sense of capability that frames positive dispositions about mathematics.

MANAGEMENT

suggestions for students, but you don't want to tell them what to use. You might say, "Today to solve this subtraction problem, you might want to consider using Unifix cubes, two-colored counters, or color tiles. Or you might decide to draw a picture. It is up to you how you show your thinking." In this example, you suggest to them some of the options, but it is up to them to decide what makes sense.

Tip #6 | Make use of student work.

Students take ownership of the learning when their work is showcased. As you debrief the lesson, showcase student work. Purposefully choose the work of a few students to discuss as an entire class during the debriefing stage of the lesson (see Facilitate a Lesson, p. 66). The work you choose should show differences in strategic thinking, representations, interpretations, and solutions. Ask questions about how the different examples are similar and different. Help students make connections between approaches. And be sure to have students share their thoughts and responses to your questions about their work rather than posting student work and describing what they did to the class.

Tip #7 | Support their thinking without taking over.

You will find yourself in situations where a student is stuck on a problem. It will be difficult to not tell the student what to do or how to solve the problem. You might even be tempted to take the student's pencil and show them how to do the problem! Instead, provide guidance, asking them questions to prompt what they might try next. Or refer them to strategies they can use when they are stuck (see Stuck Students, p. 116). These two moves support students but call for them to take action to move forward, making the interaction more student centered.

Tip #8 | Have students work together.

Students benefit from working collaboratively during math lessons. It exposes them to diverse thinking and helps them develop social and emotional skills. There are some things you need to consider for students to work collaboratively:

- *Think location:* First, think about where students can work in the room (at tables, on the carpet, in the corners of the room, on vertical surfaces, etc.).
- *Assign partners:* Think about partner assignments. While there may be some situations where you let your students decide who they want to work with, it is typically more beneficial to assign groups so you can intentionally match student strengths.
- *Use threes and fours:* Use triads (three students) or quads (four students) for collaborative work. Two students can be problematic, especially if the match isn't a good fit. We have found that grouping three students often creates the best balance and that more than four becomes unproductive.
- *Keep them together:* Creating new partner groups challenges efficiency and effectiveness. Each time a new group is formed, students have to restart building relationships, figuring out how their partners work, and so on. We suggest assigning triads or quads to work together for a few days or even a week before making new assignments.
- *Remember norms:* Remind students of the norms for working together that you and they established so everyone is aware of the expectations and is productive (see Community, p. 19).

What Is Whole-Group Collaborative Math Instruction?

Rich, high-quality math tasks take time. They require students to productively engage, collaborate with classmates, persevere, share their reasoning, and react to the reasoning of others. A whole-group, collaborative model is a good structure for realizing all of this. This whole-group model isn't a lecture-style approach. Instead, it is a model in which you introduce a task, provide time for students to engage with it, and then bring the class together to discuss their strategies and solutions.

> I ONCE THOUGHT SMALL GROUPS WERE THE BEST AND ONLY CHOICE FOR MATHEMATICS. BUT GREAT TASKS, EXPLORATION, COLLABORATION, AND DISCUSSION TAKE TIME. I CAN DO ALL OF THOSE THINGS WITH A WHOLE-GROUP MODEL.
>
> —FOURTH-GRADE TEACHER

Launch
- **You:** Introduce the task.
- **Students:** Share observations about the task and/or ask questions about the task.

Engage
- **You:** Circulate to monitor progress and ask questions.
- **Students:** Engage in the task with their partner or group.

Debrief
- **You:** Bring the class together to discuss strategies, questions, representations, challenges, and solutions.
- **Students:** Share their strategies including what worked and what didn't work.

During the engage portion of this structure, students work collaboratively on the task, and you monitor and select which ideas you'll want to feature during the class debrief. During the debrief, you select and sequence the student ideas to discuss, and you help students make connections between strategies and concepts. Read more about monitoring, selecting, sequencing, and connecting student ideas (see Plan for Discourse, p. 146).

You want your whole-group structure for the lesson to complement your intent of the day. No one lesson structure, whole group or small group, will satisfy you and your students' needs every day during the year. Know that structures may not be used equally. Over the course of the year, you might use whole-group structures 60% of the time and small-group structures 40% of the time. That is okay! What is important is that you choose grouping structures that align with your intent and purpose.

It is helpful to find a common "flow" to your lesson with an opening and closing. The middle component is the whole- or small-group part (see Small-Group Instruction, p. 56) that can be swapped out as needed. Familiarizing students with two or three common structures (small-group rotation, small-group breakout, or whole-group collaborative) will help you find order, efficiency, and positive outcomes. And most important, an established, familiar set of structures allows you to plan more easily, and you and your students can move between structures from day to day with ease and efficiency.

HOW DOES WHOLE-GROUP COLLABORATIVE INSTRUCTION WORK?

This model begins with the whole class engaged with an opening routine (see Begin Class, p. 59). Then, the centerpiece of the lesson follows a model of launching the task, engaging students in the task, and debriefing the task (see Facilitate a Lesson, p. 66). Note that the engagement time is when students should be working collaboratively with partners. After the debrief, and a possible extension, the whole class comes together for reflection and lesson closure.

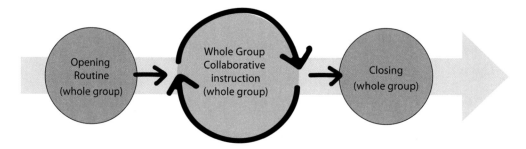

WHEN IS A WHOLE-GROUP INSTRUCTIONAL MODEL A GOOD CHOICE FOR MY LESSON?

Whole-group instruction is especially good for the following reasons:

- Providing more time for students to work with rich tasks and problems
- Providing more time for using tools, representing, and sharing strategies
- Developing collaborative skills among students
- Exposing students to a greater variety of perspectives and reasoning
- Giving students opportunities to explore mathematics and make sense of it on their own
- Limiting your opportunities to intervene when student strategies don't work, requiring them to come up with their own ideas about how to proceed
- Introducing concepts through rich problems
- Building student stamina with high-quality tasks

WHAT DO I NEED TO KEEP IN MIND ABOUT A WHOLE-GROUP LESSON STRUCTURE?

With a whole-group model, you have to keep the following points in mind:

- Remember that you might not be able to visit each partner group as they work. So you will have to find ways to balance who you visit and think about how you can include those individuals in the full-class debrief. Or consider modifying your approach to use a "catch-and-release" model (see Facilitate a Lesson, p. 66).
- Be prepared for students who finish early while other groups are still working. You can extend the problem for these students or have independent activities ready for them.
- Be careful not to stay with one partner group for too long.
- Be mindful of groups who might sit idle because they are stuck while waiting for you to visit them. You have to be sure that students have strategies for getting unstuck (see Stuck Students, p. 116).
- Consider pausing the group during the engage stage for a group discussion and then having them reengage in the task (see Facilitate a Lesson, p. 66).
- Remember reteaching or enriching, though still possible, can be more challenging. You might need to reserve it for the next day, using a small-group structure.
- Find ways to capture information about student progress, reasoning, or misconceptions (see Find Out What Students Know, p. 168) so that you can address it during the debrief or a follow-up lesson.
- Be sure to provide closure (see Close the Lesson, p. 75) to the lesson so that the class can process what they did and what they learned.

Notes

How Do I Use Small-Group Instruction?

Small-group instruction is a model that supports an intentionally differentiated approach to the same content for groups of students. In this model, you work with some students in a group while others work on their own or in other small groups in stations or centers. The number in that group depends on your intentions and student needs. You can use small groups as part of a rotation model or to pull a breakout group of students who would benefit from additional instruction, practice, or extension of a skill or concept. Keep in mind that using more than two groups can be problematic because it limits how much instructional time (teacher facetime) students can access. An increase in the number of groups also creates more transitions, movement between groups, which challenge engagement and time management. And also know that increasing the number of groups increases the number of students not working with you, meaning that there are more students you have to monitor indirectly and more who might be able to disengage from their task.

HOW DOES SMALL-GROUP INSTRUCTION WORK?

You should group students flexibly, meaning that you select students for small groups intentionally and based on their mathematical learning needs. There are two general approaches to small-group structures: (1) the rotation model and (2) the breakout model. Both models start with a whole-group number sense or warm-up routine (see Instructional Routines, p. 63) and end with a whole-group closure. Where the core instruction happens differs between these models.

SMALL-GROUP ROTATION MODEL

This option splits the class into two groups for the main content lesson. You work with one group (group A), while the other group works independently (group B). Then, students switch, and you now work with the group that first worked independently (group B). Students in both groups may work with the same content or a similar task, but you may provide different numbers or scaffolds to support students.

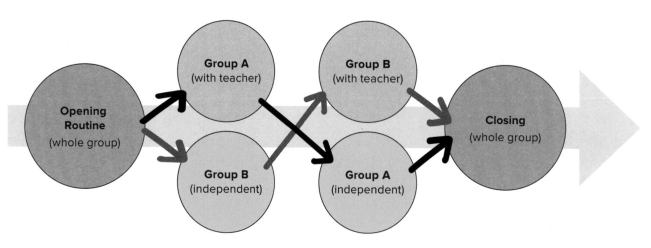

SMALL-GROUP BREAKOUT MODEL

This option begins with teaching a skill or concept with the whole group before breaking into smaller groups for the latter part of the lesson. One group will meet with you for more work with the skill or concept of the lesson. The other group will practice the skill or concept independently. For some lessons, you might choose to extend or enrich the concept with the students in your group rather than always focusing on reteaching or reinforcing.

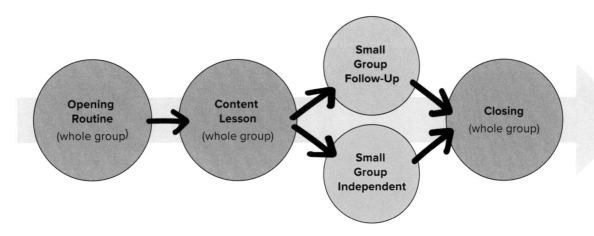

WHEN IS A SMALL-GROUP MODEL A GOOD CHOICE FOR MY LESSON?

Small-group instruction is especially good for

- revisiting skills and concepts with specific students or groups,
- extending or enriching skills and concepts with specific students or groups,
- focusing your observation on students in your small group to determine how well they understand a skill or concept,
- providing independent practice time for students not working with you,
- easing the burden of not having enough materials or manipulatives for a lesson, and
- making use of a shorter amount of time to work with a group.

WHAT DO I NEED TO BE MINDFUL OF?

With a small-group model, you have to do the following:

- Be sure that students understand their independent work.
- Maximize efficiency because you have less time to work with students directly.
- Remember that you may not be able to finish a task.
- Balance focusing on your group and monitoring the independent students.
- Be aware of your independent students' engagement with their assigned work.
- Prepare for your independent students to play a game or work on a center if they finish early—you should have the materials ready and make sure they know how to play the game or do the center (see Centers p. 119).
- Plan two, shorter lessons.

> I WAS REALLY STRUGGLING TO FIND TIME FOR RETEACHING. I FOUND SMALL GROUPS TO BE THE WAY I COULD RETEACH THE STUDENTS WHO NEEDED IT.
>
> —FIFTH-GRADE TEACHER

- Be aware that having shorter lessons for small groups challenges building the student stamina needed for working with more complex tasks, explorations, or problems.
- Be mindful to balance the time spent with each group.

Flexible Learning

For remote learners, you can use breakout rooms for small-group instruction. Or you might have students who are working independently mute themselves but still have access to you in the chat box in case they have questions. Some teachers have students log off completely for independent time while others stay online for their small group.

Notes

How Do I Begin the Math Class?

The first few minutes of math class give you a chance to set the tone for the entire lesson. Students are most fresh and ready during the first moments of mathematics, so it's a good time to engage them in meaningful thinking, reasoning, and idea sharing. Your opening activity is also a chance to connect with students and create a benchmark moment that you might refer to during your lesson discussions. Ideally, you want an opening activity that is structured and familiar to students so that you can get started quickly and ensure that students know what to do. There are two different ways to open your math lesson effectively: (1) number sense or fluency routines and (2) daily math meetings.

MANAGEMENT

NUMBER SENSE OR FLUENCY ROUTINES

An opening number sense or fluency routine is a highly recommended approach to starting math class. These engaging activities help students practice important number concepts, or develop computational fluency, and practice discussion techniques before getting into the content focus of the lesson.

Great Resources

SanGiovanni, J. J. (2019). *Daily routines to jump-start math class.* Corwin; Parrish, S. (2010). *Number talks.* Math Solutions; Bay-Williams, J., & SanGiovanni, J. (2021). *Figuring out fluency: A classroom companion.* Corwin; Shumway, J. (2011). *Number sense routines in K–3.* Stenhouse; Wyborney, S. (n.d.). *New esti-mysteries and number sense resources every day for the rest of the school year.* www.stevewyborney.com

HOW DO I FACILITATE A NUMBER SENSE OR FLUENCY ROUTINE?

While the details of number sense and fluency routines differ, they all fall into a similar structure. First, you pose a number situation. Then, students think about possible strategies and solutions to respond to your prompt. Students share their thinking with their partners before you bring the whole class together for discussion.

HOW LONG SHOULD A NUMBER ROUTINE LAST?

Number routines should be 5–10 minutes long. Students need about 1–2 minutes to think independently and another 1–2 minutes to share with a partner, and then you need about 3–6 minutes to discuss as a class.

SHOULD I ASSIGN PARTNERS FOR ROUTINES?

Yes. Assign partners for your opening routine so that when class starts, students find their partners and get ready to start the routine. Consider assigning the same partners for an entire week so that students have time to get comfortable with each other and build relationships over time before working with new partners the following week.

SHOULD I USE PAIRS OR SMALL GROUPS FOR A ROUTINE?

The choice is up to you, but we recommend triads. Two students can be problematic if one dominates the discussion or can't access the conversation. Four students can be too many. We have found that three students assigned as a group for a week works well.

WHAT IF THE ROUTINE RUNS LONG?

A good conversation may take a few more minutes. It's okay if the routine occasionally runs long, but be careful to avoid letting the routine spill over too often because it cuts into time for your lesson. Remember that you control the activity. If you are only able to use one of the prompts during the routine, you can stop and save the others for the next day. If you finish the entire routine in a short amount of time, don't feel compelled to extend it. Instead, get started with the lesson.

DAILY MATH MEETING

An opening math meeting calls all students together to check in as individuals and collectively. This is a great time for you and your students to quickly share celebrations and announcements—an important aspect of building community. It is a good time to ask students how they are feeling or to share how they recently used mathematics elsewhere in school or at home. The opening math meeting is also a good time to talk about classroom norms and remind students that they should work together or what to do when they're stuck. This isn't the traditional skills-based practice approach to beginning math class. That's okay! Instead, it is an opportunity to revisit and strengthen student identities and your classroom community.

LESSON OPENINGS TO LIMIT OR AVOID ALTOGETHER

Remember, you want the opening to be a springboard into your lesson focus for the day. You want a controlled beginning that engages students but not one that could unravel into an extended mini lesson that overruns your lesson time. Some types of openings to avoid include the following.

CALENDAR ACTIVITIES

Calendar activities recite the day of the week, the date, and the weather, and usually incorporate some collection of number activities associated with the date or the number of days you have been in school. They may appear useful for helping students make connections with numbers while practicing or reviewing important number concepts. However, they lose appeal and instructional value by quickly becoming mindless rituals. This can happen more quickly as students repeat the same calendar ritual year after year.

TRADITIONAL WARM-UPS OR BELL RINGERS

These are three to five written practice problems that review prior content with the intent that practicing a skill is a way to get ready for the lesson. Though the ideas of review and practice are important, leveraging prior knowledge isn't that simple. Also, beginning mathematics with a paper-pencil practice inadvertently sends the wrong idea about what it means to do math. These techniques present other challenges to the positive start you want for your class. Students finish the work at different rates, so from the very start of class, you have students who begin to disengage because they are finished or can't keep up. Then, as you go over the answers, you may feel tempted to teach a mini lesson on the skill or topic that your students didn't do well with, which then hijacks your instructional time. Practice is a good idea. There are just better ways to go about it (see Practice, p. 123).

GOING OVER HOMEWORK

Instructional time is precious, and going over homework jeopardizes your lesson in a variety of ways. Some students may not have done their homework, so for them, going over the answers is a complete waste of time. Others might not have understood it or have had help at home, which disrupts the value of revising the work. As with warm-ups, going over homework can potentially hijack your lesson as you begin to reteach problems that weren't done correctly. There are better ways to check or review homework (see Homework, p. 78).

DISCUSSING WHAT HAPPENED YESTERDAY

This start to the lesson asks students about what they did the day before. It is a good idea to make connections between lessons and concepts. But starting this way can be problematic for a few reasons. First, student learning may be unfinished, making it difficult to recall what they learned or why they learned it. Second, students may be distracted by the context of a problem, which can spark discussion about a tangent that has no instructional bearing. It's also sometimes difficult for adults to think about the details of the previous day, so it's reasonable to think the same is true for students. If the conversation stalls, interest and enthusiasm for the daily lesson can wane. It can even cause frustration, which is not the tone you want to set.

SHOWING A VIDEO ABOUT THE CONTENT

Videos that demonstrate mathematics may seem engaging, but bad videos distract, show misconceptions, or overly focus on procedures. Showing how to do the math to start the lesson undercuts your goal of having students develop their own understanding. Videos are likely best reserved for the end of the lesson so that students can decide how the ideas presented in them compare with their interpretation and understanding of the mathematics they have learned.

Notes

What Are Instructional Routines?
How Do I Use Them?

Instructional routines are familiar, structured experiences that are adaptable to a range of math content. They provide a framework for making sense, reasoning, and discussing. Routines set expectations for engagement and participation, support productive relationships, and foster a community of math doers. Having a collection of routines helps you plan more efficiently because you have "go-to" activities that you and your students are familiar with. Routines naturally complement any textbook series or curriculum that you use. Popular examples of routines include number routines, fluency routines, problem-solving and reasoning routines, and mathematical language routines.

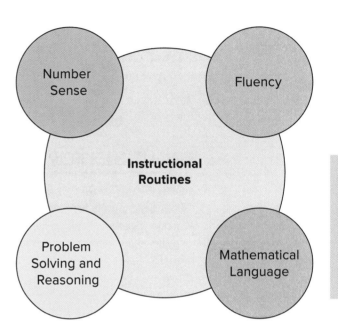

MANAGEMENT

NUMBER ROUTINES

Number routines or number sense routines develop understanding of number concepts and relationships. There are routines for breaking apart numbers, for determining where numbers might go on a number line, or for estimating quantity. Number routines are a great choice for starting your lesson each day (see Instructional Routines, p. 63).

IS THIS THE END?

Is This the End (SanGiovanni, 2019) is a routine for helping students think flexibly about how numbers are related. For the left example, the endpoints could be 630 and 640, 634 and 636, 535 and 735, and so on. The right example is a version with decimals.

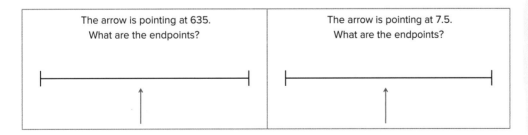

| The arrow is pointing at 635. What are the endpoints? | The arrow is pointing at 7.5. What are the endpoints? |

FLUENCY ROUTINES

Fluency routines are similar to number routines but lend themselves more to computational fluency. Fluency routines develop skill with manipulating numbers and operations so that students become flexible, efficient, and accurate. A fluency

Great Resources

SanGiovanni, J. J. (2019). *Daily routines to jump-start math class.* Corwin; Shumway, J. (2011). *Number sense routines in K–3.* Stenhouse; Wyborney, S. (n.d.). *New esti-mysteries and number sense resources every day for the rest of the school year.* stevewyborney.com

What Are Instructional Routines? How Do I Use Them?

63

routine might focus on a specific computation strategy, estimate, or determine reasonableness. Fluency routines provide quality practice and can also be good choices for starting math class.

THAT ONE
Which expression is best for solving with the make-a-ten strategy? Why?

34 + 57	21 + 64	95 + 44

THAT ONE
Which expression is best for solving with an algorithm? Why?

1,499 + 423	1,577 + 5,587	2,602 + 2,816

ROUTINES FOR PROBLEM SOLVING AND REASONING

Routines for problem solving and reasoning help structure student thinking so that they can make sense of problems. These tools help students persevere and develop productive habits for solving problems that can be used time and time again. These routines are used each time students engage with word problems and other high-quality tasks.

Great Resources

Kelemanik, G., Lucenta, A., & Creighton, S. J. (2016). *Routines for reasoning: Fostering the mathematical practices in all students.* Heinemann; Ray-Riek, M. (2013). *Powerful problem solving activities for sense making with the mathematical practices.* Heinemann.

MATHEMATICAL LANGUAGE ROUTINES

Mathematical language routines provide access to developing understanding of math content and language. They provide structure for all students to participate in mathematical discussions. When we tie in language routines, we are providing access to conversations for students who may not have the language skills yet but have the understanding. These routines are temporary scaffolds for students to use for long-term, independent methods of making sense of and doing math.

Great Resources

The Stanford Center for Assessment, Learning, and Equity captures seven must-know language routines for math instruction. You can find them at http://ell.stanford.edu.

Equity and Access

Familiar routines provide structure so that each student has the opportunity to participate and discuss.

USING INSTRUCTIONAL ROUTINES

Tip #1 | Teach the routine.

Students have to understand how routines work, meaning you have to take the time to teach them. Teach students so they know what to do for the routine, how to interact with one another, and so on. Once taught, routines almost "run themselves."

Tip #2 | Practice, and be patient.

After you teach a routine, it can take some time for it to become familiar. Unfortunately, the exact number of exposures isn't set. Be patient. And remember that sometimes a routine might not go well for a slew of reasons—for instance, the numbers used in a number routine or the contexts used in the word problem. It's okay if they don't always work. Reflect on what didn't work and why. Tinker and modify as needed.

> WHEN I BEGAN, MY ROUTINES WERE MESSY. I WANTED TO SCRAP THEM, BUT MY TEAMMATE TOLD ME I SHOULD KEEP DOING THEM TO SEE IF THEY GOT BETTER. I'M GLAD I DIDN'T GIVE UP. THEY SMOOTHED OUT, AND I HAVE A GREAT SET OF TOOLS IN MY TEACHER TOOLBOX.
>
> —FIRST-GRADE TEACHER

Tip #3 | Modify them.

Routines are structured but still pliable. You can (and should) make adjustments to meet the needs of you and your students. It might mean adding a fourth read to the Three Reads routine. Or you might add a turn-and-talk move to a Number Talk.

Tip #4 | Take note.

Take note of which routines your students are most receptive to. Find a few "go-to" reasoning or language routines that you can remind students to use when they are stuck with a problem. Think about number sense or fluency routines that students enjoy doing. Leverage them to spark engagement and excitement for mathematics that day.

Tip #5 | Mix them up.

Don't let a routine become stale. Even routines that students love shouldn't be overused. You want to keep mathematics fresh, interesting, and stimulating. You want students to develop a collection of approaches they can use for problems or language. So you will have to mix in a variety of routines over time.

How Do I Facilitate a Math Lesson?

A math lesson includes an opening (see Begin Class, p. 59), focused instruction, and a closing (see Close the Lesson, p. 75). The middle portion of the lesson takes most of the class time, focused on teaching new topics. You will have to explicitly teach skills, concepts, and procedures. But a good math lesson first gives students an opportunity to think, try, and make sense of the mathematics on their own. It provides an opportunity for students to share their thinking and listen to the ideas of others. It all starts with selecting a good task (see Tasks p. 91). But then what? How should a math lesson play out?

AVOID GRADUAL RELEASE

You are likely familiar with the gradual-release model of teaching. It is often referred to as "I do, we do, you do." In the "I do" phase, the teacher shows how to do the math. In the "we do" phase, the class does the math together. In the "you do" phase, students do the math on their own. You may have experienced this kind of lesson as a student yourself. *Do not do this*. This approach compromises students' opportunities for making their own meaning of mathematics. It compromises their identity and their agency. It does not allow individuals to think about mathematics critically and to develop their own understanding. It is a mimicking approach that simply instructs someone to do math the way another person does it, which in mathematics does not usually lead to very long-lasting or deep learning. This is not what you want for your students. Instead, you want to reverse the process (Seeley, 2017). You want students to do the math and then to bring the class together to discuss; then, you might explicitly teach a skill or concept if it hasn't been developed by the group. Perhaps you will connect another, possibly more traditional approach to the thinking that students already have.

> MY MATH COACH SUGGESTED I TURN MY TEACHING "UPSIDE DOWN," AND BOY DID IT MAKE A BIG DIFFERENCE! MY STUDENTS WERE MORE ENGAGED IN LEARNING.
>
> —FIFTH-GRADE TEACHER

LAUNCH-ENGAGE-DEBRIEF

The launch-engage-debrief (L-E-D) structure for teaching a math lesson is considered to be much more student centered. It begins with launching a task.

Answers to Your Biggest Questions About Teaching Elementary Math

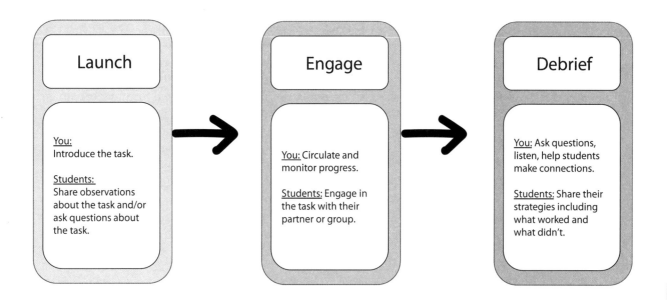

LAUNCH

At this stage, you ask students what they might know about the context of a problem or task. You help them think about personal experiences they have had with the context of the problem. You call for their observations about a prompt or what they notice about it. You can ask them about the possible questions the prompt might be setting up, or you can ask what they wonder about the task. The launch stage is also an opportunity to remind students about how to work with one another or to discuss what they might do if they get stuck during the task (see Stuck Students, p. 116).

ENGAGE

This is when students work with the task. They might work in pairs, triads, or small groups. As students work with the problem, you circulate around the class observing what they are doing, taking notes about their strategies and approaches, or asking groups questions to probe their thinking.

DEBRIEF

After students have engaged with the task or problem, you bring the whole class together to debrief the task. You discuss strategies, approaches, representations, challenges, and potential solutions. This is when students have the opportunity to share their thinking and see how their approaches compare with their classmates'. You can build on their ideas to establish the skill or concept and offer, if needed, another (familiar) way to go about it.

Flexible Learning

Breakout rooms are a good way for students to work collaboratively.

Flexible Learning

You can have each student post a solution or thought in the chat box and have others look for an idea they want to discuss. Or you can display different examples of student work and have students choose which one they want to talk about.

CATCH-AND-RELEASE

The L-E-D model works well to provide opportunities for students to engage in the task in order to develop their own understanding and strategies. However, as the engage stage unfolds, you might find that you are unable to check in with each group of students. Students may disengage because they are at an impasse and you aren't able to get to them. Or you may find that different groups have the same questions, observations, or challenges, which could have been addressed all at once. And sometimes the debrief is too late for lifting up an important idea. Catch-and-release (SanGiovanni et al., 2020) modifies the engage stage of the L-E-D model. This enhancement enables you to be more responsive and to position students as the authors of ideas in the classroom.

Catch-and-Release

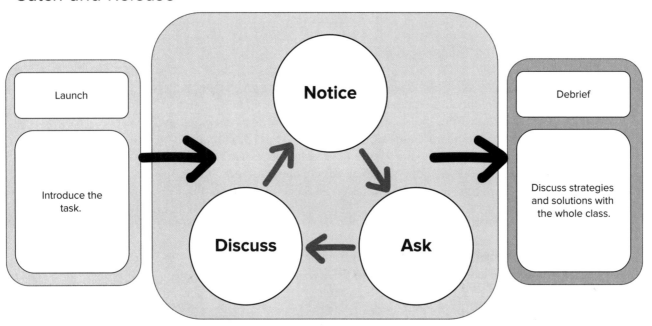

Catch-and-release is carried out as you circulate around the room observing what students are doing. It begins when students ask you a question or you notice something that is useful for the whole class to discuss in the moment.

NOTICE

As students are working, you observe an interesting strategy, representation, or emerging challenge. Or a group of students asks you a question. You get the attention of the whole class to pause engagement.

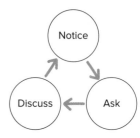

ASK

You share your observation or the group's question with the entire class.

DISCUSS

Then, the entire class discusses the observation or question. Ideas are shared among the groups. You offer insight or direction as you see fit. Then, you ask all the groups to get back to work. You resume circulating to notice something to discuss again or to solicit a question from another small group, which initiates the catch-and-release cycle all over again.

CATCH-AND-RELEASE EXAMPLES

- A teacher observes two groups that used different operations for a two-step problem, stops the class and says, "I noticed that Kelly's group added and that Colbi's group subtracted. Which operation did your group use? Why?"
- A group tells the teacher they are stuck. The teacher asks them how they represented the problem. They share that they don't know how. The teacher pauses the class and says, "Jesse's group isn't sure how to show the problem. How did your group represent it?"
- A teacher notices a group's emerging struggle, pauses the class and says, "Just checking in with everyone. Does anyone have a question to ask the whole class?"
- A teacher sees a variety of approaches that groups would benefit from and says, "Let's stop and take a look at another group's work."

KEEP THE FOCUS ON THE STUDENTS

The L-E-D model and the catch-and-release modification might feel uncomfortable because they are different from the way you might have experienced math lessons. They might feel awkward because you aren't doing all of the talking or you aren't "teaching." This is okay because a good math lesson is about what your students are doing. That is, they should be engaged, thinking, reasoning, representing, struggling, talking, and asking questions. They should be positioned to make sense of the mathematics for themselves before acquiring a specific understanding or approach. And most important, remember that a good math lesson is about thinking rather than simply getting answers.

Notes

How Do I Plan for Diverse Learners?

Students bring a variety of strengths, experiences, and learning needs to your class. You must avoid a one-size-fits-all approach. To do this, you must know each and every student as individuals and as learners (academically). This intimate knowledge shapes the action you need to take to meet their needs. Your goal is to make grade-level learning accessible. This includes unpacking vocabulary and supporting language acquisition. It also means scaffolding instructional activities so that students can acquire the math concepts. An example of a scaffold is to provide a number chart to a second grader as they learn to skip, count, or add within 100. In fourth grade a multiplication chart might be used to scaffold multidigit multiplication or finding equivalent fractions. There are many, many different ways to enhance access. The guiding principle is that you want to support access without lessening the rigor of the math content. The strategies and tips we highlight are some of the most practical and important ones for improving access to grade-level math content. As you read, you may think that these strategies and tips are good for all students. You're right! They are. But while they are good for all students, they are essential for some students, especially multilingual learners and students with special learning needs, including those who are ready for additional challenges.

There are certain strategies, such as giving more time to complete work, having students sit in the front of the room, or enlarging text, that we don't include here. But you are likely to find that these are written into a student's learning plan.

Great Resources

Chval, K., Smith, E., Trigos-Carillo, L., & Pinnow, R. (2021). *Teaching math to multilingual students, grades K–8: Positioning English learners for success.* Corwin. This is an excellent tool for learning more about how to support multilingual students.

Tip #1 : Incorporate their interests.

Connect students' interests, hobbies, favorite movie characters, favorite books, and community contexts to the math tasks you use. Knowing students and being familiar with their home communities (Ladson-Billings, 1995) enable us to plan instruction that represents students' experiences, which creates relevancy and supports access by providing a familiar anchor for the skills and concepts you teach. It also makes mathematics relevant, helping students realize that mathematics lives outside the classroom too!

Tip #2 : Position all students as leaders.

Be sure that each student has opportunities to share their perspectives and strategies with the class. This means you have to be careful not to rely on students who typically have the right answer or a traditional approach to be the featured discussion leader. It also means that students whose families have learned mathematics in other countries come with knowledge and approaches that may be different from what is traditional in the United States.

✳ Tip #3 ¦ Use and connect representations.

The value of diverse representations, especially visual representations, cannot be understated (see Representations, 156). Making connections between representations enables students to add more to their cognitive network, helping them access and use the mathematics more freely. A common misconception is that visual representations muddy the math waters for students who "just need" straightforward steps and procedures.

✳ Tip #4 ¦ Modify tasks.

Modify tasks to improve access through different entry points (see Tasks, p. 91). For example, instead of having a first grader compare 81 and 95 (which they may be challenged to do), modify the task for them to choose any two numbers to compare within 100. Find the numbers they can compare successfully, and move toward 81 and 95 as the lesson unfolds.

✳ Tip #5 ¦ Use graphic organizers.

Graphic organizers are powerful tools for presenting the relationships between concepts to help students comprehend and make connections between concepts (see Visual Tools, p. 103). These tools help students organize their thinking, support strategy use, and acquire the steps within processes for problem solving.

✳ Tip #6 ¦ Provide talk time.

Language and vocabulary develop through discussion. Each and every student must have access to unmitigated discussions with their peers to expose them to language and others' ideas, and to strengthen a community of inclusion. Provide students with structured opportunities or language routines to help them talk with one other. Having clearly defined protocols for engaging in discussions with peers and using tools such as sentence frames are helpful for students to communicate their mathematical thinking and build on the thinking of their peers (see Plan for Discourse, p. 146). Table tents that feature sentence starters or targeted vocabulary for the unit of study can be used to support student talk time.

> LAST MONTH I TRIED A STRATEGY SUGGESTED BY MY MATH COACH. INSTEAD OF USING MAINLY WHOLE-GROUP DISCUSSIONS, I INTRODUCED MY STUDENTS TO SENTENCE STEMS AND ALLOWED THEM TO SHARE THEIR THINKING WITH A PARTNER FIRST. NOW, MANY OF MY STUDENTS WHO IN THE PAST DIDN'T PARTICIPATE IN DISCUSSIONS FEEL COMFORTABLE SHARING WITH WHOLE-GROUP DISCUSSIONS.
>
> —SECOND-GRADE TEACHER

Great Resources

Zwiers, J., Diekmann, J., Rutherford-Quach, S., Daro, V., Skarin, R., Weiss, S., & Malamut, J. (2017). *Principles for the design of mathematics curricula: Promoting language and content development.* http://ell.stanford.edu/content/mathematics-resources-additional-resources. This is a great tool for learning mathematical language routines.

MANAGEMENT

Tip #7 | Revoice.

Revoicing involves repeating, restating, or clarifying students' responses using precise mathematical language while emphasizing the mathematics in their response. Use revoicing to clarify students' responses and to reinforce vocabulary and language. Revoicing models this but maintains the student's own ideas.

Tip #8 | Use and reinforce vocabulary.

Use word banks, interactive word walls, and personal math dictionaries organized by content for introducing and reinforcing math vocabulary. You can call attention to specific words as they come up during discussion and as you revoice. You can also incorporate these tools into your vocabulary instruction (see Vocabulary, p. 160).

Tip #9 | Leverage the home language, and build on it.

This tip is specific to multilingual learners. Encourage students to use translation software or glossaries to help them translate their mathematical thinking from one language to another. Work to provide opportunities for students to use their home language when possible. Consider partnering multilingual learners with classmates who speak the same language so they can discuss their ideas in both languages. Engage families to partner in this work, inviting them to reinforce meaning and concepts through both languages if possible.

SUPPORTING MATHEMATICALLY ADVANCED LEARNERS

Great Resources

Johnson, S. K., & Sheffield, L. J. (2012). *Using the Common Core State Standards for mathematics with gifted and advanced learners.* NCTM.

When we talk about mathematically advanced learners, it's important to note that this description is not limited to students who have been identified as "gifted" or "talented" based on a formal intelligence assessment or an educational IEP (individualized education plan). There is a wide range of students who exhibit high achievement and talent in the area of mathematics, including multilingual students and those with special needs. Moreover, some students can show advanced needs with certain skills or concepts rather than an entire grade-level curriculum.

You want to be sure that you don't simply give mathematically advanced learners more problems to keep them busy if they finish early. This frustrates those students and can challenge their passion for or interest in doing math. We note this because often teachers aren't sure what else to do. These tips can help:

Tip #1 | Use independent logic puzzles and strategy games.

This tip is more about early finishers than advanced learners, but it still applies. Simply have independent games, centers, and puzzles available for these students. When they are finished with their work, they don't have to do more of the same. Instead, they can practice logic and strategic thinking in a different way. The activities can be related to the skills and concepts you are teaching but don't have to be. While Sudoku is a somewhat famous example, we encourage you to look into the many options beyond it.

Tip #2 | Feature conceptual understanding, problem solving, and communication.

A common mistake is to skip or rush through topics because often, advanced students do great with procedural and computational skills. Yet the underlying conceptual understanding may be fragile or absent altogether. Advanced students can also be challenged to apply their skills to problems in different contexts or to communicate their understanding or methods. For them, the mathematics "just works." Challenge them to develop communication skills to work collaboratively with others.

Tip #3 | Provide choice.

Providing choice gives an opportunity for students to think about how they want to express their thinking and creates a self-paced element that advanced learners benefit from. Incorporate opportunities for choice in the curriculum—for example, allowing students to select a product to demonstrate their learning at the end of a unit, such as giving a presentation, using art to showcase their work, or submitting a written product. Choice boards and menus are excellent tools for student choice.

Tip #4 | Extend tasks.

As an advanced student finishes a task, ask, "What if?" This triggers a natural extension that can develop the problem into a multistep problem and so much more. Over time, the student begins to think "What if?" as they work on a task. You can encourage them to jot down some of their what-ifs and use them after the initial task is completed. This opens the door to new explorations, novelty, and student interest. For example, a student might be working on multidigit division. They solve 728 ÷ 7. The teacher asks, "What if you were dividing by 6 or 9? How would the quotient change?" Or the teacher might ask, "What if there were different problems that had the same quotient? What could those problems be?" Good extensions ask students to generalize (does that always work?) or to create new situations or problems that are similar.

Tip #5 | Enrich the content.

Provide students who show mastery of grade-level concepts with activities and assignments that enrich the content. Allow them to explore a topic in depth for deeper understanding or learn about other applications of the topic. For example, after learning about comparing fractions through a baking context, ask students to investigate the different ways in which fractions are used in carpentry or medicine. Have these students explore how the topic applies to their interests, and then have them share their findings with you and the class.

Tip #6 | Accelerate.

Acceleration is a common practice often used in gifted education programs, where students move through grade-level concepts at a faster rate than their grade-level peers. If choosing to accelerate, it is imperative to ensure that important concepts aren't skipped or rushed. Data to support this move are critical because acceleration from one grade level to another can create situations where students miss entire topics necessary for future work.

Keep in mind that this tip would be carried out most often through a unit or concept. Acceleration as in skipping to the next grade is a school-based decision that involves other teachers, administrators, and families. However, you can accelerate content when all other options are exhausted. For example, a second-grade teacher who is teaching addition and subtraction within 1,000 might accelerate an advanced group to addition and subtraction within 10,000, which is a third-grade standard. In another example, a fourth-grade teacher might have students find equivalent fractions beyond the target denominators of 2, 4, 8, 10, and so on.

COMMUNICATE YOUR MOVES

Meeting student needs is a charge of each and every teacher. Regardless of the tips you use, it is important that you communicate to the next year's teacher what you have done so that they can build on your work. This is especially true in situations where you extend or accelerate a concept, as just mentioned. But it is also helpful when you find techniques that work well with certain students.

Notes

Answers to Your Biggest Questions About Teaching Elementary Math

How Do I Close a Lesson?

Closing a lesson does not mean to pack up and push in your chair. It is a critically important cognitive activity that helps students focus on and consolidate what they have learned. For teachers, closing a lesson can be hard. Sometimes, the lesson activities, transitions, and discussions take more time than anticipated, and there is no time for closure. To avoid this, plan to end your lesson five to eight minutes early each day so that you can spend some time providing closure. Remember, you can always pause a task, provide some closure for the day, and pick up and continue the task the following day. Rushing to complete it, with or without closure, creates the likelihood of fragmented or incomplete understanding.

> SOMETIMES, MY CLOSURE WAS "PUT AWAY YOUR THINGS" BECAUSE I RAN OUT OF TIME. THEN, I STARTED SETTING A TIME TO END EARLY ENOUGH TO HAVE TIME FOR A GOOD CLOSURE.
>
> —FOURTH-GRADE TEACHER.

Sometimes, an exit ticket or similar assessment is used as closure. While this approach will give *you* information about how well your students understood the content, it doesn't necessarily help *them* make sense of it. Remember, closure is an opportunity for students to make meaning of the lesson for themselves. It is a time for them to think about what they have learned, why they learned it, and how it can be useful (Phillips, 1987). Students can also use this time to think about what happened during the lesson, what they did, or what others did that can be useful for future experiences. Notice that it is important to make meaning of the *experience*, not just the content. Connecting content and experience increases the likelihood that content will be remembered (Sousa, 2008). The highest form of closure helps students reflect, while informing you about what they understand.

ROUTINE ACTIVITIES FOR CLOSURE

Another challenge with closure can be the lack of "go-to" strategies or activities for closing the lesson. Here are some to get you started. Practice them. Make them routine. Find the ones that you and your students like best, and use them most often. Identify those that can be done somewhat quickly, and use them when the lesson runs long. Identify closure activities that take a bit longer, and reserve those for days when you have more time at the end of the lesson. Adapt routines so that they are appropriate for your students. Young students might benefit from sentence starters, modeling, or other modifications. But know that each and every learner can and should have opportunities to unpack in their own way what they have learned and reflect on it.

Identity and Agency

Giving students opportunities to reflect on their learning and their experiences helps shape their math identity and helps them process what they can do as mathematicians.

THREE FOR ONE OR ONE FOR THREE

This closure asks students to think of three things. They can identify three ideas about one of the bullets or share one idea about each of the three bullets. You can have students record their ideas in their math journals or create a recording sheet.

- Something I learned . . .
- Something I wonder . . .
- Something I might do next . . .

ONE WORD

In this closure, students identify one word that summarizes their experience (SanGiovanni et al., 2020). Students can choose to write a word about the content or vocabulary, with examples like fraction, sum, or equal. Students can also write about their actions or feelings. For example, a student might write "asked" because they asked a question when they were stuck. It's a good idea to provide examples through a word bank the first few times you use this closing activity.

Source: Ask Post-it Note by iStock/-slav-.

THAT'S WHAT

This activity prompts students to think about a "what" from the lesson. First pose a question for students to respond to, like those in the following bulleted list. After the students think of their responses, have them share. After a student shares, the class calls out together, "That's what!"

- What did you learn today?
- What was important about _____ today?
- What do you think we will do with this tomorrow?
- What if we added in chunks rather than by singles? (after a count-up lesson)
- What if we used fraction circles instead of fraction tiles? (after an equivalency lesson)
- What if we wrote the sum to a problem on the left side of an equal sign?

Have fun with it. Create more "whats" for students to think about. There is no wrong "what" to ask because the ultimate goal of this closure is to shift from thinking, "So what?" about the lesson.

GLOW AND GROW

Students are given a small sheet of paper, which they fold in half. They record what they feel confident about (their glow) and what they need additional practice with (their grow). After time to reflect and record, the students share their ideas with the class. The class celebrates glows and can be asked to share ideas about how to support classmates' grows. You collect the papers for review to inform yourself about student insights and how you might plan in the future.

Answers to Your Biggest Questions About Teaching Elementary Math

JOURNAL PROMPTS

Closure can be an independent activity without having students share out. The prompts below are just some of the journal prompts you might have students write about. Remember that these reflections should not be graded. But reading them and providing feedback is important.

- How does something you learned today connect with something you already knew?
- What are two things you learned today?
- What was your favorite part of the lesson today? Why?
- How did you use tools today in mathematics?
- What questions do you still have about today's lesson?
- What did you like about mathematics today? What didn't you like about it?
- If your parents asked what you learned today, what would you say?
- What are three math vocabulary words you used today?
- If you had to explain to a friend who is absent today, what would you tell them we did in mathematics today?
- How would you explain the mathematics you learned today to your younger brother/sister?
- Describe what you did well in mathematics today.

WHIP-AROUND

For this closing activity give students a few moments to think of something they learned or experienced during the lesson. Have them share their idea with a partner. Then, have the whole class participate in a whip-around as many students share ideas quickly. Using a ball, the student holding the ball shares their thought and then tosses the ball to another student to share their idea.

MATH DOODLES

Doodling is an excellent way to reflect. In this closure, students make a quick doodle to capture a big idea from the lesson. They might doodle the context of a word problem or the bar diagram they used to solve a problem. They might draw a ruler after a measurement lesson, a double ten frame after working with numbers to 20, or an array after a multiplication lesson. Students might also doodle something from their experience, such as playing a game with a partner, working with a group to solve the problem, or the class sitting on the carpet discussing solutions.

Notes

What Do I Need to Consider About Math Homework?

Homework and formal schooling seem inseparable. In recent years homework debates have popped up in school communities across the country. Your school district may provide explicit guidance about homework, or it may allow you to use professional judgment on whether to assign it and how much to assign. As you consider homework, here are some questions to reflect on.

HOW DOES HOMEWORK AFFECT STUDENT ACHIEVEMENT?

The research about this is rather inconclusive—especially in elementary schools. Some factors are the nature of the homework assignments, how well students learned skills and concepts before attempting the homework, and students' access to resources and support for doing homework at home. But it's hard to argue that practicing a skill or concept like addition, comparing fractions, or solving word problems isn't a good idea.

WHAT SHOULD I ASSIGN FOR HOMEWORK?

Historically, a homework assignment has been connected to the lesson of the day. However, that doesn't always make the most sense, especially when students haven't yet fully learned the skill or concept just presented. Instead, consider the following:

Homework should be . . .	Homework should not be . . .
A risk-free way to practice something that has already been taught and is somewhat understood. Spiral reviews, math puzzles, or basic-fact practice might be good options.	A tool for reteaching a skill or concept.
A purposeful way to practice a recently learned or critically important skill.	Just something to do.
An activity students can complete independently. While multiplayer games can be engaging, not all children will have a partner who is able to join them.	Something that requires significant help, teaching, or access to certain resources or adults' time at home. This isn't equitable for every child.
Minimal in quantity and maximum in quality, even if it means just one high-quality task.	Just a large number of problems to complete. If a student has incomplete understanding, repeated practice only cements misconceptions.
One of many forms of practice (see Practice, p. 123).	The only form of practice.
Additional information for you about how students are doing with a skill or concept, guiding your planning decisions.	A measure of a student's capability.

SHOULD I GRADE HOMEWORK?

Before deciding whether you should grade homework, think about some of these aspects:

- Homework should be a risk-free opportunity to practice. Grading it for accuracy undermines students' ability to practice without fear of making mistakes or being penalized for trying something they are still learning to do.
- Incomplete or inaccurate homework shouldn't jeopardize academic grades. Grades should communicate how well someone has learned something, not how thoroughly or accurately they practice and refine a new skill that will be formally assessed in the future.
- You can't be sure that any student did their homework independently. If used for an academic grade, you may be grading the work of a sibling, parent, or caregiver rather than the student.

Access and Equity

Grading homework becomes inequitable when students have varying levels of support at home.

SHOULD I GO OVER HOMEWORK IN CLASS? WHAT CAN I DO INSTEAD?

Instructional time is precious, and naturally you want to maximize it. Avoid beginning class by going over homework (see Begin Class, p. 59), because this rests on the assumption that each student completed it and did so independently. It also risks losing engagement and momentum. If you need to assess whether students completed their homework, you may opt to

- collect the homework and correct it outside of class or have a co-teacher, para-educator, or volunteer record completed homework or
- assign a student to the classroom job of checking to see if homework was completed.

> WHEN WE USED TO CHECK HOMEWORK TOGETHER AT THE BEGINNING OF CLASS, IT SUCKED UP SO MUCH TIME THAT I DIDN'T HAVE ENOUGH TIME LEFT FOR MY LESSON. NOW I LOOK OVER HOMEWORK AT ANOTHER TIME SO I CAN USE THE ENTIRE CLASS TIME TO TEACH.
>
> —FOURTH-GRADE TEACHER

If your goal is for students to determine how they have done or to receive feedback and guidance, you may want to address homework as a portion of small-group discussion or during independent time elsewhere in the lesson. To do this, you could

- go over a small subset of problems by asking students to vote on one or two problems they would like to discuss;
- post answers to the homework questions and tell the students that two answers are incorrect, then ask them to determine which ones and to share their thinking with a partner;

- have students share with a partner answers for particular questions (your choice or theirs) and explain how they found the solutions; and
- have students self-assess by reviewing the homework answers displayed on the board or with a completed copy.

WHAT DO I COMMUNICATE ABOUT HOMEWORK WITH FAMILIES?

Homework is a form of communication with caregivers. It gives them insight into what students are doing and how they're doing it. But remember, adults have done homework themselves as students and might have misconceptions about it. Here are some helpful tips to keep families and caregivers feeling engaged, informed, confident, and competent (Kreisberg & Beyranevand, 2021):

✓ Communicate the purpose of homework, and state clearly that it should be done independently and that there is no penalty for incorrect or incomplete work.

✓ Provide questions adults can use to help children if they get stuck, such as the following:
  - What don't you understand? What isn't working?
  - What have you tried to do? What else could you try to do?
  - What tools could you use to help you?
  - How are these problems like other problems you have done?

✓ Offer a suggested time limit, and encourage families to communicate to you if the homework took longer and/or why it wasn't completed.

✓ Encourage parents to communicate with you if they see student fatigue or irritability caused by homework. Ask for specifics about what may be causing the tension (e.g., the content, number of problems, type of problems).

✓ Identify one or two alternative activities (e.g., basic-fact practice) that students can do instead of homework if they are finding a certain assignment confusing or beyond their current reach.

✓ Use Google Translate to send assignments or directions to families in their first language.

Notes

chapter THREE

HOW DO I ENGAGE MY STUDENTS IN MATHEMATICS?

We've learned that engagement is not about how busy you are as a teacher during the lesson but about what your students do during the lesson. If they're not engaged, all your planning and preparation are for nothing, and you leave as the most tired person in the room. Engagement is not about singing songs or completing cute worksheets that take more time to color than time doing the math. Engagement is about kids rolling up their sleeves and breaking into a "math sweat" as they solve problems, persevere, show their thinking, and talk to grow their mathematical skills.

As we have said previously, this may be different from the math learning experiences many of us had as students. You probably remember sitting in rows and columns listening to how the teacher told you to do the math. Engagement was about taking notes and practicing the teacher's way many times. Opportunities to explore, to draw, to try out the problem first, or to talk with others were missing.

Engaging students meaningfully positions them as leaders of learning. It will feel noisy at first. You may even feel like your classroom is slightly out of control when you are not leading, directing, and telling. It's okay! In fact, it's a good thing! Math learning shouldn't be about compliance but about focused thinking, and even focused work can feel messy. Rely on the norms and structures you establish to remind students how to use tools, share materials, and work with one another. Practice letting students do the math first and allowing them to lead discussions through your questions. Be patient, and give feedback, not just about their learning but also about how they work during the lesson.

Engagement relies on interesting tasks and good problems. It calls for students to actively participate. It means that students are the ones using manipulatives and that their strategies are honored, discussed, and polished. Engagement means students are more tired after math class than you are because they did most of the work. You might be thinking that this sort of student engagement is wildly different from what you experienced. You might be thinking, "Wow, that's a lot" or "How do I even begin to do this?" This chapter answers questions about how to engage students in the learning, which include the following:

- [ ] **What does it mean to "know the math"?**
- [ ] **What should I plan to avoid? ("rules," e.g., rounding with[out] understanding)**
- [ ] **How do I select high-quality tasks?**
- [ ] **What do I need to know about manipulatives?**
- [ ] **Which manipulatives should I use?**
- [ ] **What other visual tools help students learn?**
- [ ] **How do I use literature in the math classroom?**
- [ ] **How do I teach problem solving?**
- [ ] **How do I support student thinking and reasoning?**
- [ ] **What do I do when students get stuck?**
- [ ] **How do I select and use games and centers?**

As you read about these, we encourage you to think about the following:

- [ ] **What does this mean to me?**
- [ ] **What else do I need to know about this?**
- [ ] **What will I do next?**

A popular idea of what doing math means is really just successfully plugging numbers by rote into a procedure to get an answer. But truly *knowing* mathematics is an entirely different thing. Knowing mathematics means that you can understand, retain, and transfer it to new situations. You can apply it to solving different problems. Learning mathematics today means to develop a balance of conceptual understanding, procedural fluency, and application. This may be the biggest difference between how many of us were taught mathematics and how all of us are expected to teach mathematics now. Here are some examples to illustrate what this means.

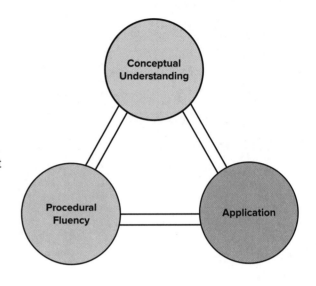

Conceptual understanding	Procedural fluency	Application
Two-digit addition (second grade)		
Students add 29 + 43 with base-ten blocks and ten frames. They understand that they are joining two quantities and see that they can also represent this joining on a number line or a hundreds chart.	To add 29 + 43, a student chooses to add up from 29, using one of several methods: • Partial products (20 + 40 + 9 + 3) • Making ten (30 + 42) • The standard algorithm	A student interprets a bar graph to find the number of people who like ice cream, seeing that 29 like chocolate ice cream and 43 prefer vanilla.
Comparing fractions (fourth grade)		
A student compares $\frac{3}{4}$ and $\frac{3}{7}$ by drawing rectangles and partitioning them. From their drawings, they can see that $\frac{3}{4}$ is closer to one whole than $\frac{3}{7}$. They are able to do the same thing for comparing $\frac{2}{5}$ and $\frac{3}{7}$.	A student compares $\frac{3}{4}$ and $\frac{3}{7}$ by relating them to $\frac{1}{2}$, but they use the common denominator procedure for comparing $\frac{2}{5}$ and $\frac{3}{7}$.	A student reads a table about the fractional lengths of different butterflies to compare and order them.

WHAT DOES KNOWING THE MATHEMATICS MEAN FOR ME?

It's important to recognize these three components of teaching and learning mathematics because math instruction historically has focused more on skills and procedures than on concepts. And application was something reserved for after learning a procedure or only for certain students who seemed to be doing well. Because of this, you may need to learn more about conceptual understanding and teaching problem solving (see Problem Solving, p. 109). Knowing the mathematics should be your students' outcome from your teaching. This also means that knowing the mathematics is where you start to plan your lessons. It may sound daunting if you don't think of mathematics as your strong suit, but here are some ways to bolster your own understanding.

KNOW HOW MATHEMATICS GROWS

As the teacher, you also need to know how the mathematics grows from year to year. If this feels overwhelming, let's break it down. First, take a look at the topics taught in the grade before yours, and study how certain topics build within the year of mathematics you are teaching. You might also wonder why this matters. Knowing previous years' content will help you build on students' understanding. It can help you identify how and what to revisit, reteach, enrich, or extend. For example, adding two-digit numbers in second grade builds on adding one-digit numbers, counting within 100, skip counting, and ideas of place value developed earlier in second grade as well as in first grade.

Great Resources

Achieve the Core. (n.d.). *Coherence map.* This is an interactive tool that connects skills and concepts across grades. Your curriculum is also likely to offer something similar.

KNOW THE MATHEMATICS TO ESTABLISH THE LEARNING TARGETS

Often, the standards within your curriculum are big; they are end goals. That is, they are made up of a collection of smaller skills and strategies that come together to create the standard. Knowing how a standard can be broken up and developed over time lets you create short-term learning targets. Look back to the idea of comparing fractions in fourth grade. The actual standard might call for students to compare fractions with a set of different strategies. The image on the next page shows the big ideas embedded in that standard. Each of those becomes learning targets for individual lessons or potentially a cluster of lessons.

Great Resources

NCTM's *Developing Essential Understanding for Teaching Mathematics.* These are an informational series as they unpack big mathematical ideas.

Great Resources

Van de Walle, J., Lovin, L., Karp, K., & Bay-Williams, J. (2019). *Teaching student-centered-mathematics: Developmentally appropriate instruction for grades pre-K–2.* Pearson. This book, which is often referred to as "the Van de Walle book," is an exceptional resource for helping you develop a deep understanding of the mathematics you are teaching.

ENGAGEMENT

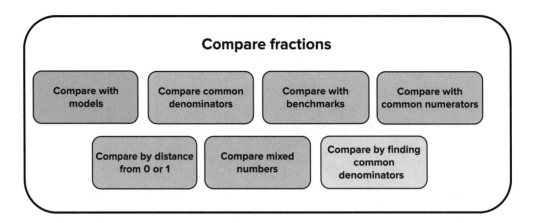

KNOW THE MATHEMATICS TO ANTICIPATE STUDENT THINKING

This is possibly the most important part of knowing the mathematics. Anticipating what students might do with a task or a problem is an important teaching skill to develop. You will see it pop up throughout this book. When anticipating, you think about the strategies students might use, the representations they might draw, the reasoning they might share, and even the errors they might make. Anticipating these prepares you to respond to them intentionally. It helps you think about which ideas you would want students to discuss and the order in which you want to discuss them (see Plan for Discourse, p. 146). Anticipating might feel overwhelming too, because you can't possibly predict everything they might do. You're right. You can't. But these tips should help with anticipation:

> NO ONE EVER TAUGHT ME TO ANTICIPATE, BUT ONCE I STARTED TO, MY LESSONS WENT MUCH BETTER. I FELT LIKE I WAS BETTER PREPARED FOR WHAT MY STUDENTS COULD DO.
>
> —FOURTH-GRADE TEACHER

Tip #1 | Do the task first.

This helps you think about how you would solve it, and will help you think about how they might solve it.

Tip #2 | Know your students.

Continue to learn about who they are. This will help you think about how they see things and the strategies they most often use.

Tip #3 | Consider what they know.

Think about what they have already learned this year and what they probably learned in previous years.

Tip #4 | Plan with others.

Collaborative planning will expose you to others' ideas and experiences with the content.

Tip #5 | Don't spend too much time.

There are lots of things you need to do to be a teacher. Anticipate what students will do, but don't spend too much time on it. Target a few thoughts, and know that it gets easier with practice and you get sharper with experience.

Notes

ENGAGEMENT

What Should I Plan to Avoid?

There are certain practices still commonly seen in math teaching that are actually better to stay away from. These are instructional devices or strategies that are often taught to simplify the mathematics or make it "easier." These are the rules, tricks, and catchy sayings that may help students arrive more directly at a correct answer, but they do not lead to conceptual understanding. Also, as mathematics becomes more complex, many of these devices no longer apply. Teachers use these particular instructional methods with the best intentions, and they may produce short-term gains, but they also have the potential to cause more harm than good for students over time, especially when they reduce the need to reason and problem solve.

STAY CLEAR OF SHORTCUTS

Shortcuts are what we use to get to the end result faster. One example of a shortcut in mathematics that needs to be avoided is keywords (see Problem Solving, p. 109). *Keywords* is a shortcut strategy that encourages students to look for words that serve as a "signal" to indicate what operation to use to solve a word problem. The use of keywords becomes a procedure that students apply, as it tends to follow an "if this, then this" structure. It sends an unintentional message to students to not consider the context or situation but just grab the numbers from the problem and compute according to what the keyword signals them to do. By doing so, students will not apply their own thinking and reasoning to solve problems. And many, many problems in academic mathematics and in life do not follow a pattern. This shortcut and others too often lead students to jump to the wrong conclusions.

STAY CLEAR OF RHYMES AND CATCHY SAYINGS

Rhymes and catchy sayings are often utilized as a novel way for students to remember something. In mathematics, these quick phrases tend to proceduralize the mathematics, without emphasizing conceptual understanding. Students repeat the phrases and carry out a set of steps, often not understanding the "why" behind what they are doing. Here are some commonly used phrases to avoid:

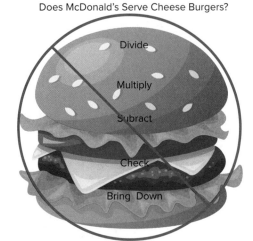

Source: iStock/Valentina Semenovich.

- *Five and Above Give It a Shove!* (rounding; regrouping in multidigit subtraction)
- *Ask your MOMA* (two-digit by two-digit multiplication)
- *Does McDonald's Serve Cheese Burgers?* (steps for long division)
- *Please Excuse My Dear Aunt Sally*, or PEMDAS (order of operations)

Instead of using rhymes or sayings that don't promote sense making, consider ways to help your students construct understanding through the use of manipulatives (see Manipulatives, p. 95), representations (see Representations, p. 156), and discourse (see Plan for Discourse, p. 146).

STAY CLEAR OF RULES THAT DON'T ALWAYS APPLY

It is sometimes tempting to overgeneralize a mathematical rule in an attempt to make the mathematics easier for students. This is often done with the good intent of helping students get to the correct answer in a more simplistic way. However, a number of these rules break down in different situations. For example, one overgeneralized rule used with students is "To multiply any number times 10, add a 0." While this rule may work for 35×10, it doesn't for a problem such as 0.86 $\times 10$. Another rule that doesn't hold true is "You can't subtract a bigger number from a smaller number." In the case of $10 - 30$, the answer is -20, so this rule falls apart once students learn about negative numbers. Another overgeneralized rule is "You have to start on the right to add." For a problem like $538 + 275$, students can be very successful when adding the hundreds, the tens, and then the ones, followed by adding the subtotals together to find the sum. This method, which begins with adding the digits that are on the far left first, contradicts the aforementioned "rule." The rules mentioned here, and others, become "hit-or-miss" rules and do not encourage students to apply their thinking and reasoning to the mathematical contexts.

STAY CLEAR OF IMPRECISE OR INCORRECT VOCABULARY

Mathematicians use precise mathematical vocabulary. It is important that you and our students do the same. If not, students may end up using multiple different terms for one, single mathematical word as they progress through elementary school. Just think what might happen if students' first-grade teacher calls the "greater than" and "less than" signs an alligator, their second-grade teacher calls them a shark, and their third-grade teacher calls the symbols a crab whose claw grabs the larger number. Over three years, most likely the students will come to believe that "greater than" and "less than" have something to do with water animals that eat the larger number, but they will not fully understand the meanings of the "greater than" and "less than" symbols. This becomes problematic when these students encounter an expression such as $n > b$ in middle school, as they won't be able to draw generalizations about the value of n or the value of b.

Make sure to use the correct vocabulary and use it frequently so that students come to understand what the term means. Students are capable of learning precise vocabulary at a very young age, so feel free to start using precise mathematical language from the start.

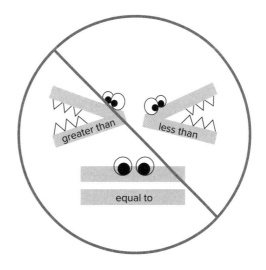

Here are some examples of imprecise terms to try not to use in your classroom:

- "Take away sign" for a minus sign
- "Borrow" for trading or regrouping when subtracting multidigit numbers
- "Diamond" instead of rhombus
- "Slanted square" instead of parallelogram

STAY CLEAR OF CHECKLISTS FOR PROBLEM SOLVING

In an effort to make problem solving easier, checklists were developed to lead students through a series of steps to solve a problem. One example of this is the CUBES strategy. Each letter stands for a step the student should follow: C = circle the numbers, U = underline the question, and so on. This strategy fails to promote understanding and has the potential to fall apart when there are different interpretations of what each letter stands for. There are other variations of checklists that have been created to guide students through thinking about a problem. All of these lists of steps fail to support the type of thinking students need to take part in as they solve math problems. It is important to remember that students need to be engaged in authentic thinking about the problem situation and context, rather than be encouraged to robotically complete a series of steps to arrive at the answer (see Problem Solving, p. 109).

> I THOUGHT IT WAS USEFUL TO GIVE MY STUDENTS A LIST OF STEPS TO FOLLOW WHEN THEY SOLVED PROBLEMS. I REALIZED THIS DIDN'T HELP THEM MAKE SENSE OF THE PROBLEM, SO NOW I HELP THEM DO *THAT* INSTEAD.
>
> —FIFTH-GRADE TEACHER

Notes

How Do I Select High-Quality Tasks?

When selecting a task, it is important to select rich tasks in which all students can engage in relevant, rigorous, and meaningful mathematics. Not all tasks are equal. A high-quality task piques students' curiosity while also provoking productive struggle. It is in this struggle that you are pushing their thinking and helping them work through authentic problem solving.

> EARLY IN MY CAREER I DIDN'T THINK ABOUT THE QUALITY OF A TASK. I FIGURED IT WAS MY JOB TO MAKE A DULL TASK FUN AND ENJOYABLE. I DIDN'T REALIZE THAT THE TASK SPARKED THE LEARNING.
>
> —THIRD-GRADE TEACHER

To determine if a task is a worthwhile rich task, consider the following criteria:

Characteristics of rich math tasks	What it means to you
Has a meaningful context	• Your students can relate to the context of the problem. • It relates to mathematics used in the real world.
Aligns to the math standards	• It is aligned to grade-level essential standards. • Opportunities to assess those standards formatively are provided throughout the task.
Encourages use of multiple representations	• Students can understand the mathematics through various representations. • It doesn't dictate which representations to use. • See page 156 for more about representations.
Provides opportunities to communicate reasoning	• It asks students to justify their thinking (but not in formulaic words or sentences). • See pages 146 and 153 for more about student reasoning.
Has multiple entry points	• It offers different ways to access, represent, begin, or solve the problem.
Has multiple solution paths	• There are different ways for students to solve the problem or complete the task.
Requires cognitive effort	• Thinking or reasoning is needed to solve the problem or complete the task. • It requires more than basic recall.

HOW WILL I KNOW IF THE TASK HAS A MEANINGFUL CONTEXT?

Putting math concepts and problems in context helps students make sense of the mathematics by anchoring it to a familiar, real-world setting. If students struggle to understand the context, they will not ever get to the mathematics. Typically, the most

ENGAGEMENT

engaging and relevant tasks connect to your students' interests and experiences. At every grade level, taking the time to do an interest survey on topics students both enjoy and are curious about helps in your task selection process. Tasks need to be age appropriate for students so that they have some background knowledge to bring to the table. Another opportunity for relevancy is to connect tasks to the cultures of your students (see Culturally Relevant, p. 22). Knowing your students helps you find culturally related tasks or adapt existing tasks to fit your community of learners. Here are some prompts to think about when selecting tasks:

1 What do you know about the communities your students live in, and how can you connect them to mathematics?
2 What careers exist in your community, and what mathematics do they involve?
3 How do students already engage with mathematics at home or with their families?
4 What experiences have your students had in previous grades that they can connect new math learning to?
5 What trends in pop culture do your students love that you can connect to mathematics?

WHAT DOES IT MEAN FOR A TASK TO HAVE MULTIPLE ENTRY POINTS?

High-quality tasks are often said to have low floors and high ceilings, which means that they allow for all students to have an entry point (low floor) but are rigorous enough for all students to have to grapple with some complexity in the mathematics (high ceiling). Here is an example:

The 1,2,3,4 Challenge: Using only the numbers 1, 2, 3, and 4 once, write equations that equal the numbers 0 through 20. You only need one equation for each of the numbers to complete this challenge. You can use any mathematical operations or symbols that can help you. For example, $3 \times 4 + 1 - 2 = 11$.

WHAT DOES IT MEAN TO HAVE MULTIPLE SOLUTION PATHWAYS?

When you were a student, your teacher may have shown you how to solve a problem, and your job was to replicate the process. There was seemingly only one correct way and one right answer. This is a form of mimicking and is a very common experience in learning mathematics in school. But it requires very little thinking, if any. When using high-quality tasks with students, the goal is to get them thinking and reasoning, and you will see that there are many ways to solve the problem. Some may be more or less efficient than others, but they all are viable solution paths. Consider this example:

Giselle says 23×45 is greater than 1,000. Do you agree or disagree with her? Explain or show your thinking.

This example shows different solutions and representations for $23 \times 45 = ?$. You see an area model in the upper left, equal groups in the upper right, partial products in the lower left, and the standard algorithm in the lower right.

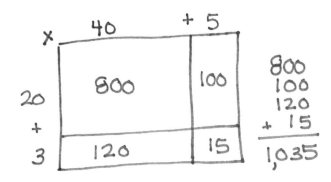

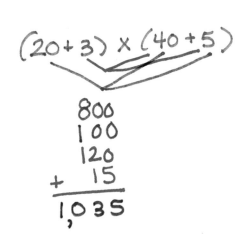

WHERE DO I FIND HIGH-QUALITY TASKS ALIGNED TO MY GRADE-LEVEL STANDARDS?

High-quality tasks are embedded in high-quality curriculum materials. The richest tasks are often set at the beginning and at the end of a unit within your curriculum materials. You can also find high-quality tasks in books and on some online resources that we have listed in the reference list at the end of this book.

Great Resources

Classroom-Ready Rich Math Tasks series (Corwin, 2021).

Use the examples below to evaluate the tasks in the resources you currently have to help you select:

Not a high-quality task	High-quality task
Miguel wanted to have a fundraiser to buy new carpeting for his school library. The library is 25 feet long and 45 feet wide. How many square feet of carpeting will he need? Use the standard algorithm to show how you arrived at your answer.	Your class wants to hold a fundraiser to buy new carpeting for your school library. 1 How much carpeting would you need for the whole library? 2 What will it cost? 3 How will you go about raising the money?
• One way to get to the answer • A one-step problem • Unrelated to the students	• Has a meaningful context (solving a problem within their school community) • Aligns to the math standards (students use measurement, fraction, and decimal computation) • Encourages the use of multiple representations • There are multiple entry points to start this problem • Provides opportunities to communicate student reasoning (students will discuss size, cost, and fundraising ideas) • Requires cognitive effort

But remember, you need to make use of high-quality tasks every day, and elaborate tasks like the school library task should be balanced with less elaborate but still high-quality tasks that focus on specific skills and concepts. You can do this by turning what may appear in your resources as somewhat low-level activities into higher-quality tasks. The table below gives you an idea of how to modify tasks to increase thinking, reasoning, struggle, and discussion.

Great Resources

Smith, M., Bill, V., & Steele, M. D. (2020). *On-your-feet guide: Modifying mathematical tasks.* Corwin.

Original task	Modified task
Ten problems of two-digit addition (e.g., 49 + 32)	The sum of two numbers is 91. What could those numbers be?
Complete the pattern in each. 5, 10, 15, _____, 25, _____, _____, 40 30, 40, _____, _____, _____, 80, 90 100, 200, 300, _____, 500, _____, _____	Make a pattern that counts by fives, tens, or hundreds. Make a pattern that begins with 31 and counts by fives, tens, and hundreds.
Write the fraction each figure represents. *(figures: square divided in fourths, rectangle divided in fifths, triangle divided into four parts)*	Represent $\frac{3}{5}$ in four different ways. Label your representations to tell how they show the fraction.
Find the sum of each. 3,128 + 5,750 = _____ 7,034 + 2,355 = _____ 8,790 + 1,014 = _____	Jake found the sum of 3,128 + 5,750 by adding 3,000 + 5,000 + 100 + 700 + 20 + 50 + 8 + 0. Gina found it by adding 3,128 + 5,000 + 700 + 50. How are their two strategies the same? How are they different?

What Do I Need to Know About Manipulatives?

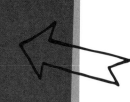

Manipulatives help students see the mathematics. They allow students to explore ideas, and they enable the math practices (see Math Practices, p. 33) to come alive as students use these tools to solve problems, model concepts, and explain their thinking. It is easy to overlook their value if you already understand the mathematics abstractly or if you didn't use them when you were a student. You might be teaching upper elementary grades and believe that manipulatives lose value as students get older. They don't! You might be unfamiliar with them or how to use them. That's okay! Or you might be unsure how to introduce, organize, or manage them. Here are a few "manipulative must-knows."

Tip #1 Students must be the ones to use them.

Manipulatives can inadvertently become teacher demonstration tools, which undercuts the purpose of supporting student exploration of concepts. They should be in the students' hands.

Tip #2 They are tools for making sense of the mathematics.

The manipulatives themselves have no answers in them. Students have to make their own meanings and find their own solutions, using manipulatives as a tool to help them "see" the problem.

Tip #3 They are not a "crutch."

Manipulatives are sometimes viewed as a tool for someone who isn't capable of doing paper-and-pencil, or abstract, mathematics. This isn't true. Manipulatives help students make sense of abstract mathematics so that they understand it, remember it, and use it.

> WHEN I FIRST STARTED TEACHING, I DIDN'T USE MANIPULATIVES BECAUSE I THOUGHT THEY WERE A NIGHTMARE TO MANAGE! NOW I REALIZE HOW IMPORTANT THEY ARE IN HELPING STUDENTS MAKE SENSE OF MATHEMATICAL IDEAS AND USE THEM ALL THE TIME.
>
> —SECOND-GRADE TEACHER

Tip #4 Avoid using connection making as a linear process.

You may hear about a concrete > representational (semiconcrete) > abstract process for learning a concept, in which students learn something with manipulatives, then with pictures and diagrams, before moving to abstract or symbolic representations.

ENGAGEMENT

Today, we know this process isn't linear. Instead, let students use all representations and make connections among them.

Tip #5: Learn how they work.

Great Resources

Hands-On Standards: Teaching Math With Manipulatives [Hand-2-Mind, 2021]; Moore, S. D., & Rimbey, K. A. (2021). *Mastering math manipulatives, grades 4–8.* Corwin.

Take a few minutes to play with them, and use them for a problem before your students do. This is especially helpful if you didn't have access to them when you were a student. Read about them online or in the many math resources that include them. Ask a trusted colleague about how certain tools work and how that person uses them. Be careful not to create rules for using manipulatives that may limit understanding. For example, ten frames don't have to be filled from left to right and top to bottom. Eight is eight no matter how it is represented.

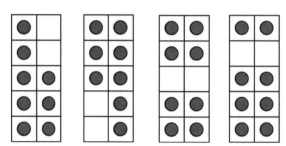

Tip #6 Introduce them through play and exploration.

Give students time to play with a manipulative before they use it. As they explore, ask them these questions:

- What might you use this tool for?
- How do you think the manipulative works?
- What do you notice about it?
- What do you wonder about it?
- Have you ever used this tool before?

Keep in mind that even though some tools are used in different grades, you still want to give students this opportunity to explore them the first time you use them each year. Another way to provide exploration time is to make the tools available during indoor recess and independent, center time.

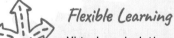

Flexible Learning

Virtual manipulatives are perfect alternatives that can be used for distance learning as well as in-person learning. You can search online for virtual manipulatives or visit the Math Learning Center, Didax Virtual Manipulatives, or Toy Theater sites. Introduce these in the same ways you would physical manipulatives.

Tip #7 Make them available and accessible.

Make sure your students can access manipulatives whenever they decide the tools are needed. Use bins or plastic tubs to store them. Label those tubs, and try to keep them in a place where students can find them and reach them. Make sure students know that they can leave their seats and get a tool if they deem it useful. If possible, create personal manipulative kits for students that they can house in pencil boxes or something similar and keep in their desks or take home to support homework.

Tip # 8 Provide choices.

Most manipulatives can be used in a variety of ways, and most skills and concepts can likewise be modeled in a variety of ways. Let students choose the tools that best help them understand. During class debriefing discussions, highlight how the different tools used connect to the concept or problem. This discussion helps students see mathematics from different perspectives.

Tip #9 Encourage them, don't require them.

Ultimately, you want students to develop an abstract, symbolic understanding of mathematics. As students progress toward this, don't require them to keep using manipulatives when they aren't needed. Instead, monitor for student struggle and encourage them to use a tool. Using manipulatives is likely more necessary when first learning about a concept; allow students to continue to use them as often as they like to revisit mathematical ideas.

Tip #10 Expect responsibility.

Develop classroom norms (see Community, p. 19) with your students that set expectations for how students are to work with manipulatives. Ask students to identify what it means to use tools well and what it doesn't mean. Be sure that the norms include cleaning up when done, putting the manipulatives in their correct buckets, only taking what you need, taking care of the tools, and using them!

Tip #11 Be clever with limited supplies.

You might have limited supplies of manipulatives. Have students work with partners or in small groups for tasks and problems that will likely require certain tools with limited supply. Reach out to other teachers in other teams. Most manipulatives can be used with a variety of topics in different grades. It's likely that a teacher in another grade can lend your class what they need.

Tip #12 Examine them carefully.

Even though manipulatives have common names, different brands may come in different colors or slightly different sizes. Any of them can be used. Just be careful not to mingle different sets, as the differences may confuse students.

Tip #13 Print and cut, or make your own.

Many manipulatives, like pattern blocks, fraction tiles, and even base-ten blocks, can be printed and cut when they are in short supply. Use cardstock or heavy bond paper so that they can be used more than once. Enlist parent volunteers to help cut them out, or have students do it themselves. Also know that you can make many manipulatives. For example, a ten frame can be made from an egg carton, and base-ten blocks can be made by gluing beans on a craft stick.

Identity and Agency

Giving students choice about when to use manipulatives as well as about what manipulatives to use fosters their math identity and agency.

Tip #14 | **Send them home.**

Those printed versions can be sent home to help students as they work on homework or play games with their families. Make sure you don't assign homework that requires specific manipulatives unless you can supply a take-home version.

Tip #15 | **Show parents how to use them.**

It's likely that parents and caregivers are unfamiliar with manipulatives too. Encourage your students to teach their families how to use them. Make manipulative conversations a focus of Mathematics and Muffins (see Engage Families, p. 45), or work with colleagues to create a manipulative-based Math Night.

Notes

Which Manipulatives Should I Use?

Manipulatives are concrete representations that help students visualize and make sense of mathematics. Manipulatives can be used by themselves, or you can pair them with dry erase boards so that students can redraw or diagram what they see and think. You might also use them with work mats and other organizers (see Visual Tools, p. 103).

Flexible Learning

Virtual manipulatives are excellent for distance learning and in-person learning. You can search online for virtual manipulatives or visit the Math Learning Center, Didax Virtual Manipulatives, or Toy Theater sites.

GO-TO MUST-HAVE MANIPULATIVES

There are many, many types of manipulatives. You likely don't have them all, nor do you need them all. These are some go-to or must-have manipulatives you should be familiar with:

Manipulative	Useful for (grade range)	What you should know about it
Ten frames and two-color counters *Source:* From Moore and Rimbey (2021).	Representing numbers (K–2) Breaking apart numbers (K–2) Addition and subtraction (K–1) Basic facts (K–1)	Use two-color counters to show how to decompose a number. Use a double ten frame to work with numbers up to 20. Vary how numbers are represented.

(*continued*)

ENGAGEMENT

(continued)

Manipulative	Useful for (grade range)	What you should know about it
Rekenrek *Source:* From Moore and Rimbey (2021).	Number concepts (K–2) Addition and subtraction (K–1) Basic facts (K–1)	Rekenreks work well to show numbers up to 10 and 20. You can pair them with ten frames to reinforce different ways to show a number.
Bead strings *Source:* iStock/Roman Prysiazhniuk.	Number concepts (K–2) Addition and subtraction (1–2)	Bead strings work well with numbers within 100. Each color is a group of 10. Use them to help students count on or back by 10.
Assorted counters *Source:* From Moore and Rimbey (2021).	Number concepts (K–1) Addition and subtraction (K–1)	You can have students use assorted counters to sort by color, shape, or object. The counters are useful for counting and representing addition and subtraction.
Dominos *Source:* iStock/Michael Burrell.	Number concepts (K–1) Addition and subtraction (K–2)	Dominos are great for representing numbers. Students can find the total or the difference between two parts of the domino. Dominos can be sorted to find those that have the same total or the same difference.

Manipulative	Useful for (grade range)	What you should know about it
Base-ten blocks *Source:* From Moore and Rimbey (2021).	Place value (1–5) Comparison (1–5) Addition and subtraction (1–5)	Have students explore how to make numbers in different ways with base-ten blocks. For example, 37 can be shown as 2 tens and 17 ones. Know that the tens don't have to be shown to the left of the ones. A challenge with base-ten blocks is that the tens (and hundreds) don't separate. It can be challenging for students to recognize that 10 ones is the same as a rod.
Connecting cubes *Source:* From Moore and Rimbey (2021).	Counting (K–1) Making tens (1–3) Addition and subtraction (K–3) Measurement (K–4) Fractions (3–5)	Connecting cubes can be used to make measuring sticks. They can be bundled to make groups of tens and ones. They're useful because the groups of 10 can be broken apart. Use two different colors to show combinations of numbers. These cubes are also great for modeling fractions. A stick of three blue and five yellow cubes is three-eighths blue.
Pattern blocks *Source:* From Moore and Rimbey (2021).	Geometry (K–5) Fractions (3–5)	The yellow hexagon can represent one whole. Two hexagons can be put together to make a whole. When doing this, the red trapezoid changes from a half to a fourth.
Place-value discs	Place value (3–5) Comparison (3–5) Addition and subtraction (3–5) Decimals (4–5)	Place-value discs are good for showing larger numbers that would require too many base-ten blocks. Often, they're more appropriate for upper grades than in lower grades.
Color tiles *Source:* From Moore and Rimbey (2021).	Geometry (K–5) Area and perimeter (3–5) Fractions (3–5)	Color tiles are 1-inch-square tiles, which makes them ideal for measurement activities. In addition to being used as game pieces, they can be used for pattern activities, for perimeter and area, and for modeling fraction concepts.

THERE WERE HUNDREDS OF CONNECTING CUBES IN MY CLASSROOM WHEN I STARTED, AND I WASN'T SURE HOW I WOULD USE THEM. IT TURNS OUT THEY WORK FOR ABOUT EVERYTHING. I USE THEM ALL OF THE TIME!

—FIRST-GRADE TEACHER

ENGAGEMENT

(continued)

(continued)

Manipulative	Useful for (grade range)	What you should know about it
Cuisenaire rods *Source:* From Moore and Rimbey (2021).	Fractions (3–5) Multiplicative comparison (4–5) Number combinations (1) Measurement (K–5) Problem solving (K–5)	Rods can be combined to equal the length of other rods. The length ranges from 10 cm (orange rod) to 1 cm (white). They work well with fractions as you can change the size of the whole and make equivalents in a variety of ways. They can be used for combinations of 10 and can even be used to show bar diagrams.
Fraction tiles *Source:* iStock/Nataliia Tymofieieva.	Fractions (3–5)	Two sets can be put together to show fractions greater than 1. Look for tiles that aren't labeled, or consider having students use the unlabeled side.
Ten-sided dice *Source:* iStock/kira_an.	Any topic (K–5)	Six-sided dice limit the numbers students can use. Ten-sided dice let them make any number. They can use two to make random two-digit numbers and three for three-digit numbers.

Notes

What Other Visual Tools Help Students Learn?

Having students diagram or sketch their thinking is an excellent way to help them make sense of the mathematics. Certain tools, like hundreds charts and number lines, are used frequently and productively to organize and support student thinking. Though students might be able to sketch and use tools on paper or in their math journals, we have found that these also become useful work mats or graphic organizers. Graphic organizers for problem solving (see Problem Solving, p. 109) would also make good additions to the collection.

TIPS FOR USING THESE TOOLS

1. Copy and laminate the tools so that they can be reused with dry erase markers.
2. Make two-sided copies to limit the number of tools needed.
3. Let students use manipulatives or draw pictures as needed with a variety of mats, such as ten frame mats, place-value mats, and more.
4. Use mats together. For example, use a hundreds chart, a number line, and/or a place-value mat together.
5. Make a large "posterized" teacher version that matches the student versions and can be used with groups of students.
6. Modify the downloadable versions provided in the following table to suit the needs of you and your students.

Flexible Learning

You can screenshot images of graphic organizers and work mats and use the image in a Jamboard or something similar so that students can interact with these resources virtually.

ENGAGEMENT

Ten frame mats: Ten frames show numbers up to 10. Use multiple ten frames to show numbers up to 20, 30, or more. Keep in mind that there are no rules for how to show a number. For example, 8 can be shown with a column of 5 and 3 ones or two groups of 4 ones.	**Ten Frames**
Hundreds charts: 1–100 charts should be in every primary class. Use 101–201, 201–301, and other charts in later grades for students to make connections. Bottom-up hundreds charts (Bay-Williams & Fletcher, 2017), like the one shown here, are also good to consider.	**Bottom Up Hundred Chart (1-100)**

Ten Frames

Bottom Up Hundred Chart (1-100)

91	92	93	94	95	96	97	98	99	100
81	82	83	84	85	86	87	88	89	90
71	72	73	74	75	76	77	78	79	80
61	62	63	64	65	66	67	68	69	70
51	52	53	54	55	56	57	58	59	60
41	42	43	44	45	46	47	48	49	50
31	32	33	34	35	36	37	38	39	40
21	22	23	24	25	26	27	28	29	30
11	12	13	14	15	16	17	18	19	20
1	2	3	4	5	6	7	8	9	10

Place-value mats:

Place-value mats help students see the number of hundreds, tens, or ones. They can be adjusted for more place values and can include decimals.

Place Value Mat

Hundreds	Tens	Ones

Part-part-whole mats:

These mats are perfect for showing number decomposition and also serve as good models for solving addition and subtraction word problems.

Part-Part-Whole Mat

Part	Part

Whole

Number bonds:

Number bonds are a way to show how to break apart a number. For example, 100 can be broken into 99 and 1, 50 and 50, or 70 and 30. In later grades, they can be used with fractions or decimals. And know that students can (and should) break numbers into three parts, which would add another circle to the model.

Number Bonds

Decimal charts:

Decimal charts are adaptations of hundreds charts that show the hundredths between 0.01 and 1.00. They can be adjusted in the same ways as mentioned for hundreds charts, including bottom-up versions and 2.01–3.00 versions.

Decimal Chart (.01-1.00)

.01	.02	.03	.04	.05	.06	.07	.08	.09	.10
.11	.12	.13	.14	.15	.16	.17	.18	.19	.20
.21	.22	.23	.24	.25	.26	.27	.28	.29	.30
.31	.32	.33	.34	.35	.36	.37	.38	.39	.40
.41	.42	.43	.44	.45	.46	.47	.48	.49	.50
.51	.52	.53	.54	.55	.56	.57	.58	.59	.60
.61	.62	.63	.64	.65	.66	.67	.68	.69	.70
.71	.72	.73	.74	.75	.76	.77	.78	.79	.80
.81	.82	.83	.84	.85	.86	.87	.88	.89	.90
.91	.92	.93	.94	.95	.96	.97	.98	.99	.100

Number lines:

Number lines are essential for understanding number relationships and showing strategies for computing. Number lines can be ticked by ones or tens for younger students. Empty number lines and number lines for fractions are also good tools.

Number Lines

Decimal grids and grid paper:

These can be used for showing decimals but also work well to show multiplication and the area or perimeter of figures. Centimeter grid paper provides a larger area for students to work with.

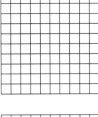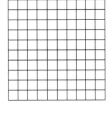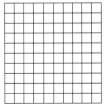

Addition and multiplication charts:

These charts have obvious applications. Individual laminated copies allow students to look for patterns, record problems, and make other notations. Consider shading out or removing sums and products of known facts so the charts are only used for facts students haven't yet mastered.

Addition Chart

+	0	1	2	3	4	5	6	7	8	9	10
0	0	1	2	3	4	5	6	7	8	9	10
1	1	2	3	4	5	6	7	8	9	10	11
2	2	3	4	5	6	7	8	9	10	11	12
3	3	4	5	6	7	8	9	10	11	12	13
4	4	5	6	7	8	9	10	11	12	13	14
5	5	6	7	8	9	10	11	12	13	14	15
6	6	7	8	9	10	11	12	13	14	15	16
7	7	8	9	10	11	12	13	14	15	16	17
8	8	9	10	11	12	13	14	15	16	17	18
9	9	10	11	12	13	14	15	16	17	18	19
10	10	11	12	13	14	15	16	17	18	19	20

Digit cards and number cards:

Digit cards or number cards are indispensable. It is wise to have a set or two for each student. They are perfect for playing games or generating numbers randomly.

0	1	2
3	4	5
6	7	8
9		

Triangle fact cards:

Triangle fact cards represent the inverse relationship between addition/subtraction and multiplication/division. These cards are good for a variety of centers and activities. Students can use a card and write related equations or draw pictures of the facts. You can remove one of the numbers or cover it with a sticker (or your finger) and ask students to find the missing number.

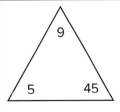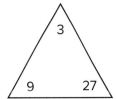

I DIDN'T KNOW ABOUT TRIANGLE FACT CARDS BEFORE I STARTED TEACHING, BUT NOW I USE THEM ALL OF THE TIME. THEY HELP STUDENTS THINK ABOUT HOW MULTIPLICATION AND DIVISION ARE RELATED.

—THIRD-GRADE TEACHER

What Other Visual Tools Help Students Learn?

How Do I Use Literature in the Math Classroom?

Identity and Agency

Using culturally diverse literature promotes student identity and agency. Through stories, students connect their own experiences to the concepts a story explores, and expand their view of who is a mathematician.

Integrating children's literature in the math classroom is a powerful way to promote, reinforce, and support student learning. This is especially important because

- students hear and make sense of math-specific vocabulary through authentic stories—particularly when learning terms that only hold special mathematical meaning;
- storytelling is a way to integrate multiple content areas and help students make practical applications and connections;
- selecting diverse literature exposes students to a variety of multicultural characters and settings and allows all students to view themselves as doers of math;
- incorporating literature in the classroom allows you to provide a nonthreatening introduction, explanation, and/or extension of a math skill or concept;
- using authentic children's literature in the math classroom also helps students experience the wonder, joy, and beauty of mathematics and emphasizes reasoning and sense making;

Using literature in the math classroom can also help you do the following:

- Introduce new topics and vocabulary
- Introduce, explain, or extend a math skill or concept in a nonthreatening way
- Pre-assess skills and understanding
- Connect with children's previous experience
- Address misconceptions
- Help students apply mathematics to the world outside of school, such as making connections among concepts, to other math topics, or to other disciplines

Great Resource

Monroe, E. E., Young, T. A., Fuentes, D. S., & Dial, O. H. (2018). *Deepening students' mathematical understanding with children's literature.* NCTM. This is a good resource for understanding how to use children's literature authentically to broaden the purposes of learning mathematics and to develop mathematical understanding.

> I USED TO THINK THAT LITERATURE BOOKS WERE ONLY FOR YOUNGER STUDENTS UNTIL I SAW MY MENTOR TEACHER USE THE BOOK *SOLVING FOR M* WITH HER FIFTH-GRADERS. I HAVE A STUDENT WHO LOVES ART AND IS A BEAUTIFUL WRITER. I WOULD LIKE TO START A BOOK/MATH CLUB TO PICK HER BRAIN AND THEN CREATE A SIMILAR JOURNAL CONCEPT.
>
> —FIFTH-GRADE TEACHER

WHAT KIND OF LITERATURE CAN I USE IN THE MATH CLASSROOM?

Integrating children's literature in your classroom starts with selecting a good book. You'll find a large number of children's books written with an obvious math focus (some even have *mathematics* in the title). Most important, you should choose a book that features mathematics or provides a context or purpose for learning a math skill or concept, such as the following:

- In *Baby Goes to Market* by Atinuke and Angela Brooksbank, the author tells the story of Baby's trip to an outdoor African market with Mom. Young students will delight in reading the beautifully illustrated book while practicing counting as they count the food treats Baby eats while riding in the basket on Mom's back. You can also use the story to explore basic addition and subtraction by finding out how many treats Baby received in all and determining how many treats are left after Baby samples one of each treat.
- *The Very Hungry Caterpillar* by Eric Carle is a popular book for primary students. Though it is not specifically about mathematics, you can use it to set a context for learning mathematics. For example, after reading the book, you might have young students determine how many pieces of fruit the caterpillar ate during the week; or you might use it to begin a geometry lesson where students create their own caterpillars using pattern blocks to practice composing shapes. You could use it to introduce measurement by having students create caterpillars on paper and then using string and rulers to measure the lengths of their creations.
- *The Doorbell Rang* by Pat Hutchins is a very popular children's book that is used often in the math classroom with students to introduce and/or explore division concepts.
- *Two of Everything: A Chinese Folktale*, retold by Lily Toy Hong, is a delightful story that introduces students to a character who discovers a magical pot that doubles everything placed inside it. This story provides a great context for exploring patterns and algebraic reasoning.

Remember to select books that are relevant and appropriate for your students. Also, encourage your students to engage in math-related discourse as they discuss math concepts.

HOW DO I WEAVE LITERATURE INTO A MATH LESSON OR UNIT?

Children's literature naturally lends itself as a tool to help students make connections to other math concepts and to other content areas. A common practice is for teachers to integrate children's literature in math lessons or units as a tool to promote problem posing and sense making. Integration of authentic children's literature in lessons or units can be used to regularly engage students in activities that help them make connections between representations, and to foster reasoning and sense making as tools for problem solving. Young and Marroquin (*Teaching Children Mathematics*, 2006) provide suggestions for using children's literature before, during, and after a lesson or unit as a tool to promote problem posing in the math classroom.

Before	During	After
• Pre-assess skills and understanding • Introduce new topics and vocabulary • Introduce manipulatives • Connect with children's previous experience	• Reinforce vocabulary • Address misconceptions • Encourage higher-level thinking • Provide multiple representations • Generate new knowledge • Make connections among concepts	• Review concepts • Prompt further questions • Make applications to the world outside of class • Encourage connections with other math topics and other disciplines • Serve as an extension or enrichment activity

Other suggestions for using literature in a math lesson or unit include the following:

- Inviting guest readers to read books to students so you can "do the math" along with your students
- Providing opportunities for students to act out the mathematics in books to help them make sense of the math concepts explored

Here are some additional resources for identifying authentic children's literature to integrate into your math classroom that also features diverse characters and contexts:

- Mathical Award Winning Book List: The purpose of the Mathical Book Prize, awarded by the Mathematical Sciences Research Institute, is to inspire a love of mathematics in the everyday world of children. The Mathical book list includes award-winning and honor books that feature and highlight mathematics for students in grades pre-K–12. The books include picture books, novels, poetry collections, puzzle books, and biographies.
- National Science Teaching Association Best STEM Books K–12: Each year, the association identifies outstanding children's literature that highlights STEM-related topics. Books on this list address criteria such as interdisciplinary integration; illustrating teamwork, diverse skills, and creativity; and exploring multiple solutions to problems.

Notes

How Do I Teach Problem Solving?

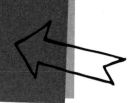

A problem is a question that needs a solution, which may not have one, single, immediately obvious solution pathway or process. "Problem solving is what we do when we don't know what to do" (Liljedahl, 2021, p. 19). Problem solving is not about simply applying a procedure to a problem to find an answer; it is a process that requires students to think, question, and make sense of the mathematics. Teaching problem solving can be hard, and you'll want to avoid teaching "answer-getting" shortcuts that cause students to simply mimic what you do without developing their own conceptual understanding. Shortcuts might offer short-term success, but they rob students of the chance to learn the critical thinking skills needed for the long term. Here is a list of helpful tips for working with problem solving across the year.

Great Resources

There are lots of resources for teaching problem solving. Two resources that have been most valuable to us: Moore, et al. (2019). *Mathematize It!* Corwin; Ray-Riek, M. (2013). *Powerful problem solving.* Heinemann.

TIPS FOR DEVELOPING PROBLEM SOLVERS

Teaching problem solving is hard. You want to avoid shortcuts, such as keywords, as they are not about thinking and don't always work. You also want to avoid proceduralizing problem solving. Real problem solving is not a set of steps that lead to the correct answer. Problem solving is about thinking and reasoning, which is what you want to help your students develop. To do this well, consider these tips:

Tip #1 Include problem solving every day.

Problem solving was once reserved for Fridays or displayed as a word problem at the bottom of a textbook page. But problems come in all shapes and sizes and involve different contexts, different operations, and varying complexity. Because problem solving is at the heart of doing math, and it requires thinking and reasoning, it should also be at the heart of every lesson; the thinking and reasoning strategies shared in the next section will help you realize this.

> I FEATURED "PROBLEM-SOLVING FRIDAY" IN MY CLASSROOM FOR A FEW YEARS. THEN, I REALIZED THAT PROBLEM SOLVING IS SOMETHING WE HAVE TO DO EVERY DAY.
>
> —FIFTH-GRADE TEACHER

Tip #2 Remember that a good problem might not be a word problem.

Good thinking problems can take on many forms. Word problems often represent the bulk of the problems we pose in elementary school. However, problems can take on other forms. Asking second-grade students to represent 437 in four different ways and to explain their thinking is a problem-solving task. Asking fourth graders to create a set of fractions close to 1 and justify their choices is another example.

Tip #3 Avoid keywords and other "tricks."

You may be familiar with an approach to solving word problems that seems to help students get to the correct answer by highlighting numbers and circling the keyword that tells them what to do. But because keywords don't always work in all situations, this approach can be misleading and set students up for errors, misconceptions, and a feeling of incompetence. Notice in the following problems that the keywords *were left* in the first problem has nothing to do with subtraction; the word *times* in the second problem signals multiplication, but division is actually needed; and there isn't a keyword in the third problem. Simply, there isn't any trick for problem solving. It is about making sense and thinking.

In October, 46 jackets were left on the playground. In November, 35 jackets were left on the playground. How many jackets were left on the playground in these two months?	Kristen ran 6 miles last week. That was four times farther than John. How many miles did John run last week?	How many legs do 12 elephants have?

> I USED TO HAVE A KEYWORD POSTER IN MY CLASSROOM, BUT I TOOK IT DOWN AND NOW HELP MY STUDENTS FOCUS ON UNDERSTANDING THE PROBLEM BY DRAWING PICTURES AND TALKING ABOUT THE PROBLEM.
>
> —FIRST-GRADE TEACHER

Tip #4 Be patient.

Teaching problem solving is about helping students learn how to think. It isn't easy, and it takes time. Students can be inconsistent when solving problems. One day they might seem able to solve any problem, and other days they may not even know how to get started (see Stuck Students, p. 116). It feels good when students get the right answer, but keep in mind that you want to dig into their thinking.

Tip #5 Use and connect representations.

Physical models and drawings enable students to visualize the problem and make sense of it. Encourage students to represent their thinking in these ways, first, and then have them write equations to go with their thinking. Most important, work to

Answers to Your Biggest Questions About Teaching Elementary Math

ensure that students are able to connect the problem, their models and drawings, and their equations to one other. For example, consider the following problem for second-grade students: Jackson scored 68 points in the first game and 73 points in the second game. How many points did Jackson score in the two games?

Physical representation	Visual representation	Symbolic representation
A student uses base-ten blocks to show 68 and 73.	A student draws sticks (tens) and dots (ones) to show 68 and 73.	A student writes 68 + 73 = ?
A student uses two bead strings to show each number.	A student draws a number line that starts with 68 and counts on.	A student records 60 + 70 and 8 + 3 to show partial sums.
A student uses a set of linking cubes with six sticks of 10 to show 60 and seven sticks of 10 to show 70.	A student uses two hundreds charts to show how they added.	A student records 68 + 2 + 71.

The examples in the chart show the different ways students might represent the problem. You want to help them make connections between their specific representation and the problem as well as between the different representations across categories (physical-visual-symbolic) and within a category (base-ten blocks–bead counters–linking cubes).

Tip #6 | Talk about it.

Learning to solve problems comes from sharing the ideas and strategies that worked and those that didn't work. Be careful to avoid conversations that simply list the steps one took to solve the problem. Focus the conversation on student thinking. Ask questions like these:

- What did you know about the problem? What were you trying to find out?
- How can you describe the problem in your own words?
- How did you represent the problem?
- How does your representation connect to the problem?
- How does your representation compare with others' representations?
- How do you know your answer makes sense?
- Why did you choose _____ (operation) to solve the problem?
- How is your strategy similar to/different from _____ (another student's)?

Tip #7 | Grow reasonableness.

"How do you know your answer makes sense?" is one of the most important questions you can ask your students. Keep in mind that checking for reasonableness is not the same as solving a problem and then using the inverse operation or steps to see if it is correct. To develop reasonableness, incorporate estimation into your math class often (see Estimation, p. 127), and talk with students about their thinking after they find a solution. Every time ask, "How do you know your answer makes sense?" And be sure to talk about how *you* know an answer makes sense—what you ask yourself to check for reasonableness. This helps them develop understanding of what questions they should consider.

Tip #8 *Use diverse problem types when using word problems.*

Not all word problems are created equal. In fact, there are different types of word problems. Consider this simplified version of problem types, and use a balanced mix of them during instruction.

Addition and subtraction		
Result unknown	**Change unknown**	**Start unknown**
There were 24 cookies on a tray. Ten were eaten. How many were left?	There were 24 cookies. Fourteen were left on a tray. How many cookies were eaten?	Ten cookies were eaten, and 14 were left. How many cookies were there to begin with?

Multiplication and division		
Product unknown	**Group size unknown**	**Number of groups unknown**
There are 6 bags of cookies with 4 cookies in each bag. How many cookies are there?	There are 24 cookies in 6 bags. How many cookies are there in each bag?	There are 24 cookies with 4 cookies in each bag. How many bags are there?

Notes

How Do I Support Student Thinking and Reasoning?

When you solve a problem, you think about it, ask yourself questions, visualize or draw it, think about it with different numbers, and consider the order of the steps you need to take. You want this for your students too. Problem solving is grounded in thinking and reasoning. Students need to learn strategies to make sense of problems, organize their thinking, plan a solution path, determine if they have solved the problem, and determine if their answer makes sense. You need strategies to develop these ideas in your students. Here are seven effective strategies for developing your students' ability to make sense of problems, think, and reason. You can make the images into reproducibles or anchor charts.

> I LEARNED YOU CAN'T DO THE THINKING FOR YOUR STUDENTS. RATHER, SET THEM UP TO DO THE THINKING!
>
> —KINDERGARTEN TEACHER

NOTICE AND WONDER

Notice and wonder gives students an opportunity to make observations about a problem or a context. Then, they identify questions they have about it. For this approach, pose a problem without the question or prompt. Ask students what they notice about the problem (including the numbers, context, etc.). Ask students what they wonder about the problem. Talk about their questions and how they might be answered. Then, reveal the question part of the problem. Consider using an image related to the problem's context before posing the written problem, as it activates prior knowledge and helps students make sense of the context of the problem.

NUMBERLESS WORD PROBLEMS

Pose a problem without the numbers. Ask students to describe the problem in their own words. Ask them to describe what is happening and how they might solve it. Have students represent the problem. Then, introduce the numbers into the problem, and discuss it again, revisiting the thinking of the problem without numbers.

THREE READS

There are a variety of ways to use *three reads* for problem solving. One way is to have students read the problem first and restate what is happening in their own words. Then, they read it a second time to identify important information, such as the numbers or actions of the problem. On the third read, they think about how to represent the problem, which may be in drawings, using manipulatives, by acting it out, or using numbers and symbols.

1st Read to **Make Sense**	2nd Read for the **IMPORTANT INFORMATION**	3rd Read to **REPRESENT the PROBLEM**
The problem is about . . .		

KNOW-WANT-STRATEGY CHART

A Know-Want-Strategy Chart (K-W-S) is a graphic organizer for organizing one's thinking when solving a problem. First, students write down what they *know* (K) about the problem and its context. Then, they write down what they are trying to find out about the problem, as well as questions they have about it or the context—what they *want* (W) to know. Finally, students identify a *strategy* (S) to solve the problem. They share their thoughts for each component before actually working to find an answer.

K	W	S
What do I **KNOW** about the problem?	**WHAT** am I trying to find out?	How can I **SOLVE** the problem?

WHAT'S THE QUESTION?

What's the question helps students develop a sense of how questions and problems vary. There are two options for this approach. One is to pose the stem of the problem without a question and ask students to generate what the question might be before revealing what the question actually is (e.g., There are 98 students in second grade. There are 114 students in third grade. What's the question?). Another option is to provide students with an answer (e.g., 24 golf balls), and they write the problem (e.g., The answer is 24 golf balls. What could be the question?).

AND THEN . . .

This approach helps with problems with two (or more) steps. Students first solve a one-step problem. Then, they tell what happened next. For example, a problem might be as follows:

> Kara gave her dog 10 bones, and it ate 6 of them. How many were left?

After solving this problem, students add an "and then" statement, such as

> And then her dog ate 2 more bones later that day. How many bones were now left?

This approach helps students think about the order of the steps they take.

COMPARE AND CONTRAST

Compare and contrast helps students think about how one problem is similar to another problem, so that they can consider how they might solve a problem in the same or a different way. To do this, pose two different problems to students, and have them talk about how the problems are the same and different and how they would solve them in the same or different ways. Here are three ways problems can be similar and different:

Same context, same question, different numbers	
Sam added 32 treats to her dog's toy. The puppy got 19 of the treats. How many more were there for the puppy to get?	Sam added 25 treats to her dog's toy. The puppy got 7 of the treats. How many more were there for the puppy to get?
Same context, same numbers, different question	
Sam added 32 treats to her dog's toy. The puppy got 19 of the treats. How many more were there for the puppy to get?	Sam added 32 treats to her dog's toy. Sam then added 19 more treats to the toy. How many treats were there in the toy?
Same context, same numbers, different numbers, different question	
Sam added 32 treats to her dog's toy. The puppy got 19 of the treats. How many more were there for the puppy to get?	Sam added 32 treats to her dog's toy. The puppy got 19 of the treats. Sam added 10 more treats. How many more treats were there for the puppy to get?

What Do I Do When Students Get Stuck?

There will be times when a student is working on a math problem and comes to an impasse or doesn't know what to do next. The way you react to the student's struggle matters. The goal is to encourage your students to do the thinking, so that over time they develop a number of strategies to draw on when they encounter difficulty with new problems or situations.

Identity and Agency

Getting unstuck develops students' sense of agency. When the teacher steps in to rescue their work, the teacher unintentionally sends a message that the student can't do the work themselves, compromising student agency.

AVOID RESCUING!

It is difficult to see one of your students not be able to make progress on a problem.

I REALIZED IT IS OKAY FOR MY STUDENTS TO STRUGGLE!

—SECOND-GRADE TEACHER

You will be tempted to step in and tell the student what to do. You may even find yourself grabbing the student's writing tool and doing the work for them! Instead of you doing all of the work to solve the problem, use instructional moves that spark students' thinking and help them develop problem-solving skills.

You may feel the impulse to . . .	Take a deep breath, and try this instead
Tell the student what to do next. *Example:* "You know how many pages the student reads each week. Now just add them up to find out how many pages they read in one month."	Ask the student to think about their next steps. *Example:* "You found how many pages the student reads each week. How might you go about finding out how many pages they read in a month?"
Show the student how to solve the problem using a math tool. *Example:* "Let's use the cubes. These five blue cubes will be the birds on the branch. I will take two away for the birds that flew away. How many birds are left?"	Suggest that the student use a math tool to represent their thinking. *Example:* "How might you use cubes to show what is happening in the math story about the birds?"
Ask questions that provide step-by-step guidance. *Example:* "How many baskets did the team make in the first game? How many baskets did the team make in the second game? How many baskets did the team make in all?"	Provide general guidance that encourages students to engage in thinking about what they know about the situation. *Example:* "Tell me what you know about this basketball problem. So how can you use what you know to help you solve the problem?"

Answers to Your Biggest Questions About Teaching Elementary Math

POSE QUESTIONS THAT ENCOURAGE STUDENTS TO DO THE THINKING

You've likely noticed that a good way to not take over a student's thinking is to pose a question. Asking good questions will encourage students to think about the math situation in a way they might not have on their own. Other questions you might consider asking a student who is stuck are as follows:

- What might you try next that you haven't tried yet?
- Does this problem remind you of a problem you've solved before?
- What strategies have you tried that didn't work?
- Have you thought about drawing a math picture to help you get started?
- Is there an answer you know has to be wrong?
- Might it be useful to ask a classmate for some help?
- What do you know about this problem so far? Where are you exactly getting stuck?
- Are you confused about any of the words in the problem?

REFER STUDENTS TO A STRATEGY CHART

Students need to try something rather than saying, "I don't get it!" when they get stuck. Take time to develop a list of strategies students can draw on when they come to a point where they are not sure what to do next. Make sure to involve students in co-creating a list of strategies so they develop ownership and will be more likely to refer to the list on their own. Display the list in the room where students can easily access it. You may find that you need to revisit the list periodically and add new strategies you observe students using. When you encounter a student who isn't sure what to do next when solving a problem, refer them to the strategy chart. Simply say, "What strategy might you try next?" This will empower students as they choose which strategy they would like to attempt. Here are some examples of what might appear on a strategy chart:

List of strategies I can try when I am stuck
▶ Use a math tool
▶ Think of a similar problem
▶ Say the problem in my own words
▶ Visualize the problem
▶ Draw a pictorial representation
▶ Use smaller numbers
▶ Ask a classmate for some coaching
▶ Take the numbers out

OFFER HELP IN SOME SITUATIONS

There may be times when asking a question to prompt student thinking or referring the student to the strategy chart doesn't seem like the right thing to do. The challenge lies in determining when to offer help and what to do, as you don't want your students to come to believe that they can rely on you for determining their next steps when solving problems. Consider a few situations where you might provide some assistance to students by giving a suggestion, offering a tool, or bringing the discussion to a close.

When might you do something other than ask a question or help the student determine a strategy to use? When . . .	A student does not understand the context of the problem. A student has tried a number of strategies and doesn't know what to do next. A student has made a simple computation error. A student is getting visibly upset and shutting down.

ACKNOWLEDGE STUDENTS' STRATEGIES TO GET UNSTUCK

Make sure to recognize students who use their strategies to overcome whatever caused them to become stuck. It might be as simple as saying, "Jordan, you didn't give up when you got to that challenging part in the problem. Instead, you drew an array to help you think about what the problem was asking. Using a math drawing is a great strategy to help you get unstuck." You might showcase a strategy a student uses to the entire class by asking them to share how they got unstuck during the closure of your lesson. Another way to publicly recognize a student's efforts is to ask them to put their name on a sticky note and place it near the strategy they used from the chart. Whatever the case, students will appreciate their efforts being celebrated. This also sends a message to all students about the importance of using strategies to navigate struggle while maintaining a growth mindset (see Growth Mindset, p. 30).

Notes

How Do I Select and Use Games and Centers?

Games and centers (also known as stations) work well in the elementary math classroom. Many teachers use these to differentiate instruction. Students often use these independently while the teacher works on specific content with a small group (see Small-Group Instruction, p. 56). Games and centers, when used regularly, can offer meaningful practice that reinforces the concepts and strategies you teach.

SELECTING GAMES AND CENTERS

The games and centers you use matter! Planning these should be kept simple. Don't get caught up in searching for the perfect activity. Tweak an instructional activity you have used before so that it becomes a game or center. Modify games and centers for other content to work with the math concepts you want students to practice. Games and centers don't need to be complicated or fancy. There are questions you can ask yourself to determine if the activities will be worthwhile.

QUESTIONS TO ASK YOURSELF WHEN SELECTING GAMES AND CENTERS

Questions	Purpose
What is the purpose of the activity?	Activities should connect to standards, learning targets, and student needs.
How well do students understand the topic of the activity?	Games and centers can be used to help students acquire a skill or concept. Or activities can be used to offer practice with a skill or concept.
Do students know how to use the activity?	Students need to know how to use the game or center to maximize its purpose. Make sure rules for the game or expectations for a center are straightforward.
Does the activity provide an assessment opportunity?	You can observe students as they play games or collect products (recording sheets, etc.) to assess their understanding.
How will students engage?	Some activities promote student-to-student discourse. Others are independent activities. You want to find a balance between the two.
Do they like the games and centers?	Find the games and centers that students enjoy doing. Use them! Modify them to practice different concepts. Be sure to ask students what they think about the activities.

ENGAGEMENT

PREPARING FOR GAMES AND CENTERS

Preparing the activities well is key to the success of these activities. Planning is about more than just selecting an activity. It's about making sure you have the materials that students will need for the activity, as well as thinking carefully about how your students will work with the games and centers. Think about whether they will use only one activity or if they will move from activity to activity. If they are to move, be sure that they know how to transition from activity to activity. Consider how you will keep your students accountable. Being mindful of all of these aspects will contribute to the success of centers and games.

ORGANIZING THE MATERIALS

Having your materials for games and centers organized enables students to maximize the time they have with the activity. You don't want students using their learning time searching for a recording sheet or a number cube. Gather the materials in advance. Consider keeping everything needed for the activity in a plastic tub, manilla envelope, or plastic bag. Then, students can grab the center or game, take it to their workspace, and get started right away. Be sure to also enlist students in cleaning up and putting materials back in the proper places. This teaches responsibility and saves you a lot of time!

INTRODUCING THE ACTIVITIES

Regardless of their grade level, students won't magically understand how to use games and centers. A brief, one-minute overview of the directions for an activity just before students get started isn't enough to achieve the productivity you are looking for. Students need to explicitly understand the activity's purpose, instructions, and expectations and get some practice with it before they can be independent. This means that you need to teach them the activity and ask them if they have questions about it.

When you introduce your students to a new center or game, start small. Introduce one activity at a time so that students don't get confused between activities. Have the students try it out right away so they don't forget what they're expected to do. Add in new activities once they get comfortable with the first one, and so on. To introduce a new activity, do the following:

1 *Teach the activity:* You can model it by playing against a student or the class as a whole.
2 *Model the thinking:* As you introduce an activity, ask questions to yourself aloud so that students hear the kind of questions they should ask themselves.
3 *Establish clear expectations for students:* Make sure they know how to fully engage with and complete the activity. Make sure they know how to use it independently or with a partner.
4 *Talk about getting stuck:* Refer students to class anchor charts, and highlight other ideas they might try so they can get themselves unstuck if possible (see Stuck Students, p. 116).
5 *Remind students of their responsibility:* Make sure students understand how they should treat and share materials, how to take turns, and how to clean up properly.

6 *Remember accuracy:* Provide tools (paper, pencil, number charts, fact charts, base-ten blocks, and/or calculators) to help support accurate practice.

ASSIGNING GAMES AND CENTERS

You will need to decide how often students will use these activities. Will you have your students take part in center activities daily or weekly? Do you want to make sure that students get to use certain activities? Consider whether students will self-select the activities or if you will regulate how they move through the centers. Some popular systems for determining what activity students will engage in are the following:

Rotation system	Self-selected system
Give students a designated amount of time to complete each center before moving on to the next (see Small-Group Instruction, p. 56). You will determine how long students engage in each center based on the amount of time you have during the day or the week. If students will attend more than one center in a day, you might want to use the timer on your phone or computer so that students know when to move to the next activity. This system works well if you want all students to engage in the same activities.	Students are given a contract, a planning sheet, or some other type of accountability form to help them record completed activities and keep track of their work. One example is a math menu. Students complete "must-do" activities before choosing from a list of optional activities. A choice board, or grid of activities, allows students to choose which activities they will complete. You might specify the number of activities the student needs to complete or challenge them to complete the activities that will make a "tic-tac-toe" design.

HOLDING STUDENTS ACCOUNTABLE DURING GAMES AND CENTERS

You will likely be working with a small group of students while the others are engaged in a center or playing a game. To ensure this time is productive and is contributing to student learning, you will want to hold students accountable in some way. Some ways to do this are as follows:

- *Use recording sheets aligned to the activity when possible:* This helps students work with the activity and provides insight into their thinking as well as their engagement.
- *Use scrap paper:* Require students to record their work on scrap paper and turn it in so that you can see what they did during the activity.
- *Use reflection questions:* After a student completes a game or center, ask them to reflect on what they did, why they think they did it, how it might help them, and what part was especially easy or tricky.
- *Have students keep a log of their activities:* Students use these to record the games and centers that they use during a week or unit.

Center Recording Sheet

Name: _____

Name of Activity	Date Completed	One thing I learned from this activity.	Is there anything you want your teacher to know about this activity?

- *Have students self- or peer-assess:* Simply ask students to report their effort during independent work. In primary grades you might use smiley faces or frowny faces to report effort and attitude. You can also ask students to assess their partner's engagement and effort.
- *Discuss as a whole class periodically how the games or centers are going:* This reinforces desired behaviors that are expected within the classroom community (see Community, p. 29).

Notes

_____

_____

_____

_____

_____

_____

_____

_____

_____

_____

_____

_____

_____

_____

What Should Practice Look Like?

Practice plays an important role in cementing the math skills and concepts students learn. It's important to note that practice isn't the same as teaching. It isn't showing students how to do a problem and then asking them to do similar problems repeatedly. First, teach a skill or concept well. Then, have students practice it after they demonstrate understanding.

The most effective practice is doable, enjoyable, and varied. It is a matter of quality rather than simply quantity. While repetition can have value, the number of problems on a page is not an indication of quality. Moreover, practice should not simply be busy work.

WHAT ARE THE DIFFERENT WAYS MY STUDENTS CAN PRACTICE?

Routines:	*Games:*
Routines are brief engagements that follow a familiar structure (see Instructional Routines, p. 63). They are opportunities for students to practice and share their thinking. A routine can be devised for practicing almost any skill or concept.	Games are great ways to develop strategic thinking, problem solving, and targeted skills or concepts. You want to use games that are interesting and easy for students to learn and play.
Centers:	*Paper-and-pencil practice:*
Centers (see Centers p. 119) are repeatable activities typically done independently. They have an element of variability so that they can be repeated with different results. For example, students might roll digits to make two-digit addends, find the sum, show how they found it, and then repeat the activity.	Paper-and-pencil practice is okay when used appropriately and in balance with other types of practice. Be sure to avoid having too many problems on any one practice sheet, timing the practice, or using such practices every day.

WHAT DO I NEED TO KNOW ABOUT PRACTICE?

Effective practice should be as follows:

- *Brief:* Long, repetitive practice can cause students to become bored, disengaged, or disruptive. More important, this type of practice can cause them to fall out of love with mathematics. Ten minutes of practice is about right for elementary students.
- *Focused:* Practice that mixes skills and concepts should happen after your students have had opportunities to learn the new skill or concept that is being taught. Once students show some understanding of the topic under focus, you can begin to mix in other topics.
- *Varied:* Offering a variety of activity types not only keeps practice fresh, but it also helps students transfer learning to new and novel situations. So mix up the activities students use to practice. Maybe you can offer popular activities

more often, but be careful to avoid the same activity over and over again. Also know that you want to vary written practice with mental practice.

- *Connected:* Students' learning is stronger when they explicitly see connections between what they know and what they are practicing. For example, second through fourth graders can play the practice game "So Close" to transfer what they know about whole-number operations to decimals.

GAME: "SO CLOSE"

In So Close to 100, players take turns rolling a ten-sided die and placing the digit in the tens or ones place and adding it to their running total. The goal is to get as close to 100 as possible without rolling the die more than seven times. Students can move up to playing So Close to 200 by starting at 100 and trying to get close to 200. These two games might be used in second grade so students can make connections between hundreds when practicing. In So Close to 1.00, students add hundredths and tenths. Fourth graders might play it after playing So Close to 100 to see how whole numbers and decimals are related.

So Close to 100

Directions: Roll a digit. Place the number in the tens or ones. Add that amount to your total. After seven rolls, get as close to **100** as possible without going over.

Start with 0

Tens	Ones	Total

So Close to 200

Directions: Roll a digit. Place the number in the tens or ones. Add that amount to your total. After seven rolls, get as close to **100** as possible without going over.

Start with 100

Tens	Ones	Total

So Close to 1.00

Directions: Roll a digit. Place the number in the tens or ones. Add that amount to your total. After seven rolls, get as close to **100** as possible without going over.

Start with 0

Hundred-ths	Tenths	Total

TIPS FOR MAXIMIZING PRACTICE

Practicing directly after a lesson may seem like a good idea, especially if there are a collection of practice problems on the next page of your textbook. But know that students may have unfinished learning for that topic and may not be ready for practice. Lessons and practice don't always unfold in a linear fashion (teach > practice > teach > practice). Knowing your students' strengths and needs is the best way to select purposeful practice. Here are a few more tips for maximizing practice outside of the lesson of the day.

Tip #1 | Make sure students think about what they practiced and why.

To make practice meaningful and more than simply a "time filler," have students reflect on and process what they did in writing or through discussion. Ask questions like the following:

- What did you practice?
- What patterns did you notice?
- How did today's practice connect to _____?
- Why do you think you need more/less practice with today's topic?

Tip #2 | Intentionally choose practice activities.

Practice time doesn't have to be relegated to exercises directly connected to the skill or topic you just taught. In fact, it's often a good idea to practice important skills and concepts from earlier in the year to keep them sharp. You might even practice things taught the previous year before an upcoming unit. Most important, practice starts with "Why?" In deciding what purposeful practice is worth the time it takes, ask yourself the following:

- What are your students learning now, and are they ready to practice it?
- What have they learned during the year that they need to reinforce?
- What have you observed in class recently where you've noticed more practice is needed?
- What is coming up in the next unit that you could prepare students for through practice?

Tip #3 | Make sure students practice with accuracy!

This cannot be said enough! Support students' accurate practice by

- providing them with calculators, number charts, or fact charts;
- having students check their opponent's accuracy when playing games; and
- encouraging families to use these tools during homework.

Tip #4 | Make sure they know how to practice.

When using games and centers, make sure that your students know how to play or use them. You can play the game as a class first, where you are one player and the class works together as the other player. Or you might use a center as a small-group instructional activity.

Tip #5 | Hold them accountable for practice.

Students have to actively engage with practice assignments. Worksheets offer a level of accountability because there is an artifact to collect. But you can also hold students accountable with games and centers by having them

- write a journal reflection about what they did or the mathematics they used;
- record their thinking to participate in or complete a game or center; and
- fill out an accountability slip for themselves or to evaluate their partner.

> Name: _____
>
> My partner(s): _____
>
> For math practice today, I worked with
>
> _____.
>
> ❑ I gave my best effort.
> ❑ I gave some effort.
> ❑ I need to give better effort in the future.
>
> Next time,
>
> _____
>
> _____

✳ Tip #6 Avoid having too many problems.

Too many problems cause fatigue, irritability, anxiety, and unproductive struggle. It obviously challenges the notion of keeping practice brief. But most important, too many problems may risk students cementing misconceptions that they may have by repeating the same action over and over again.

> I USED TO THINK THAT MY STUDENTS NEEDED TO SOLVE EVERY PROBLEM ON THE PAGE. HOWEVER, I REALIZED I COULD PURPOSEFULLY SELECT THE PRACTICE PROBLEMS TO GET THE MOST OUT OF THE PRACTICE WHILE KEEPING THEM ENGAGED.
>
> —FOURTH-GRADE TEACHER

✳ Tip #7 Don't grade practice.

Practice is just that. It is an opportunity to polish a skill. It should be unencumbered. If they are graded, students may become fearful of making mistakes and disengage from the practice activity, undercutting its value and purpose. Moreover, grading may suppress student reasoning and attempts to tinker with other strategies or approaches to the skill or concept.

Notes

Answers to Your Biggest Questions About Teaching Elementary Math

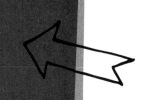

Why and How Should I Incorporate Estimation?

Estimation is a critical life skill. It is helpful for solving problems and determining the reasonableness of solutions. You want to have students estimate quantity by determining how many are in a set or collection. You also want students to practice estimating the solutions to their calculations and problems. Here are some tips and activities to get you started with estimation:

> I ESTIMATED ALL THE TIME IN MY REAL LIFE. AT SOME POINT, I FIGURED OUT IT WAS A GOOD IDEA TO START ESTIMATING IN MY MATH CLASS ALL OF THE TIME TOO.

Tip #1 Estimate often.

Students in each elementary grade need to practice generally estimating quantity frequently, so you want to work in practice as much as possible. As students begin to compute and solve problems, you also want to include activities to estimate their solutions. Your students' skill with estimation will grow as they practice and talk about their thinking. Here are five practical ways to use estimation every day:

<table>
<tr><td colspan="2" align="center">Estimate with containers (or jars)</td></tr>
<tr>
<td>Fill different-sized jars with a variety of things, including marbles, counting bears, crayons, dice, or even paper clips. Vary the amount you put into a jar. Note that the collection in the jar would be the same. Fill approximately $\frac{3}{4}$ of a jar, and tell students how many marbles are in $\frac{1}{2}$ of the jar to provide benchmarks.</td>
<td>Marbles in a jar

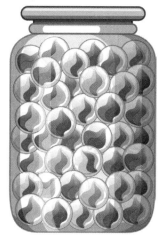

Source: iStock/blueringmedia.

- About how many marbles are there?
- Are there more or less than 100 marbles?
- About how many marbles would be in the whole jar?</td>
</tr>
</table>

Estimate with counting	
Arrange a group of students in a circle. Count around the circle using a variety of intervals, including by ones, twos, fives, and eventually fractional or decimal amounts for higher grades.	The class gets in a circle. The teacher says they will start with 31 and count by 10s. She asks, • What number will you say? • What number will we end with? Third-graders might begin counting with three-digit numbers or by multiples. Fourth- and fifth-graders can count by fraction or decimal intervals.

Estimate with pictures	
Pose a picture. Ask students to estimate something within the picture. At first, use examples where the exact answer can be found after estimating. In time, use pictures where students have to reason and may not be able to find the exact answer.	Cookies on a rack  *Source:* iStock/mikessss. Grades K–2 questions for this picture: • About how many cookies are there? • Are there more or less than 20 cookies? Grades 3–5 questions: • Each cookie has 25 chips. How many chips are in the picture? • This is half of the cookies made. About how many cookies were made altogether?

Estimate before solving problems	
Before students solve a problem, have them estimate what the answer might be, and record their estimates. After students solve the problem, have them compare their solutions with their original estimates. Talk about how their estimates compared with their solutions and what their estimates told them about their work.	The Tigers scored 68 points in game 1 and 77 points in game 2. How many points did the Tigers score in the two games? Before solving, students estimate the total points to be about 130, about 140, about 150, or more than 100 but less than 200.

Estimate before calculating	
Before students practice computation problems, have them estimate the answer and then compare the estimate with the exact answer.	$93 + 319 = $ _____ or $1\frac{3}{4} + 4\frac{1}{2} = $ The sum is about _____. The sum is exactly _____. $23 \times 14 = $ The product is about _____. The product is exactly _____.

Tip #2 | Avoid "the right answer" or "the right way."

Estimation helps us determine if our exact solutions are reasonable. Estimation is about thinking. You want to avoid insinuating that there is a right way to do it and when done correctly you'll get a "right estimate." Instead, you want students to learn to find a good estimate and to be aware that there may be a better estimate. To develop their estimation skill, you must talk about it. Ask them how they estimated and why they used a certain way to estimate. Share your thinking as well, but be sure to avoid implying that your approach is the best or preferred approach for the estimate.

Tip #3 | Teach different ways to estimate for computation.

There are different ways to estimate, as shown in this chart:

Rounding	Numbers are rounded by place value.	39 becomes 40 319 could be 320 or 300.
Range	Find a range that the actual answer will fall within.	48 + 68 will fall between 40 + 60 and 50 + 70.
Front end	Simply look at the leading place value.	721 + 819 becomes 700 + 800. 72×16 becomes 70×10.
Benchmarks, compatibles, or friendly numbers	Benchmark numbers, compatible numbers, and friendly numbers are numbers that are easy to work with.	24 rounds to 20 but is close to the benchmark of 25. So 24 + 374 can be thought of with the compatible benchmarks of 25 + 375.

Notes

How Do I Help Students Learn Basic Facts?

The students in your class might be learning basic facts for the first time. Or your students may have been introduced to basic facts but have not yet acquired automaticity, or quick recall. And if you find yourself in the latter group, know that it is completely normal and appropriate for students to have challenges with basic facts. Don't buy in to the misconception that students can't work with multidigit computation, problem solving, fractions, or any other more "advanced" concept until they master the basic facts. In fact, using basic facts in new settings (multidigit computation, etc.) opens up another opportunity for practice! You must provide access to meaningful mathematics regardless of your students' prowess in acquiring basic facts, though you can still also offer supports for accuracy and practice opportunities for students to continue to develop recall.

Access and Equity

Basic fact recall cannot be a gatekeeper, allowing some students to access meaningful mathematics and restricting others from it.

If you are teaching math facts for the first time or providing intervention to fill gaps, there are some important things you must know and take advantage of. These tips apply no matter what situation you find yourself in or what math textbook program you have.

 Tip #1 *Teach basic-fact strategies.*

The goal with learning basic facts is to develop reliable and automatic recall. It is the result of exposure and repetition. For a variety of reasons, students should learn strategies for recalling facts when they don't remember the answer quickly. Strategies develop efficiency and transfer to multidigit numbers, fractions, and decimals. Second, using strategies leads to better retention.

> I LEARNED THAT TEACHING BASIC FACTS IS MORE IMPORTANT THAN HAVING STUDENTS DO 100 PROBLEMS ON A WORKSHEET. THEY NEEDED STRATEGIES TO FIND AN ANSWER WHEN THEY COULDN'T REMEMBER IT. OVER TIME, THEY WERE ABLE TO RECALL AND NOT NEED THE STRATEGY TOO OFTEN.
>
> —THIRD-GRADE TEACHER

Fact strategies include the following:

Addition strategy	Multiplication strategy
One more, two more (e.g., $8 + 1$, $7 + 2$) – *f*	Doubles (e.g., 8×2) – *f*
Make ten (e.g., $6 + 4$, $7 + 3$) – *f*	Fives and tens (e.g., 3×5, 3×10) – *f*
Doubles (e.g., $3 + 3$, $4 + 4$) – *f*	Ones and zeros (e.g., 4×1, 4×0) – *f*
Ten more (e.g., $3 + 10$, $4 + 10$) – *f*	Break apart *(derived)*
Use ten (e.g., $7 + 9$ is the same as $6 + 1 + 9$)	• Threes (break $\times 3$ into $\times 2$ and $\times 1$) • Sixes (break $\times 6$ into $\times 5$ and $\times 1$)[a] • Nines (break $\times 9$ into $\times 10$ and $-\times 1$)[b] • Eights (break $\times 8$ into $\times 5$ and $\times 3$)[a] • Sevens (break $\times 7$ into $\times 5$ and $\times 2$)
Use doubles (e.g., $6 + 7$ is the same as $6 + 6 + 1$)	Use doubling *(derived)* • Sixes (double $\times 3$)[a] • Fours (double and double again) • Eights (double, double, double)[b]

Note: f, foundational fact.

[a]Sixes and eights can be derived in different ways.

[b]Nines take a group away.

Tip #2 | Sequence basic-fact strategies.

Teaching basic-fact strategies sequentially can improve student outcomes. The order of strategies in Tip #1 is a possible sequence beginning with foundational facts (*f*). These facts follow patterns and can be easier for students to learn and recall. In the following chart, foundational facts are shown in gray. As you will notice, these foundational facts make up the majority of the facts students need to learn. Students can then use the foundational facts to derive or find other facts.

ENGAGEMENT

+	0	1	2	3	4	5	6	7	8	9	10
0	0	1	2	3	4	5	6	7	8	9	10
1	1	2	3	4	5	6	7	8	9	10	11
2	2	3	4	5	6	7	8	9	10	11	12
3	3	4	5	6	7	8	9	10	11	12	13
4	4	5	6	7	8	9	10	11	12	13	14
5	5	6	7	8	9	10	11	12	13	14	15
6	6	7	8	9	10	11	12	13	14	15	16
7	7	8	9	10	11	12	13	14	15	16	17
8	8	9	10	11	12	13	14	15	16	17	18
9	9	10	11	12	13	14	15	16	17	18	19
10	10	11	12	13	14	15	16	17	18	19	20

Addition foundational facts

×	0	1	2	3	4	5	6	7	8	9	10
0	0	0	0	0	0	0	0	0	0	0	0
1	0	1	2	3	4	5	6	7	8	9	10
2	0	2	4	6	8	10	12	14	16	18	20
3	0	3	6	9	12	15	18	21	24	27	30
4	0	4	8	12	16	20	24	28	32	36	40
5	0	5	10	15	20	25	30	35	40	45	50
6	0	6	12	18	24	30	36	42	48	54	60
7	0	7	14	21	28	35	42	49	56	63	70
8	0	8	16	24	32	40	48	56	64	72	80
9	0	9	18	27	36	45	54	63	72	81	90
10	0	10	20	30	40	50	60	70	80	90	100

Multiplication foundational facts

How Do I Help Students Learn Basic Facts?

131

Tip #3 | Ensure that students understand the commutative property.

Deeply understanding that the order of addends (or factors) does not change the sum (or product) cuts the number of facts to learn by half. For example, if students know that $2 + 3 = 5$ or $5 \times 7 = 35$, they don't have to learn that $3 + 2 = 5$ or $7 \times 3 = 35$ as separate facts.

Tip #4 | Leverage inverse operations.

"Think addition" and "think multiplication" are powerful strategies for recalling subtraction and division facts, respectively. First, students must have a sound understanding of the relationship between inverse operations. You can then maximize this understanding by organizing your fact instruction to teach a fact set and then the related inverse fact set. For example, first you can teach and practice "make-ten" facts ($6 + 4$, $7 + 3$, etc.). Then, teach and practice the related subtraction facts ($10 - 6$, $10 - 4$, $10 - 7$, $10 - 3$, etc.). For multiplication, teach and practice doubles (7×2, 8×2, etc.). Then, teach and practice division facts ($14 \div 2$, $14 \div 7$, $16 \div 2$, $16 \div 8$, etc.). Arranging fact sets in this way reinforces the inverse relationship and improves student recall.

Tip #5 | Focus on one fact set at a time.

Introduce, practice, and assess only one new fact set strategy at a time. After students show some level of proficiency with the focus set, begin to mingle previously learned fact sets.

Great Resources

Two great resources for teaching basic facts are as follows: O'Connell, S., & SanGiovanni, J. (2011). *Mastering the basic math facts in addition and subtraction: Strategies, activities, and interventions to move students beyond memorization.* Heinemann; Bay-Williams, J., & Kling, G. (2019). *Math fact fluency: 60+ games and assessment tools to support learning and retention.* Association for Supervision and Curriculum Development.

Tip #6 | Make time, and be patient.

Fact recall can't be accomplished in two or three weeks. Spread out instruction, and practice across the year. Take time to practice appropriately (see Practice, p. 123) as often as possible.

Tip #7 | Avoid timing.

Timed assessments and timed practice activities can create unnecessary stress and anxiety for students. You do want your students to develop quick recall of facts. More practice and exposure is the way to do so; testing their speed is not.

Tip #8 | Use engaging practice.

Use centers, games, and routines to vary practice and keep it engaging. Avoid practice that isolates students or leaves them feeling incompetent. Games like "Around the World" or similar games that put students on the spot can damage their positive beliefs about mathematics and their ability to do math.

Tip #9 | Offer tools to support accuracy.

Provide addition/multiplication charts or calculators as students work to reinforce accuracy. Inaccurate practice leads to more complicated problems later. For example, practicing $3 + 4 = 9$ over and over again, without accuracy support, leads to a student "learning" that $3 + 4 = 9$.

Notes

ENGAGEMENT

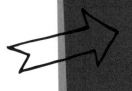

Why Teach Different Strategies for Computation?

Take a moment to solve 149 + 127. How did you do it? You may have "lined up the numbers" in your head or on paper and added vertically by place value. Or you may have given 1 to 149 to make 150 + 126, thus creating a friendlier problem (Example 1). You might have broken apart one of the addends by place value and found the partial sums, as in Example 2. Or you might have made both addends friendlier numbers (adding 1 and 3, respectively, to get 150 + 130) to find a sum and then compensated (subtracting 4) for your adjustment (Example 3). Of course, you might have done something quite different from these strategies. And the strategy you use for this problem might change as the numbers in the problem change.

> I WASN'T SO SURE DIFFERENT STRATEGIES WOULD WORK THAT WELL, BUT I DIDN'T HAVE A CHOICE. IT TURNS OUT THAT MY STUDENTS DID BETTER WITH ADDITION AND SUBTRACTION USING DIFFERENT WAYS THAN WITH THE ONE WAY I HAD ALWAYS TAUGHT.
>
> —SECOND-GRADE TEACHER

Example 1	Example 2	Example 3
$149 + 127$ $150 + 126 = 276$	$149 + 127$ $100 + 100 = 200$ $40 + 20 = 60$ $9 + 7 = 16$ $\overline{276}$	$149 + 127$ $150 + 130 = 280$ $280 - 3 = 276$

QUESTIONS ABOUT TEACHING COMPUTATION STRATEGIES

It's possible, if not likely, that you weren't formally introduced to different strategies for adding, subtracting, multiplying, or dividing. Yet it's also possible, if not likely, that you have acquired these strategies on your own through experience and your own dabbling. Your student experiences probably create questions for you about teaching different strategies for these operations.

WHY SHOULD I TEACH A VARIETY OF COMPUTATION STRATEGIES?

Fluency is the end goal of teaching computation and other procedures. Fluency is the combination of efficiency, flexibility, and accuracy (National Research Council, 2001):

- *Efficiency* = Solving a problem in a reasonable amount of time.
- *Flexibility* = Knowing multiple strategies to adapt one's approach when needed.
- *Accuracy* = Finding the correct solution.

The first two components call for students to learn different strategies so that they can move between strategies and for efficiency.

Identity and Agency

Teaching different strategies develops students' agency so that they can make decisions about what strategy to use and when to use it.

WHY NOT JUST USE THE ALGORITHM?

You may be wondering why the algorithm doesn't satisfy the different components of fluency. Well, it does sometimes. But it is not always the most efficient. Think about 200 + 517. It's easily solved by adding on by hundreds. Using an algorithm to find the sum is inefficient. The same can be said for problems like 25 × 3, 99 + 76, 587 − 124, and others. So while you want students to learn algorithms eventually, you also want them to learn when to use an algorithm. Having different strategies also supports students' accuracy as they learn algorithms. But also know that students' sense of number and reasonableness can be challenged, if not damaged, by only learning the rote procedures of algorithms.

WON'T ALL OF THESE STRATEGIES JUST CONFUSE THEM?

Strategies for computation are grounded in the conceptual understanding of operations and the properties of operations. Think about 703 − 689. Regrouping could make the algorithm quite challenging. Yet thinking about the space between these two numbers and counting up or back makes it much more doable. For example, a student might think that 10 more than 689 is 699 and 4 more from there is 703, so the difference is 14. Using different strategies makes sense to students. They offer alternatives that empower students to choose the approach that is best for them based on the numbers in the problem. Simply put, each and every student is better off knowing a set of useful strategies and when to use them (Bay-Williams & SanGiovanni, 2021).

SHOULD STUDENTS KNOW ALL OF THEIR FACTS BEFORE I TEACH STRATEGIES?

Unfortunately, the myth that students must know all of their facts before learning multidigit computation still persists today. The fact about facts is that they can create unnecessary barriers. This is not to say students shouldn't learn basic facts. They should! But mastering them should not be a prerequisite for learning other skills and concepts. In fact, learning multidigit computation provides an opportunity to practice basic facts and can improve student recall. You can provide students with addition/multiplication charts, calculators, and other tools to support accuracy as they develop fact recall.

HOW DO I TEACH DIFFERENT STRATEGIES?

Teach the strategies by posing problems in context, rather than as just "naked computation," to help students make sense of what is happening. Support student thinking by giving them tools to represent their understanding, including physical manipulatives, like base-ten blocks, as well as number charts and number lines. Help them connect their different representations to one other, the problem, and the symbolic equations (see Representations, p. 156). Follow the sequence of strategies introduced in your curriculum, and be sure to give ample time for learning and practicing the different strategies.

Great Resources

Bay-Williams, J., & SanGiovanni, J. (2021). *Figuring out fluency: A classroom companion.* Corwin; Van de Walle, J., Karp, K., Lovin, L., & Bay-Williams, J. (2019). *Teaching student-centered mathematics: Developmentally appropriate instruction for grades 3–5* (Vol. 2). Pearson; Parrish, S. (2014). *Number talks: Whole number computation, grades K–5: A multimedia professional learning resource.* Math Solutions.

ARE REPRESENTATIONS, LIKE BASE-TEN BLOCKS AND NUMBER LINES, STRATEGIES?

To put it simply, no. Strategies are ways of thinking and reasoning. Representations help us see those ways of thinking. Using a number line isn't a strategy, but the number line helps you see a strategy. For example, adding 375 + 435 can be solved by adding on (the strategy), as demonstrated with a number line (the representation).

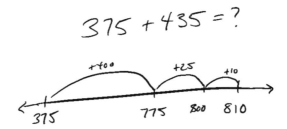

The same is true for other operations. In the following example, the area model on the left (the representation) shows the partial products strategy for multiplying 412 × 7. This strategy could also be represented through equations, as shown on the right.

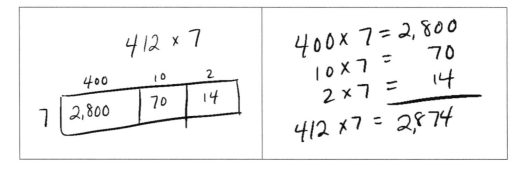

SHOULD I AVOID CALCULATORS?

No! Calculators are extremely helpful tools. They carry an antiquated stigma. The fact is that calculators help with accuracy and are readily available in our world and our students' world. They can be used during the work or after the work to confirm accuracy. Students should be empowered to use them but need to know how to use them and think carefully about when to use them. Importantly, as they learn to judge the reasonableness of their solutions, they should always ask if the results on the calculator *make sense*.

WHAT DO I SAY TO FAMILIES?

Families may wonder why these strategies are necessary. You want them to know that fluency is a matter of thinking and reasoning that serves students beyond math class. They may think that these strategies won't help them on standardized tests, but the opposite is actually true. Families may believe that this "math" is too different from what and how they learned. You can acknowledge that math instruction has changed as we have learned more about how students learn it. Share that these strategies have always worked but we just haven't always taken the time to teach them. Families may have the misbelief that the facts and procedures taught in the past no longer matter or are no longer taught. That isn't the case. Facts and algorithms are still taught. These strategies are *also* taught so that students can be flexible, efficient, and accurate. It will also be helpful to share resources and examples of the different strategies so that families can understand and support their use.

Notes

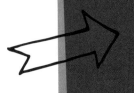

How Do I Help Students Develop Fluency With Operations?

Fluency is made up of efficiency, flexibility, and accuracy (National Research Council, 2001). Fluency is about thinking and reasoning. It is about choosing a strategy that is efficient for the problem and the problem solver. It takes time to teach and develop. You want to help students develop their ability to select an appropriate strategy, adapt a strategy, apply a strategy to a new problem, solve in a reasonable amount of time, complete strategies accurately, and get a correct answer (Bay-Williams & SanGiovanni, 2021). To do this, you need to know what to do, what not to do, and the different strategies for addition and subtraction.

DOS AND DON'TS FOR HELPING STUDENTS DEVELOP FLUENCY

> I WAS UPSET AT FIRST WHEN MY STUDENTS DIDN'T GRASP THE USE TEN STRATEGY RIGHT AWAY. BUT I REALIZED THEY NEEDED MORE TIME. NOW THEY USE IT ALL OF THE TIME.
>
> —SECOND-GRADE TEACHER

What to do	What not to do
Know how the strategies work so you can teach them, represent them, and help students think about when they are good options and when they aren't	Avoid a strategy because you aren't sure how useful it will be
Use representations, including base-ten blocks and number lines, to develop understanding	Require students to continue to use representations after they show capability in working symbolically
Practice strategies regularly through diverse, engaging experiences	Practice a strategy repeatedly using paper-and-pencil practice sheets
Talk about the different strategies you and your students use during instruction Discuss when they are efficient and when they aren't, as well as other ways to apply them (e.g., different ways to break apart numbers)	Focus on a specific strategy and feature it during discussions indicating that it is the best or preferred approach
Be patient—developing skill and utility with strategies takes time	Expect students to master a strategy within a week or two of introducing it
Assess student understanding of how the strategy works and when to use it, including whether it is carried out accurately	Assess how quickly students use a strategy
Estimate products and quotients to help students develop reasonableness—their estimation will develop the more they practice (see Estimation, p. 127)	Relegate estimation to a rounding and place-value experience—estimation plays a critical role in fluency
Use estimation skills and calculators to check for accurate products and quotients	Check for accuracy by using the inverse operation—it is unreliable if skill with an operation is fragile, and it can also cause frustration while limiting students' developing number sense

What to do	What not to do
Use area models and other representations for teaching these concepts, connecting them to related equations—let reliance on these models fade as students' comfort and skill with symbolic representations and skill, in general, develop	Skip over, or quickly move past, using representations
Connect these strategies to algorithms, helping students determine when a strategy or an algorithm is a good choice	Frame these strategies as less desirable or less sophisticated than algorithms—the algorithms are not an end goal
Help students determine when a strategy is useful	Require each problem to be solved with every strategy
Use multidigit multiplication and division work to strengthen basic-fact recall and help students make connections between basic facts (3 × 7) and related expressions (3 × 70 or 30 × 7)	Deny access to multidigit multiplication and division because fact recall isn't fully realized

WHAT ARE THE DIFFERENT STRATEGIES FOR ADDITION?

There are four significant strategies for adding whole numbers. These strategies can be applied to other number types, including fractions and decimals, later in elementary school. Though these strategies work with any set of addends, they can lose efficiency or practicality as the number of digits increases. For example, one could use partial sums to add 135,489 + 713,456, but at that point we would want students to consider alternatives including an algorithm or a calculator!

Count on	
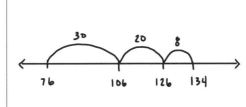	The *count on* strategy breaks apart an addend and counts on from another. The example shows one way a student might count on to solve 76 + 58. 58 is decomposed into 30, 20, and 8. The student then counted on by those amounts, finding a sum of 134. Either addend can be decomposed in any convenient way.

Use ten	
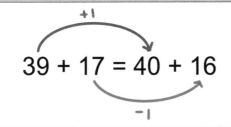	The *use ten* strategy leverages making combinations of 10 to find more efficient, friendly computations. In this example, 1 is given from 17 to 39, creating 40 + 16. The strategy develops into making a hundred, a thousand, and so on. In a problem like 355 + 380, 20 is given to 380, creating 335 + 400.

Partial sums	
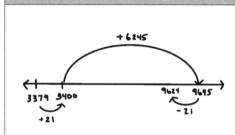 $$242 + 658$$ $$200 + 600 = 800$$ $$42 + 58 = 100$$ $$800 + 100 = 900$$	*Partial sums* is a strategy where each addend is broken apart, usually by place value, and the sum of the parts is found, and then all of the partial sums are added together. In this example, the student chose to break apart the hundreds while leaving the rest of the number "together," likely because they recognized that 42 and 58 make 100. Another student might have thought of it as 200 + 600, 40 + 50, and 2 + 8 before finding the sum of all of those partials.

Compensate	
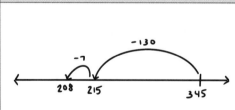	*Compensation* is a strategy for manipulating numbers to find a friendly computation and then compensating for that manipulation. In this example, the student was adding 3,379 + 6,245. The student thought of 3,379 as 3,400 and added 6,245 to find 9,645. Then, they compensated for the 21 they added to the original addend. In a problem like 47 + 48, a student might add 50 + 50 and take away 5.

WHAT ARE THE DIFFERENT STRATEGIES FOR SUBTRACTION?

There are three significant strategies for subtracting whole numbers. Like addition strategies, these strategies work with other types of numbers including fractions and decimals. And like addition strategies, these always work, but they lose efficiency and practicality as the number of digits is increased.

Count back	
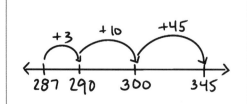	Subtraction can be thought of as takeaway, leading to this strategy. This example shows the *count back* strategy for solving 345 – 137. First, the student counts back 130, finding 215 and then 7 more to 208. Of course, students can decompose the subtrahend (137) in many different ways that are convenient to them.

Think addition	
	Subtraction can be thought of as the difference between two numbers. And one can *think addition* to count up from one number to the other, establishing the difference between the two numbers. Here, a student finds the difference of 345 – 287 by counting up from 287 to 345 in chunks and then adding up the jumps. 3 + 10 + 45 = 58. The difference of 345 – 287 is 58.

Partial differences

$47 - 34$ $40 - 30 = 10$ $7 - 4 = 3$ $10 + 3 = 13$	*Partial differences* is similar to partial sums. The numbers are decomposed, usually by place value, and the differences of each partial are found. Then, the differences are joined. In the example $47 - 34$, $40 - 30 = 10$ and $7 - 4 = 3$, the differences of 10 and 3 are joined. The difference of $47 - 34$ is 13. Note that partial differences always works but is a bit more complicated when regrouping would be needed (e.g., $73 - 38$).

WHAT ARE THE DIFFERENT STRATEGIES FOR MULTIPLICATION?

Like other computation strategies, multiplication strategies work with whole numbers, decimals, and fractions. But these strategies do begin to lose efficiency and practicality as the number of digits increases in the factors. The strategies will still work, but they can become cumbersome. At that point, an algorithm or a calculator becomes a better approach to the problem.

Break apart to multiply	

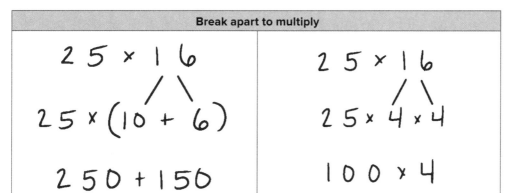

You can break apart factors to multiply more efficiently. Factors can be broken apart with addition through the distributive property. 25×16 can be thought of as $25 \times 10 + 25 \times 6$. It could also be thought of as $25 \times 10 + 25 \times 4 + 25 \times 2$.

The factors in a problem can also be broken apart by factors. The second example shows this. 25×16 becomes $25 \times 4 \times 4$. $25 \times 4 = 100$ and $100 \times 4 = 400$, so 25×16 equals 400. You could also think of 16 as 2×8, creating $25 \times 2 \times 8$, or you could break apart 25 into 5×5.

Halve and double

Halve $\left(\begin{array}{c} 14 \times 15 \\ 7 \times 30 \end{array} \right)$ Double $7 \times 30 = 210$	You can halve one factor and double the other to find a product. In the example 14×15, 14 is halved and 15 is doubled, creating 7×30, which is a much friendlier problem. This strategy is useful with other numbers too, such as 7.5×12, which becomes 15×6. And the strategy can be repeated because 15×6 can be thought of as 30×3.

ENGAGEMENT

Compensation	
8×398 $8 \times 400 = 3,200$ $-8 \times 2 = 16$ $8 \times 398 = 3,184$	Compensation is a useful strategy when a factor can be easily changed to create a friendlier problem. Here, 8 × 398 can be thought of as 8 × 400, which is 3,200. But that is two groups of 8 too many. So 16 is subtracted from 3,200. 8 × 398 = 3,184. Compensation is a good strategy for problems like 39 × 5, 97 × 12, or even 5.8 × 6.

Partial products	
25×38 $20 \times 30 = 600$ $5 \times 30 = 150$ $20 \times 8 = 160$ $5 \times 8 = \underline{40}$ 950	25×38 $30 \times 25 = 750$ $8 \times 25 = \underline{200}$ 950

Partial products is a special break-apart strategy using place value. Students first learn to break apart both factors, as shown in the left example. In time, you want students to break apart only one factor when possible. In the example on the right, this student's experience helped them recognize 25 × 8 as 200, so they were able to break apart just one factor.

WHAT ARE THE DIFFERENT STRATEGIES FOR DIVISION?

Like subtraction, division is limited to a few strategies. And these strategies are reliant on a sound understanding of the concept of division and its inverse relationship to multiplication. Division strategies also require a better-developed sense of number and basic-fact recall. But know that neither is required for learning these strategies and both will improve as students work with these division strategies.

Think multiplication	
Dividend Divisor $240 \div 30 = ?$ Factor $30 \times \boxed{?} = 240$ $3 \times 8 = 24$ $30 \times \boxed{8} = 240$ $240 \div 30 = 8$ Quotient	Dividend Divisor $154 \div 7 = ?$ Factor $7 \times \boxed{?} = 154$ $7 \times \boxed{20} = 140$ $7 \times \boxed{2} = 14$ $154 \div 7 = 22$ Quotient

The "think multiplication" strategy makes use of the inverse relationship between multiplication and division. Often, it also pulls in recognition of basic facts. In the example on the left, the student considers 240 ÷ 30 as a multiplication problem with an unknown factor, thinking, "What times 30 equals 240?" Their work shows how they arrived at their quotient.

This strategy can also be used to find quotients when a dividend is decomposed into the products of the divisor. In 154 ÷ 7, the student recognizes 154 as the sum of two products of 7, 140 and 14. So the student thinks, "7 times 'what' equals 140," and "7 times 'what' equals 14?" The student then combines those two, finding 154 ÷ 7 to be 22.

Partial quotients	

Partial quotients is a step toward the long-division algorithm. Many of us use a partial quotients strategy when we divide mentally. The strategy centers on taking out manageable groups of the divisor. On the left, the student finds 10 groups of 3 (30) and removes it from the dividend. The student then removes another group of 10 before taking out 50 groups of three.

On the right side, the student takes out 50 groups of 3, followed by 20 groups of 3, and so on. Both examples are fine applications of the strategy. You want to help students work toward taking out the most sizable, but manageable, chunks. In this problem you might have a student who goes straight to removing 70 groups of 3, whereas someone else takes out 10 groups of 3 seven times (because they don't know or recognize 50 groups at any point).

Notes

chapter FOUR

HOW DO I HELP MY STUDENTS TALK ABOUT MATHEMATICS?

We have learned that discussion is not about what you tell students but what they tell you and, more important, what they tell one other, because those doing more of the talking are also doing more of the thinking. Mathematical discourse helps cement learning because discussion exposes students' ideas to you and their classmates to give feedback on. It helps them sharpen their thinking and learn to communicate clearly and precisely. And most important, discourse exposes students to the strategies of others, causing them to think more deeply about their own ideas and helping them add to their knowledge.

This may be different from the math learning experiences most of us had as students. In those classrooms, the teacher explained what the students were supposed to do. The teacher asked closed questions and called on students quickly, often singling out either the student who could raise their hand the fastest or someone they thought had tuned out. Sometimes the teacher asked students if they agreed with something someone else said, but no one was ever brave enough to disagree. On occasion the teacher publicly interviewed a student to ask what they did and why they did it, or asked them to demonstrate what they did, while classmates sat by passively.

In a student-centered math class, talking about mathematics is a focal point and should involve a vibrant exchange of ideas in which students get to share *their* thinking first. In other words, math discussion is not done *to* students but rather *with* students. This doesn't happen by randomly calling on names written on popsicle sticks. You have to be very intentional with it as a vehicle for helping students develop their mathematical vocabulary and ideas through questions and connections. Discussion doesn't happen organically at first but must be fostered over time through community building, developing a sense of trust and safety, and co-creating discussion norms with students.

This isn't always easy, and it may feel clunky sometimes. It takes practice to do well, and even then there are days when discussions go sideways. That is okay! What is most important is that you work to position students as the leaders of the discussion. It doesn't mean that you never tell them, show them, or explain to them how something works in mathematics. You do. But first, you let them talk about it to share their observations, attempts, setbacks, and questions. You use their ideas to craft the message that you want to ultimately deliver. And you just might find that, often, students will harness the mathematics and make it their own before you ever need to tell them a thing. Granted, you might need to help them polish those ideas, but you can be confident that they won't have trouble remembering someone else's way to do math because through discussion they have made the mathematics their own.

This chapter answers questions about how to help your class talk about mathematics, such as the following:

- [ ] **How do I plan for mathematical discourse?**
- [ ] **How do I plan the questions I will ask?**
- [ ] **How do I debrief the learning?**
- [ ] **How do I use representations to support understanding and discussion?**
- [ ] **How do I develop math language and vocabulary?**
- [ ] **How do I use math journals?**

As you read about these, we encourage you to think about the following:

- [ ] **What does this mean to me?**
- [ ] **What else do I need to know about this?**
- [ ] **What will I do next?**

How Do I Plan for Mathematical Discourse?

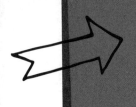

Identity and Agency

Intentional, well-planned, student-centered discourse is instrumental in developing positive dispositions about mathematics, belief in one's ability to learn mathematics, and value for others' perspectives and reasoning.

Great Resources

Smith, M. S., & Stein, M. K. (2011). *5 Practices for orchestrating productive mathematics discussions.* NCTM; Smith, M. S., Bill, V., & Sherin, M. G. (2020). *The 5 practices in practice: Successfully orchestrating mathematics discussions in your elementary classroom.* Corwin.

Every set of math curriculum standards calls for students to make mathematical arguments and to critique the arguments of others. They call for students to talk about mathematics using mathematical language and to support or oppose the work of others as they actively engage in this practice. Discussions are a vital component of learning mathematics. They must be intentional, well planned, and student centered and must allow students to express and share their ideas freely yet purposefully. Discourse should be centered on the mathematical goal of the lesson, and you'll want to be sure you've selected a task that not only meets the goal but also leaves plenty of room for exploration. Note that discourse also includes written and visual forms of expression.

STUDENT DISCOURSE IN CLASSROOM ACTIVITIES

In *5 Practices for Orchestrating Productive Mathematics Discussions,* Smith and Stein (2011) describe five practices for effectively using student responses as a tool to facilitate student discussions, which are briefly summarized here.

Anticipate
- Do the task and consider what your students might do.

Monitor
- Observe, take notes, and ask questions as students work on the task.

Select
- Identify which student work samples and ideas to share with the class.

Sequence
- Order selected student work and ideas to build understanding.

Connect
- Help students make connections between ideas and other math concepts.

These five practices explain that meaningful discussion is not organic, nor does it happen by chance. Sure, there is some level of responsiveness that you bring to the conversation, but highly effective discussion is intentional, and you play a significant role in orchestrating it. Here's what you as the teacher should do:

1 *Anticipate*
   - Examine the task prior to introducing it to the students, and anticipate possible student responses.
   - Solve the task in as many ways as possible to generate a variety of possible solution strategies (correct and incorrect).
   - Draft a set of questions to ask the students in order to gain insight into their thinking based on the anticipated responses.

2 *Monitor*

   - Facilitate and observe the students as they work on the task.
   - Circulate while the students work, asking questions to assess and gather evidence of student understanding, move their thinking forward, and/ or help students clarify their thinking. (The questions you drafted in the anticipating stage will be helpful at this stage.)

3 *Select*

   - Strategically select students to share their work with the class based on your observations from the monitoring stage.
   - Select students' work to share that
     - highlights mathematical ideas/solutions guided by the lesson goal,
     - plays a pivotal role in making the mathematics visible, and
     - helps advance the learning of the class. (This can include both correct and incorrect solution strategies.)

> I USED TO RANDOMLY CHOOSE STUDENTS TO SHARE THEIR WORK. NOW I AM MORE PURPOSEFUL BY CHOOSING THE WORK I THINK WILL BEST HELP THE STUDENTS LEARN.
>
> —FIFTH-GRADE TEACHER

4 *Sequence*

   - Make deliberate decisions about the order in which you want students to share or tell a story that will help make the mathematics visible for all learners. As part of the anticipate step, create a plan for how to sequence anticipated responses to support the mathematical goal of the lesson. Here are some possible sequences:
     - Have students present solutions from concrete to abstract.
     - Allow students to present the most common solution strategies first before moving to strategies used by fewer students.
     - Address solution strategies based on a common misconception first before moving to more successful strategies.

> • Help students connect their solutions to the solutions of their peers and to the mathematical goal of the lesson
> • Ask yourself, "How can I put the pieces of the puzzle together so that the students see coherence and connections in the math concepts explored in the lesson?"

TOOLS TO SUPPORT DISCOURSE

Students should have numerous opportunities to engage in activities that promote active engagement in mathematical discourse. Mathematical language routines that support student discourse are noted in Chapter 2 in the section "What Are Instructional Routines? How Do I Use Them?" Here are some additional teacher moves that you can easily incorporate into your classroom to support discourse:

> • *Turn and talk:* "Turn and talk" is a structured move where you divide students into pairs or triads to foster discourse. This routine allows students to learn the nuances of speaking and listening to a peer as they share their mathematical thinking. This move is good for preparing students to share their thinking with the whole group. It also provides an opportunity for each student to talk, which isn't possible in the whole-group setting. Remember to give students a moment to think before talking with their partners.
> • *Question stems:* Question stems are tools to help you plan and pose critical thinking, higher-order, probing questions to facilitate math discussions (see the next section, "How Do I Plan the Questions I Will Ask?" for sample question stems).
> • *Sentence starters:* Sentence starters, also known as sentence stems, provide students with a scaffold to help structure classroom discussions. You can use sentence starters to help your students explain and clarify their mathematical thinking, actively engage in partner and whole-class discussions, and critique the reasoning of others. The table below includes sample sentence starters:

<table>
<tr><td>To help students explain/clarify their mathematical thinking</td><td>
• I noticed . . .
• I know the problem is asking me to _____ because . . .
• The strategy I used was . . .
• I selected this strategy because . . .
• When I checked my work, I noticed . . .
• I used _____ to help me find the answer</td></tr>
<tr><td>To help students engage in partner talk and whole-class discussions</td><td>
• I agree/disagree with _____ because . . .
• Your reasoning makes sense because . . .
• I like _____ answer, but I solved the problem in a different way. I solved the problem by . . .
• My strategy is similar to/different from _____ because . . .
• I made a connection with what _____ said because . . .
• Another strategy you could use is . . .</td></tr>
</table>

Great Resources

Sztajn, P., Heck, D., & Malzahn, K. (2020). *Activating math talk: 11 purposeful techniques for your elementary students.* Corwin.

How Do I Plan the Questions I Will Ask?

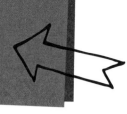

Posing purposeful questions is an important component of effective discourse in the math classroom. "Purposeful questions allow teachers to discern what students know and adapt lessons to meet varied levels of understanding, help students make important mathematical connections, and support students in posing their own questions" (NCTM, 2014, p. 35). The questions you ask your students can play a pivotal role in the direction of math discussions. Well-planned questions are an important component of rich classroom discourse; they

- provide opportunities for students to explain their thinking and build on the ideas of their peers,
- help students to think and reflect,
- deepen student understanding,
- encourage students to make connections among concepts, and
- help students arrive at new understandings of complex materials.

TYPES OF QUESTIONS

Questioning is an important instructional tool; however, just asking questions isn't enough to ensure that students are making important mathematical connections. The types of questions posed in the classroom and the patterns of questioning used are critical to ensuring that students make sense of mathematics and advance their reasoning. To promote learning of mathematical concepts, plan to use questions that promote higher-order thinking, and invite students to engage in discussions with one another as well as the teacher. Stay clear of closed-ended questions, such as those that can be answered only with a "yes" or a "no." Instead, plan ahead to pose a variety of question types during classroom discussions. The table below describes two question types (gathering information and probing thinking) and provides examples of each type based on the sample tasks:

Grades K–2 task	Grades 3–5 task
Ciara has three red toy cars and five blue toy cars. Akeem has three red toy cars, five blue toy cars, and one yellow toy car. Draw a picture and number sentence to show Ciara and Akeem's toy cars. Who has more toy cars? Use pictures, numbers, or words to show how you know.	Jose ate $\frac{1}{2}$ of a pizza. Ella ate $\frac{1}{2}$ of another pizza. Jose said that he ate more pizza than Ella, but Ella said that they both ate the same amount. Use words and pictures to show that Jose could be right.

Great Resources

NCTM. (2014). *Principles to actions: Ensuring mathematical success for all.*

DISCUSSION

Question type and description	Question examples	Question examples
Gathering information: Students recall facts, definitions, or procedures. (NCTM, 2014)	What do you know about Ciara's toy cars? How many toy cars does she have? What do you know about Akeem's toy cars? How many toy cars does Akeem have?	In the fraction $\frac{1}{2}$, what is the numerator? What is the denominator? What does $\frac{1}{2}$ mean?
Probing thinking: Students explain, elaborate, or clarify their thinking. (NCTM, 2014)	How did you figure out how many toy cars Ciara has and how many toy cars Akeem has? How do you know that Akeem has more toy cars? How did your picture and number sentence help you solve the problem?	How would you explain to Ella that Jose could have eaten more pizza than her? Can you explain how you used words and pictures to show that Jose ate more pizza than Ella?

Additional question types include the following:

- *Making the mathematics visible:* Students discuss mathematical structures and make connections among mathematical ideas and relationships (NCTM, 2014).
- *Encouraging reflection and justification:* Students reveal deeper understanding of their reasoning and actions, including making an argument for the validity of their work (NCTM, 2014).

While the types of questions posed to students during classroom discussions are important, the patterns of questions used during teacher-student interactions are equally important to promote meaningful discourse between teachers and students. *Funneling* and *focusing* are two patterns of questioning (Herbel-Eisenmann & Breyfogle, 2005; Wood, 1998).

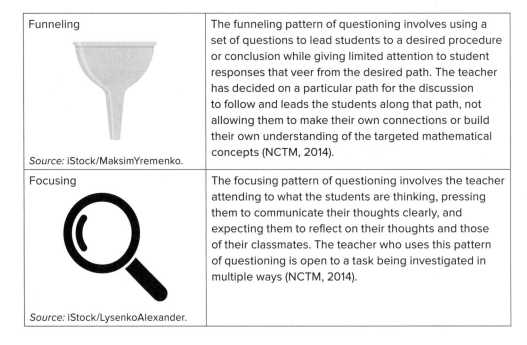

Funneling *Source: iStock/MaksimYremenko.*	The funneling pattern of questioning involves using a set of questions to lead students to a desired procedure or conclusion while giving limited attention to student responses that veer from the desired path. The teacher has decided on a particular path for the discussion to follow and leads the students along that path, not allowing them to make their own connections or build their own understanding of the targeted mathematical concepts (NCTM, 2014).
Focusing *Source: iStock/LysenkoAlexander.*	The focusing pattern of questioning involves the teacher attending to what the students are thinking, pressing them to communicate their thoughts clearly, and expecting them to reflect on their thoughts and those of their classmates. The teacher who uses this pattern of questioning is open to a task being investigated in multiple ways (NCTM, 2014).

PLANNING FOR QUESTIONING

To promote effective classroom discourse, the majority of your questions should be designed to encourage reflection and to help students build on their thinking and make connections. In addition to planning the types of questions to pose to students, also plan patterns of questioning that focus on and extend students' ideas to advance student understanding and sense making. Prior to teaching a lesson or introducing a task, plan and prepare to pose probing questions that allow students to explain, clarify, or justify their thinking. It may be helpful to use a process such as the one described below from Smith and Stein (2011) in *5 Practices for Orchestrating Productive Mathematics Discussions*:

1. First, complete the task yourself.
2. Anticipate what students might do. Be sure to include both correct and incorrect responses.
3. Brainstorm a list of possible questions to ask based on each of the anticipated student responses.
4. Based on the lesson goals, develop intentional questions that help make the mathematics more visible during student discussions, provide opportunities for students to ask and respond to one anothers' questions, and build on student thinking.
   a. Develop questions designed specifically to assess student understanding. These questions help students clarify their work and explain their work to demonstrate their understanding.
   b. Develop questions to advance student thinking. Use evidence from student work products as a foundation to build proficiency on the lesson goal(s), build on students' current thinking, and help students extend their understanding to new concepts.

Great Resources

Smith, M. S., & Stein, M. K. (2011). *5 practices for orchestrating productive mathematics discussions.* NCTM.

Some teachers find it helpful to use question prompts such as the examples given on the next page to help them develop and plan questions that assess student understanding and advance student thinking.

> STICKY NOTES WERE MY BEST FRIEND! I FOUND IT USEFUL TO WRITE MY QUESTIONS ON THEM AS I PLANNED A LESSON. I PLACED THEM RIGHT IN MY TEACHER'S EDITION SO I DIDN'T FORGET TO ASK THE QUESTIONS AS I TAUGHT THE LESSON.
>
> —KINDERGARTEN TEACHER

DISCUSSION

Sample question prompts	
Question type	**Sample questions**
Questions to help students get started on a task or problem	<ul><li>How would you describe the task in your own words?</li><li>What do you know about the task/problem? What do you need to find out?</li><li>Is there anything you know that isn't in the task/problem?</li></ul>
Questions to help you monitor students' progress and support perseverance	<ul><li>Can you explain what you have done so far?</li><li>Is there a strategy that you used in the past on a similar task that may help you?</li><li>Is there anything else you can do?</li></ul>
Questions to ask to help students make connections among ideas and applications	<ul><li>Can you tell me something we learned before that you found helpful in solving this task?</li><li>How does what we did today relate to . . .? (e.g., a previous concept, yesterday's lesson)</li><li>What did you notice when . . .?</li><li>Do you see a pattern? Can you explain the pattern?</li></ul>
Questions to ask to help students make sense of mathematics during class discussions	<ul><li>Does anyone have the same answer as yours but you can explain it differently or used a different method/strategy?</li><li>Tell me how your strategy is different from the one used by a classmate.</li><li>Find a classmate who used a different strategy from yours. Can you explain your classmate's strategy?</li><li>Is your answer reasonable? Why or why not?</li></ul>
Questions to ask to support the use of representations	<ul><li>How might a picture, table, or diagram help you support your work?</li><li>How does the picture, table, or diagram help explain your answer?</li><li>Could you tell me how you chose to organize your work?</li><li>Can you make a model to show your work?</li></ul>

Notes

Answers to Your Biggest Questions About Teaching Elementary Math

How Do I Debrief the Learning?

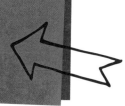

The debriefing discussion is a vital component of using math tasks during your lesson. It is the conversation after a task that provides students with the opportunity to discuss what they've learned and how they learned it, and it summarizes their mathematical ideas about a particular task. Summarizing and synthesizing foster sense making. Debriefing not only informs you of what students know and are able to do mathematically based on the learning goals, but it also gives you insight about the next steps for your students. The debrief occurs after the engagement of a lesson, but you can have mini debriefings as students work, using a catch-and-release model (see Facilitate a Lesson, p. 66.). A task debriefing could also be part of the lesson closure. The slight difference is that the lesson closure looks at the entire math lesson or block, and it can do more than debrief the task by having students reflect on other aspects, such as how they worked together or how they got unstuck.

DEBRIEF THE LEARNING

Debriefing discussions are about the students. They should have the first crack at sharing their thinking, strategies, and solutions. Toward the end of a debriefing discussion, you can then add your own approach or begin to explicitly teach the skill or concept. Enlist students to carry the conversation by inviting them to respond to one another. Provide feedback to the ideas that are shared, and probe them further as needed so that they are clear to all. Use the discussion as another piece of evidence to monitor and assess student learning.

TIPS FOR DEBRIEFING DISCUSSIONS

Tip #1 | Purposefully plan for the debriefing.

Examine your learning target(s) and lesson activities, and make a plan for how you want students to demonstrate their understanding of the lesson concepts. Be sure your plan devotes enough time to debriefing. Often, a discussion takes no less than 10 minutes. Use the strategies for discourse to frame your debriefing discussion (see Plan for Discourse, p. 146), which include monitoring what students do during the activity and identifying or selecting student work or strategies to feature during the discussion.

> I THOUGHT THE LESSON CLOSURE WAS THE ONLY TIME TO DEBRIEF WITH STUDENTS. NOW THAT I INCORPORATE OPPORTUNITIES TO DEBRIEF WITH MY STUDENTS WHILE THEY'RE WORKING ON A TASK, MY STUDENTS SHARE THEIR THINKING, HELP EACH OTHER MAKE CONNECTIONS, AND I CAN USE THE INFORMATION TO PROVIDE IMMEDIATE FEEDBACK DURING THE LESSON.
>
> —FOURTH-GRADE TEACHER

Tip #2 | Have students prepare for the debrief.

Consider ways in which you can organize their thoughts before the debriefing discussion. The following list isn't comprehensive, but it contains a few activities you can use to help students summarize and synthesize their thinking.

Activity	Description
Traffic light cups	This is a quick tool to formatively assess student understanding and prepare for a discussion: red = *having a challenge*, yellow = *unsure but think we're okay*, and green = *got this*. Give stackable party cups to students to use as the lesson unfolds. Monitor how the students use the cups to identify where you visit and what you might discuss during a debrief.
3-2-1	Students can use this reflection tool to share their thoughts about their learning. Students respond to three reflective prompts, providing six ideas in total (three for the first prompt, two for the second prompt, and one for the third prompt). Those ideas are then used to support the class discussion that follows.
Journal entries	At a pivotal point in the lesson, give students a journal prompt, and ask them to respond using numbers, pictures, and/or words (see Math Journals, p. 163).
Student reflection before discussion	At designated points in the lesson or as part of the debriefing discussion, have students complete a quick self-reflection before you begin the whole-class debriefing discussion. ☺ I understand and can explain _____ to a friend. 😐 I sort of understand but would like to talk about _____. ☹ I don't understand _____.

Identity and Agency

Label the strategies recorded on the board to honor the individual or group who shared and to empower them as the thinkers and doers in the classroom.

Tip #3 | Record strategies using the whole board.

Record student thinking on the board, or display it with a document camera to anchor the discussion. You want to find a way to capture the thinking so that it can be referred to or connected to as new ideas are shared during the debriefing.

This means, you likely need a clean space to record all of the ideas. It is not uncommon for an entire board to be filled with ideas during a debriefing discussion.

Tip #4 | Connect anchor charts.

Connect anchor charts (see Anchor Charts, p. 42) to a debriefing discussion in two different ways. Use the debriefing discussion to create a new anchor chart that the class can refer to in future lessons. Or use a previously created anchor chart to support the debriefing discussion as it unfolds.

Tip #5 | Provide feedback.

A high-quality debriefing discussion is not a parade of students sharing how they did a problem. Instead, it is a critical opportunity for an exchange of thoughts and ideas to advance student understanding. For this to happen, feedback must be part of the debriefing discussion (see Give Feedback, p. 185). The characteristics of effective feedback (Shepard, 2008) can help you think about how to craft your debriefing discussions by

- pointing out strengths and offering specific information to guide changes,
- addressing partial understanding,
- connecting the ideas of different students or groups of students,
- not doing the thinking for students, and
- directing attention to the intended learning.

Notes

DISCUSSION

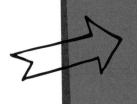

How Do I Use Representations to Support Understanding and Discussion?

Identity and Agency

Students who connect representations deepen their understanding of concepts and are able to make sense of and do the math.

When someone shows you a picture of a birthday party, you get a general sense of the party. When you see additional photos of the same party, you get a richer perspective of what the party entailed. The same idea applies to mathematical representations. Representations are learning tools used to "show" the mathematics. Representations have a lot of benefits. They

- help students access abstract mathematical ideas through visualizing or "seeing" mathematical relationships;
- deepen students' understanding as they bring mathematical ideas to life;
- create connections, helping students see mathematics as a web of interconnected, rather than separate, ideas (Skemp, 1978); and
- help students retain what they have learned.

Mathematical representations come in many forms:

Type of representation	K–2 example	3–5 example
Contextual	"There is one blue balloon and two red balloons. So there are three balloons."	"There are three rows of chairs and 4 chairs in each row. So there are 12 chairs altogether."
Visual		
Physical (using manipulatives)		
Symbolic	1 + 2 = 3	3 × 4 = 12
Verbal	"One plus two equals three."	"Three times four is twelve."

USE REPRESENTATIONS DURING MATH LESSONS

Students should use representations during their math lessons to help them access the mathematical ideas they are exploring. Your students will have deeper understanding when they are able to represent, discuss, and make connections among mathematical ideas in different forms (Fuson et al., 2005; Lesh et al., 1987). Here are some tips for using representations effectively:

Tip #1 | Encourage multiple representations.

While one representation is beneficial, students will develop a richer, more detailed view when they see the same concept through multiple perspectives. Choose tasks that invite the use of different representations and consider the big mathematical idea you want your students to make sense of. Encourage students to draw more than one representation and use a variety of manipulatives if they are able to do so.

You will find that students represent their mathematical ideas in different ways. Some will come up with ways to represent their ideas that you haven't even thought of! Accept all of these representations, and reinforce the many ways in which a mathematical idea can be represented. This can be done by showcasing student work during class discussions and asking questions to help your students find similarities and differences between the different representations.

Tip #2 | Don't ask students to copy you.

Some curricula materials suggest the use of certain representations when students are initially building understanding of a concept. An example would be when students are using ten frames to build understanding of a unit of 10. Once students have used representations in this way to construct understanding, resist the temptation to tell them to replicate the model or tool you believe best represents the mathematical idea when they are applying their understanding to new situations. Similarly, avoid "rules" such as "When you see problems like this, you will always want to use this model." Rather, allow students to choose which representations they want to use. The goal is for students to utilize whatever representation makes the most sense to them, not replicate the one you might have used that they don't understand.

If a student gets stuck or does not have an idea of which representation to try, it is okay to offer a suggestion, which might sound like this: "You might consider using a drawing or a math tool to help you think more about the problem." Offering the student a few options allows the student to do the decision-making and determine which representation might be the most helpful to them.

Tip #3 | Remember, representations are not strategies or concepts.

Representations are ways to demonstrate mathematical understanding, but they are not the same thing as a problem-solving strategy. A representation helps a student better visualize the abstract strategy they choose to use. For example, when a student solves 24 + 15, they might use a number line. They begin at 24 and break apart 15 by adding 10 to the 24 and then adding 5 more to arrive at 39. The number line is the representation, while counting on is the strategy.

Tip #4 | Remember, concrete-representational-abstract (C-R-A) is not a linear process.

It is important for students to use concrete models, representations, as well as numbers and symbols when they do math. C-R-A (also known as C-S-A or concrete-semiconcrete-abstract) doesn't necessarily follow a rigid linear process, but rather, students benefit when there is fluidity among all three.

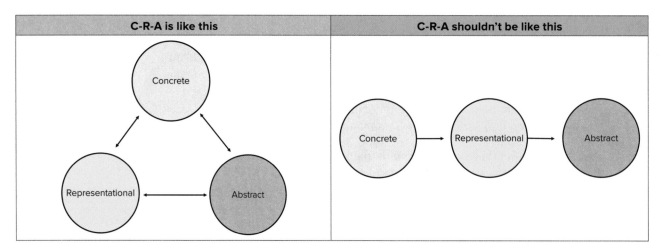

C-R-A is like this	C-R-A shouldn't be like this

For example, a student shares their drawing of three shaded and two unfilled circles for 2 + 3. You might begin with the expression and ask the student to show where in the drawing the 3 is represented. In other words, you don't always have to begin with the image or physical manipulatives. You can start with an equation or any representation. Just make sure connections are made between the different ways.

Tip #5 Be intentional with the representations you showcase.

During the lesson debrief, purposefully select and use representations to move the class toward the intended goal. Guide students to make direct connections among and between the representations they use and those used by others. Choosing which representations to highlight or use during the class discussion will be more beneficial than randomly calling on students. An unsystematic plan may not necessarily lead your class to your desired outcome for the lesson.

Tip #6 Display student work during discussions.

Representations give students something they can talk about and refer to as they explore mathematical ideas and as you debrief a lesson (see Debrief, p. 153). Put the manipulatives or work under a document camera, re-create a drawing on the board, or display it through a device or shared screen. The important thing is that every student in the class can see the representation being discussed and the student refers to their representations as they share their thinking publicly so that the other students in the class can make sense of what the student did.

Tip #7 Use representations to expose student understanding and misconceptions.

Representations may reveal a student's fragile or not fully developed understanding. For example, if a student uses base-ten blocks to build 43, and uses 3 ten rods and 4 unit cubes, it is an indication that they do not fully understand place value and how this tool represents groups of 10. The same is true if a student doesn't recognize that 2 ten rods, 3 ones, and then 2 more ten rods show 43 as well. A representation can also show a student's deeper understanding of a concept. For example, if a student shows 2 tens and 23 ones, they demonstrate that they have a flexible understanding of the composition of numbers.

Tip #8 | Help students connect representations.

In this image, you can see how connections can be made among the different representations, shown by the arrows.

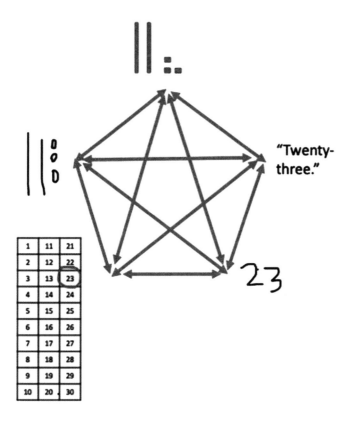

Think about young students making connections between the physical representation of base-ten blocks, a drawing of sticks (tens) and dots (ones), the number on the hundreds chart, and the symbolic representation of written digits on the board. They make further connections by saying the number out loud. Frequently making connections like this deepens students' learning.

It will take time before students start making these connections on their own. As students debrief a lesson, ask questions to guide them in making connections between their representations and the other representations you showcase. You might say, "Can you show me where the 23 is represented in your math drawing and how that looks different in the number your friend wrote on the board?" or "Where do you see the 3 from 23 in the base-ten blocks?" Eventually, students will start noticing and making these connections independently.

> MY MATH COACH SUGGESTED I ASK, "WHERE IN YOUR WORK DO YOU SEE . . . ?" TO HELP MY STUDENTS MAKE CONNECTIONS IN THEIR WORK AND TO THE WORK OF OTHERS. IT WORKS REALLY WELL! THEY EVEN STARTED ASKING EACH OTHER THAT QUESTION!
>
> —SECOND-GRADE TEACHER

How Do I Develop Math Language and Vocabulary?

If a kindergarten student can say "brontosaurus," then they can say "rhombus"! Students love big new words, so don't shy away from using the real math words. The key to introducing new or unfamiliar math vocabulary is to explore it with examples, nonexamples, and images, and in context so that students understand how to use the terms and have concrete examples of appropriate use. Whenever possible, connect it to words that they already know and other math concepts too.

If there are words that have dual meanings (e.g., *right*) or are homophones (e.g., *sum* and *some*), be sure to clarify which word you are using. Use anchor charts (see Anchor Charts, p. 42) to capture the meaning of these words, and be sure to use them during discussions. Developing math vocabulary will be critical to math discussions, and you want your students to feel empowered by a strong foundation in mathematical language.

THE DOS AND DON'TS OF MATH VOCABULARY

Dos	Don'ts
Use precise math language yourself.	Make up words for math concepts or replace proper math vocabulary.
Post words with student-friendly definitions with images and examples.	Post only the word by itself.
Introduce words after students have explored the concept.	Preteach all the math vocabulary.
Encourage the use of math words in student discussions.	Lead discussions in which you are the only person using the math vocabulary.
Provide sentence stems for students who need them.	Provide no language supports.
Use interactive word walls that are developed over the year.	Use premade word walls with all of the math terms posted at the beginning of the year.
Catch and correct yourself when you are imprecise.	Require students to use math vocabulary when you don't.

TALK ABOUT MATHEMATICS

Studies suggest that the number of repetitions needed to learn a word is about 10–15 times, with lots of variation (Shanahan, 2016). Most of the words we use in mathematics are unique to mathematics or have different meanings outside of the classroom.

This means that to enable math vocabulary to become a regular part of students' speech, you must intentionally provide plenty of opportunities for discourse. These opportunities may include the following:

- Math debates about an interesting topic
- Vocabulary-teaching strategies from language arts classes
- Small-group discussions in class or in breakout rooms
- Student recording of math vocabulary and their mathematical ideas on Flipgrid or Seesaw
- Number routines that include math vocabulary during discussion
- Math language routines (see Instructional Routines, p. 63)
- Student sharing of new words they are learning with their family

Be sure to hold students accountable for using correct math vocabulary once it has been introduced.

WRITE ABOUT MATHEMATICS

Students learn the language of mathematics when they write about it. There are many opportunities to include such writing (see Math Journals, p. 163). The key is to be sure students are using math vocabulary once they have a clear understanding of the meaning of the word. Writing, along with drawing an image or creating an example, helps cement the word in their long-term memory. Students can write about mathematics during all stages of a math lesson and when they go home. Some prompts for developing math vocabulary through writing include the following:

- Draw a picture about a new math word.
- Write about your favorite new math word.
- How are the words _____ and _____ connected?
- Write about the math word that is most confusing to you.
- Write a summary of today's lesson using three math vocabulary words.
- Write a text to a friend explaining a math vocabulary word you learned today.
- Write a short math poem about math vocabulary.
- Write a song lyric with math vocabulary words to summarize the concept.

USE WORD WALLS

Having an organized math word wall provides a place for students to go and look up words they are unsure of. Word walls should also be interactive, which means that you refer to them often and also have activities like "Guess My Word" to revisit the vocabulary. Write the word on one side of the card and the definitions on the other side. Write definitions with student-friendly language and images to help students understand the word. For example, when first talking about triangles, students may write, "three corners and three straight sides." As they become more familiar with the concept, we would want them to say, "A closed figure with three straight sides and three vertices." As they develop a better understanding, you want to replace the student-friendly language with the precise vocabulary on your word wall. Here are things to consider as you set up your word wall:

- Keep it in a place where students can reference it (and reach it) easily.
- Only include words that you have introduced and used in class discussions.
- Organize the words by topic so that students see connections between them.
- Keep common words on the wall all year (e.g., number, sum, difference, product, quotient).
- Post student examples by words to help them make meaning of the words.

WORD WALL ACTIVITIES

Here are some things you can have students do to keep a word wall interactive:

- Match the word to a picture.
- Choose a word, and write a definition of it or draw pictures and examples.
- Find words to complete sentence frames or starters.
- Connect ideas about words using a Frayer model.

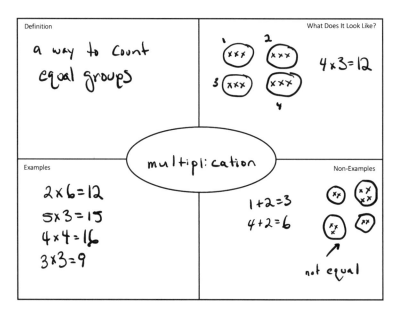

- Make a word web with a variety of details and information about the word at the center.
- Use word walls to create personal math dictionaries.
- Pick words to create math graffiti (decoratively write all the math words you know, including visuals and examples for each one, on chart paper).

Flexible Learning

You can use online gaming tools, like Kahoot, to play vocabulary games. You can use Jamboard and similar tools to create a virtual work mat of a Frayer model or something similar that students can use on their devices.

How Do I Use Math Journals?

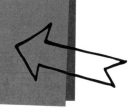

Getting your students to talk about mathematics is really about getting them to communicate about mathematics. They can do this through discussions and representations. Journal writing is another effective tool for getting your students to communicate mathematically.

> Writing in math class supports learning because it requires students to organize, clarify, and reflect on their ideas—all useful processes for making sense of mathematics. In addition, when students write, their papers provide a window into their understandings, their misconceptions, and their feelings about the content. (Burns, 2004, p. 30)

A good journal prompt is simply a good question. They are open-ended questions that naturally differentiate and provide different entry points.

Identity and Agency

Journals are a great way to learn about who your students are and what they think about themselves as math learners.

TIPS FOR USING MATH JOURNALS

Journaling in mathematics might not be something you have experienced before. There is no right or wrong way to use math journals, but we have found that there are certain things you may want to consider as you plan:

Tip #1 Journals are for all students.

Any student in any grade can journal, even if they aren't proficient writers yet. To support student journaling, you might use sentence starters (e.g., How would you describe _____ in your own words . . . ?) and make use of instructional strategies that would be used in a language arts class (e.g., have students brainstorm ideas first or doodle an image before writing). You might even offset some of the writing with drawings or voice recordings.

Tip #2 Make time to journal.

There is no right or wrong time to have your students journal. They can do it during independent work time, at a station or center in your classroom, as part of your closure (see Close the Lesson, p. 75), or even as homework. One useful approach is to provide one prompt for an entire week that students add on to when they finish the work early.

Tip #3 Make journaling reciprocal.

You want to see what students think and feel about mathematics. And your students want to know what you think as well. Read their prompts, and write a note back. Balance the workload by reading one or two each day. Or have students flag entries that they especially want you to respond to. Keep in mind that you don't have to write a lot back, but "Good job" and "Me too" are not the quality responses your students are hoping for. Instead, a note like "Good job using representations to show how the fractions are equivalent. Your diagrams go well with your writing" will be more effective. You can provide feedback (see Give Feedback, p. 185) in the form

DISCUSSION

of a question, such as "You added by counting on with ones. Can you show me what it would look like if you counted on by groups or tens?"

✳ Tip #4 | Avoid grading their entries.

Grading a journal entry implies that certain thoughts or feelings might be incorrect, not valued, or just plain wrong. That's not what you want. Reading their ideas and giving them feedback convey to them that engaging in the activity is valued and expected. If you must give credit, keep it about participation, awarding a point for completing the activity.

✳ Tip #5 | Don't get hung up on spelling or grammar.

Journaling is about content and quality. Encourage correct spelling and grammar, but try to avoid giving feedback about this specifically. Focus on their message and the ideas they want to share.

✳ Tip #6 | Look back along the way.

At the end of a unit, month, quarter, and school year, have students look back at their writing. Ask them to think about how they have grown and changed as learners. Look back through their journals yourself to take note of this and to help you reflect on the great work you have done.

✳ Tip #7 | Create a separate section for notes about content.

Math journals have clear applications as tools for taking notes about content, strategies, and so on. You might have your students keep this work separate from their math reflections. When doing this, find a structure that helps students archive their learning. This might include recording the topic or learning target at the top along with the date.

✳ Tip #8 | Use a table of contents.

If you use your math journals to create a content log as described, think about having students make a table of contents for the content portion of their journals. This will help them revisit ideas.

TYPES OF JOURNAL PROMPTS

While you want to use journals to learn about students' understanding of the content, you can actually use a variety of prompts to learn about them through other lenses as well. Here are some prompts that can help you learn about their dispositions and identities, their understanding of content, their math behaviors, and their insights and feedback about math instruction.

Dispositions and identity	Math content
• My best-kept secret about mathematics (this week) is . . . • If mathematics could be a color (shape, sound), it would be _____ because . . . • I want to become better at mathematics so that I . . . • People who are good at mathematics . . . • When it comes to mathematics, it is difficult to . . . • When I hear someone say "mathematics," I think . . . • Tell how you're a mathematician. • What kind of math figure are you? (circle, square, triangle, parallelogram, etc.) Why did you choose that figure? • My goal for mathematics this week/month/quarter/unit is . . . • My math superpowers are . . . • My family thinks mathematics is . . .	• How is _____ the same or different from _____? • I think a _____ is _____. I thought a _____ was _____. • How would you describe a _____? • How do you use _____ in your life? • How would you describe _____ in your own words? • Tell all you know about . . . • Describe how _____ is used in our everyday lives. • Explain everything you know about . . . • Tell how you compare numbers, subtract numbers, and so on. • Why is it important to know . . . ? • Which is your favorite strategy for . . . ? • One thing you have to know about _____ is . . . • What are you still wondering about . . . ?

Math practices	Class feedback
• What do you think about as you solve a problem? • What can you do when you get stuck with a problem? • How do you know if your answer is reasonable? • How do you participate in a mathematical argument? • How do you use tools in mathematics? • What tools do you use? How do you know when to use them? • What does it mean to be precise in mathematics? • What important words have you used in mathematics this week? What do they mean? • What patterns did you use in mathematics this week? How do those patterns help you understand? • How can you use patterns to help you solve problems? • Find a shortcut for . . .	• How should we use class time to the best advantage? • What has helped you the most with mathematics this week? • What did you like the most about your previous math class? What did you like the least? • One math activity I really enjoy is _____ because . . . • Write a letter to a student who will be taking this class next year, giving some advice about this class.

HOW DO I KNOW WHAT MY STUDENTS KNOW AND MOVE THEM FORWARD?

We have learned that there is so much more to knowing what students understand than points, percentages, and test scores. Though district and state assessments have some value summatively, the information that drives daily instruction comes from observing, listening, and reading about student thinking every day. We have come to agree with a popular notion that student understanding is like an iceberg. High-stakes assessments tell us something about students, similar to what is seen of an iceberg above the water line. But the true depth and complexity of their thinking and understanding constitute so much more, and it lies below the waterline. And that is the information a teacher must know about their students, and it is learned through daily assessment.

Daily formative assessment is about collecting evidence of understanding. It isn't focused solely on the right answer. It also examines the reasoning behind answers and the communication of those ideas. Evidence comes in many forms and is collected in many ways. The evidence you collect informs what you do in the next moment or the following day. Remember that no one piece of evidence tells the whole story about student understanding, and so you must collect and use multiple data points. It is this work of teaching, gathering, and interpreting evidence of understanding that ultimately shapes performance on high-stakes assessments.

Teaching mathematics well and in a student-centered way means not simply moving from page to page, lesson to lesson, as outlined in your curriculum guide. You aren't teaching mathematics, you are teaching students. Formative assessment then holds the key. It is about making your instructional decisions about how and when to move forward—and when not to—based on what you know about what they know.

This chapter isn't about multiple-choice tests, Friday quizzes, or grading because those don't necessarily give you detailed information about what students know or how to move forward. Instead, this chapter answers questions about how to find out what students know and how they think and behave, and how you decide to move forward, including the following:

☐ **How do I find out what students know?**

☐ **What should I look for as students work?**

☐ **What math behaviors do I look for?**

☐ **How do I assess student thinking?**

☐ **How do I help students self-assess?**

☐ **How do I give feedback?**

☐ **How does assessment inform my next steps?**

☐ **How do I celebrate my students' progress?**

As you read about these, we encourage you to think about the following:

☐ **What does this mean to me?**

☐ **What else do I need to know about this?**

☐ **What will I do next?**

How Do I Find Out What Students Know?

Tests and quizzes are traditional ways to assess students. But there are many more ways by which you can collect evidence of student understanding during class. To do this well, know what you are looking for. Have a sense of what it will look like when a student has mastery of a concept, as well as what it might look like when they aren't quite there yet. Think about possible, even common, misconceptions, such as adding numerators and denominators when adding fractions $\left(\text{e.g.,} \ \frac{1}{3}+\frac{1}{2}=\frac{3}{5}\right)$. To anticipate what students might do, do the task first yourself. This will give you a better picture of what students' work might look like, thus better preparing yourself to identify evidence during the lesson.

DIFFERENT WAYS TO ASSESS

As you consider the different options to assess, think about what ways might best fit with a particular lesson. There is no one right way. All the information you gather will contribute to a clearer picture of student understanding, guide your future instructional decisions, and provide information that you can share with parents regarding their child's progress.

OBSERVATIONS

Observing a student as they work provides valuable information about where they are in the learning progression. Visit students as they work. Look at their work, and listen to what they are saying. As you visit, record information about their thinking that you can refer to for debriefing discussions, determining understanding, making instructional decisions, and communicating with families.

> MY TEACHING PARTNER GAVE ME THE WONDERFUL IDEA OF ALWAYS HAVING A CLIPBOARD WITH ME SO I COULD RECORD NOTES AS I OBSERVED STUDENTS WORKING. THIS HELPED ME KEEP MY OBSERVATION NOTES ALL IN ONE PLACE.
>
> —FIRST-GRADE TEACHER

INTERVIEWS

One of the best ways to get a window into a student's thinking is through a brief interview. You can plan for them as other students work with independent assignments, centers, or games. Have students solve a problem, and ask them about the strategy they used. A useful aspect of an interview is that you can tailor your questions to probe student thinking. This will help you get a richer picture of their understanding and reasoning.

Examples of interview tasks:

- Pose a two-digit number to a first grader. Ask them to identify numbers that are greater or less than the number. Ask them what is 1 more, 1 less, 10 more, and 10 less. Ask them to put it on a number line or to identify other numbers with the same number of tens.
- Give students some digit cards. Ask them to arrange them to make the largest number. Then ask them to make the smallest number.
- Pose a problem for students to solve, such as $70 - 59$ (grade 2), $399 + 1{,}254$ (grade 3), or 34×12 (grade 4). Watch how they solve it. Ask them questions about their strategy and if there are other ways to solve it.
- Have students compare two fractions, and ask them how they compared them. Give them two new fractions, and ask them if their approach would still work or if they would do something else and what that would be.

STUDENT WORK SAMPLES

You can gather samples of students' written work to analyze after the lesson. Students can work on printed copies, on loose leaf, or in their journals. Good prompts for work samples ask students to represent and explain their thinking.

Examples of prompts for student work samples include the following:

Grade 2	Grade 3	Grade 4
Tell how you can compare 239 and 932.	How can you use $5 \times 5 = 25$ to find 7×5?	Show $\frac{3}{4}$ in three different ways. Tell how you know each shows $\frac{3}{4}$.

HAND SIGNALS

There will be times when you want to quickly know what a group of students is thinking. Hand signals work well in this situation, letting you see individual responses and the group overall. Have students give a "thumbs up," "thumbs down," or "sideways thumb" to indicate, respectively, if they agree, disagree, or are not sure about a statement. You might ask students to reveal their hand signal in front of their chest or stomach to keep their response private or to avoid influencing others' responses.

EXIT TICKETS

Exit tickets can be used at the conclusion of a lesson, asking students to solve a problem, give examples of the topic, or write about what they learned. Often this is done on an index card or sticky note. Students then turn in their work as the lesson ends and they leave the class. While the information on an exit ticket is useful for making decisions about the next lesson, sometimes it is information that you needed to address during the lesson, such as a misconception that was repeated during the lesson but wasn't addressed and now may be more challenging to undo.

SELF-ASSESSMENTS

Students of all ages are capable of self-assessing. This may be as simple as a kindergarten student drawing a smiley face or frowny face. Older students may write a few sentences on how they are feeling in relation to learning a particular concept.

Flexible Teaching

Tools like Pear Deck are good for collecting work samples in an online setting. You can also use screengrabs of virtual manipulatives and virtual whiteboards.

ASSESSMENT

Or they might choose a number from 1 through 4 that best indicates their perception of how they're doing or how well they understand. There isn't a right or wrong way for students to self-assess, and the power of the activity lies in having the student assess their learning.

TIPS FOR COLLECTING EVIDENCE

Tip #1 Assume competence.

You may feel the urge to focus on what your students can't do yet or the errors they are making. Instead, look for strengths in your students' work rather than deficits (Kobett & Karp, 2020). Rather than jotting a note that says, "Doesn't use the Count On strategy," frame the evidence as something the student can do. This might be better phrased as "Uses the Count All method repeatedly—ready to move on to Counting On." Capturing evidence in this way will help you recognize what your students are doing successfully and provide guidance for where you want to help them go next.

Tip #2 Vary your methods.

It is likely that you will find one way of collecting evidence that feels most comfortable for you. While it is fine to use this method most often, push yourself to try other ways. You will find that different ways of collecting data will come together to paint a better, fuller picture of your students' understanding.

Tip #3 Look beyond just understanding.

Assessment isn't limited to content knowledge. Gather information about how your students behave mathematically (see Math Behaviors, p. 174) and their dispositions or how they perceive themselves as mathematicians. Leverage a rubric (see Assess Student Thinking, p. 177) that helps you make sense of the evidence you collect and determine student performance.

Tip #4 Small-group interactions.

Observations are not limited to students working independently. You can gather valuable information about student understanding as well as their mathematical behaviors while they are working in groups. You can do this as students work collaboratively on a task or play games together. You can even ask groups to self-assess.

Notes

What Should I Look for as Students Work?

To learn what students know, you must observe them as they work on tasks, complete centers, or play games. Be aware that observing does not mean circulating around the room making sure the students are on task. Instead, you want to understand what they are doing and thinking. That means you are watching and asking questions. You are taking notes. You are actively listening. You are identifying strategies or planning what you want to highlight during a debriefing discussion. And while observing, you can also assess student performance and determine what you need to do next.

WHAT SHOULD YOU LOOK AND LISTEN FOR?

Obviously, you want to see if students are acquiring, applying, and retaining the skills and concepts you are teaching. While in many cases you are looking at the accuracy of the work, you are also looking for much more than correct and incorrect answers.

These are some of the questions to ask yourself as you observe the students:

Content knowledge	Mathematical behaviors
• Do they apply understanding accurately? • Are there signs of misconceptions? • Do they repeat a flawed process? • Do they repeat an inefficient approach (e.g., counting on by ones when adding two- or three-digit numbers)?	• Do they attempt to make sense of the task and show perseverance? • Do they manipulate numbers? • Do they explain their thinking to partners or when asked?

Strategies	Dispositions
• Do they use a reasonable strategy? • Do they rely on the same strategy each time? • Do they change strategies when a preferred strategy is inefficient? • Do they attempt a strategy and adjust when they recognize their work is leading them in the wrong direction?	• Do they show interest in the topic? • Do they show interest in the activity? • Do they show frustration when encountering a challenge or obstacle? • How do they engage with their partners?

RECORDING INFORMATION DURING OBSERVATION

You want to record what you observe in the moment because as the lesson and the rest of your day unfold, you can easily forget what happened in math class. These notes are valuable tools for assessing, determining your next instructional steps, making grouping decisions, and even communicating with families. Don't feel pressure to collect notes about every student, in every class. Instead, work to gather information over time. Target the individuals you want to observe during a given lesson. Try to get multiple measures of each student over longer periods of time.

ASSESSMENT

> # EACH OF THE TEACHERS ON MY TEAM RECORD WHAT WE OBSERVE A LITTLE DIFFERENTLY. WE HAVE OUR OWN SYSTEM. BUT WE EACH LOOK FOR HOW STUDENTS THINK ABOUT THE PROBLEM.
>
> —FIFTH-GRADE TEACHER

INDEX CARDS OR STICKY NOTES

A simple, low-tech way to record notes is to make use of index cards or sticky notes. There is no single tried-and-true method for using these. Fiddle with your approach to find one that works best for you. Record the strategies students use, the insights they have, the misconceptions they show, or confirmation that they understand. You can also record evidence of learning behaviors. Another way to use sticky notes is to record the student's name on the top and write down what you noticed about the student's thinking and work on the sticky note. Then after the lesson, you can organize the sticky notes to make decisions about instructional next steps and how you might potentially group students.

Flexible Learning

You can use Google Forms or something similar to create a recording sheet on your phone or tablet. Simply create a rubric (see Assess Student Thinking, p. 177) or recording sheet on the Google form. Save the link to the form on the home page of your phone or tablet. Then, simply click on the home page button to go straight to the form during class observations.

Here are some examples of the notes you might take:

- While students work on a problem, you might note if they draw a picture, use manipulatives, write an equation, or don't know how to get started.
- While students are working to solve a multidigit addition problem, you might note who counts on by ones, who counts on by chunks, who uses partial sums, and who uses an algorithm.
- While students are working on a problem, you might note who is unsure how to get started, who changes strategies as they work, or who has ideas on what to do when they are stuck.

TAKE A PHOTO

Snapping a photo with your smartphone or tablet is a great way to capture the moment. It also serves as an artifact to support your determination of student progress. You can take a picture of written work, representations, or how the student uses manipulatives. Once you have a digital file, you can create folders for each student or folders arranged by math concept. The great thing about using photos is that you have a record of student work but don't have to sift through a stack of papers when it's time to analyze it! Photos are also very helpful for communicating progress to families.

CLIPBOARD NOTES

Jot down quick anecdotal notes on a clipboard while you are observing. The way you organize these notes is up to you. You might have a clipboard with an individual paper for each student where you record evidence of their understanding. Or you might make a table that has a list of student names, followed by the activity and date. Here you can record quick notes regarding the student's work and have a page full of notes for the lesson.

CLASS OBSERVATION SHEET

A class observation sheet is another way to record notes or assess student progress. Again, there are a variety of ways to do this. A good observation sheet includes student names, the date, and a title or note about the task or activity. It can feel daunting to have to record information about every student. But there are ways to overcome this. For example, if you are recording performance with a 3 (*got it*), 2 (*making progress*), or 1 (*not yet*), you can record only the 2s and 1s, making comments only about what they do. You can choose to collect data only for those students you need information about. You can rotate through students collecting evidence about a smaller set of students each day. Or you can target a specific strategy you want to look for, such as using make tens. Then as students work, take note only of those students who use that strategy (see Fluency Strategies for Operations, p. 138).

WHAT SHOULD YOU ASK AS YOU OBSERVE?

Observation is not a passive teaching move. You are thinking about what they are doing, why they are doing it, and how you will respond. It should also be an interaction that can potentially give you even more information. There is no set of questions you have to ask as you observe. But in general, you want to ask questions like the following:

- Can you tell me more about your thinking?
- Can you describe your strategy out loud?
- How is _____ like _____?
- What would happen if _____?
- Is there another strategy you might use to _____?

These questions are examples of how you probe student thinking and reasoning. More important, they give you direct, specific information as to what students are doing and why. They enable you to draw better conclusions because you don't have to guess what they did or why they did it. And there is yet another added benefit in asking questions as you observe. These questions model those you want students to ask themselves while they work. Your questioning helps develop the metacognitive skills of the student you're talking with and the students who are watching the exchange.

Another way to ask this question is "Should I assess anything other than math content?" The answer is a resounding yes! Mathematics is more than content. Mathematics is about doing and thinking. We want our students to learn concepts and procedures so that they can apply them to problems and their everyday life. But we also want them to develop mathematical behaviors that transcend the discipline and grade level. These behaviors have to be taught and should be assessed. Doing so will tell you much about who your students are as learners and mathematicians.

MATH LEARNING BEHAVIOR CHECKLISTS

The math learning behaviors in these checklists are developed from the Common Core Standards for Mathematical Practices (National Governors Association Center for Best Practices & Council of Chief State School Officers, 2010; see Math Practices, p. 33). Some of the practices have been combined. These tools can be easily transferred to the math "processes" or "practices" in your curriculum standards. It's challenging, if not impossible, to determine these behaviors through paper-and-pencil assessments. You have to observe your students in action, during routines, lessons, centers, games, and explorations. You can look for each behavior, but it's probably more practical to focus on one or two behaviors at a time. You can create a class observation sheet to record when students demonstrate behaviors. The checklists provided here are intended more as a reporting tool. F stands for "frequently demonstrates the behavior," O means "occasionally," and N means "does not yet demonstrate the behavior."

Makes sense of problems and perseveres when solving them	F	O	N
Explains the meaning of the problem			
Engages in problem solving (develops, carries out, and refines a plan)			
Persists when solving problems			
Considers if answers make sense and adjusts if needed			

Reasons abstractly and quantitatively	F	O	N
Represents a problem with equations and can explain how they are connected			
Uses numbers flexibly			
Examines the reasonableness of their answers/calculations			

Makes arguments, critiques others' arguments, and attends to precision	F	O	N
Justifies solutions			
Listens to the reasoning of others			
Compares and asks questions about others' ideas			
Uses math vocabulary			
Looks for accuracy within their processes and thinking			
Is aware of units and necessary math labels			

Models with mathematics and uses tools strategically	F	O	N
Represents concepts and problems			
Uses equations appropriately			
Selects appropriate tools			
Uses tools accurately			

Looks for and uses patterns	F	O	N
Looks for patterns and relationships			
Uses patterns and relationships to acquire new concepts			
Use patterns and relationships to solve problems			
Uses patterns and relationships for efficiency			

Alternatively, you might choose to report on the behaviors holistically. The chart below shows what this might look like:

Mathematical practices	F	O	N
Makes sense of problems and perseveres when solving them			
Reasons abstractly and quantitatively			
Makes arguments, critiques others' arguments, and attends to precision			
Models with mathematics and uses tools strategically			
Looks for and uses patterns			

> IT WAS USEFUL TO HAVE EVIDENCE OF MY STUDENTS' MATHEMATICAL BEHAVIORS TO SHARE WITH PARENTS DURING CONFERENCES. THEY LOVED HEARING ABOUT HOW THEIR CHILD'S MATH BEHAVIORS WERE DEVELOPING. IT ALSO HELPED THEM KNOW THERE'S MORE TO MATH THAN JUST THE CONTENT.
>
> —FIFTH-GRADE TEACHER

OTHER STUDENT BEHAVIORS TO LOOK FOR

There are other behaviors that may not connect as cleanly or directly to the math practices or processes in your standards but are worthy of notice. These include behaviors that signal strengths and development.

Great Resources

Kobett, B. M., & Karp, K. S. (2020). *Strengths-based teaching and learning in mathematics: Five teaching turnarounds for grades K–6.* Corwin.

Look for students who

- show a positive disposition toward mathematics;
- like solving puzzles and playing games;

ASSESSMENT

- enjoy building with blocks and Legos, which develop spatial awareness that transfers to number relationships and magnitude;
- show curiosity about how things work;
- find different ways of doing things and solving problems;
- connect their lives and experiences with concepts and contexts in mathematics;
- like to share mathematical experiences outside of the classroom;
- share observations of logic and reasoning outside of math class/school;
- innovate their own approaches or strategies;
- like to design things and tinker;
- show comfort with making mistakes;
- connect concepts and procedures without being told to or shown how;
- gravitate to tools, technology, or coding; or
- connect mathematics to other subjects (English language arts, social studies, science, etc.)

Notes

How Do I Assess Student Thinking?

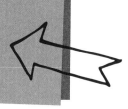

Determining student understanding is much more than identifying right and wrong answers. What evidence do you have that your students are able to reason, solve, and communicate? As you collect evidence, through observation or student work, how do you evaluate it? This can be difficult because understanding comes in many forms and is communicated in a variety of ways. And though a wrong answer can indicate some kind of challenge, it doesn't tell the whole story about what students know about a skill or concept. A reliable, practical tool like a rubric can help you determine how well students understand.

RUBRICS

A rubric is an evaluation tool that qualitatively describes performance or understanding and guides your assessment. You can use rubrics summatively to score student work or formatively to identify students who need reteaching, need reinforcement, or need to move on. Rubrics can be written specifically for every task you want to collect data about, though that can become overwhelming and cost you time that is better served planning instruction. We recommend a general or versatile rubric that you can apply to a wide variety of, if not all, standards and tasks you teach. We also recommend that your rubric uses only three, or at most four, levels because creating discernible differences in evidence becomes more and more challenging as more and more levels are used in a rubric (Liljedahl, 2021).

Demonstrates Understanding	Demonstrates Some Understanding		Not Yet Demonstrating Understanding
Answer/Solution is correct and	Answer/solution is correct and	Answer/solution is incorrect and	Answer/Solution is incorrect and
❑ Justification is clear and mathematically accurate.	❑ Justification is incomplete, slightly flawed, or task-unique.		❑ Justification is mathematically incorrect, missing, or irrelevant.
❑ Representation is mathematically accurate.	❑ Incorrect answer is the result of imprecision though the justification is accurate.		❑ Representation is mathematically incorrect, missing, or irrelevant.
❑ Strategy is appropriate and valid.	❑ Representation is relevant but mathematically flawed.		❑ Strategy is mathematically incorrect, missing, or irrelevant.
	❑ Strategy is valid but inefficient, inappropriate, or task-unique.		

When using a rubric like the above, remember the following:

- Right answers can happen for the wrong reasons, so always consider them with at least one of the conditions listed.
- Not all components need to be checked. One or more should suffice.
- Students can justify their thinking using representations such as equations, drawings/diagrams, physical models, and/or words.
- Strategies should be appropriate relative to the grade level, what has been taught, and the unique ways students think about mathematics. For example, it is appropriate for a first grader to prove that $5 + 7 = 12$ using a ten frame, a number line, a drawing, or something similar. However, it is likely inappropriate to expect a fifth grader to prove that $5 + 7 = 12$ when adding the ones place of $12,985 + 33,707$.
- *Task-unique* describes a strategy that works for the specific task but is not generalizable or would not work in all math situations. For example, a student says that $\frac{3}{4}$ is greater than $\frac{2}{4}$ because it is missing fewer pieces. Comparing the number of pieces is a strategy that does work for these two fractions, but simply counting the number of missing pieces wouldn't work in the case of comparing $\frac{7}{8}$ and $\frac{3}{4}$, or $\frac{7}{8}$ and $\frac{11}{12}$.
- *Irrelevant* means that the response has nothing to do with the task or prompt.

You can adjust the levels of a rubric from three to four. Yet even this four-level rubric yields some similarities. Most notably, student performance falls into three categories of understanding (Got It, Getting There, Not Yet), but the subsequent actions are slightly different as the middle section is broken into reinforcing versus reteaching. You can learn more about what to do next instructionally in the section "How Does Assessment Inform My Next Steps?" (page 188).

Got It	Getting There		Not Yet
Advance Extend Enrich	Reinforce Practice	Reteach	Reteach
Student demonstrates full understanding of the concept. • The solution is correct. • Reasoning is provided through pictures, words, or numbers/equations. • Justification is complete. • Minor errors may be present but do not impact the response.	Student demonstrates understanding of the concept. • The solution may be incorrect but can be attributed to a computational error rather than flawed logic. • Reasoning is provided but may not be complete.	Student demonstrates some understanding of the concept. • The solution may be correct but it is situational or coincidental. • Reasoning is based on flawed logic or misconception of the concept yielding a correct answer.	Student demonstrates no understanding of the concept. • The solution is incorrect. • There is no justification or reasoning. • Numbers or terms are disconnected from the prompt or the prompt is restated.

TIPS FOR WORKING WITH RUBRICS

Tip #1 Work for consistency.

Rubrics help you evaluate student work equitably through consistency and clearly defined levels. Yet there is still an element of subjectiveness. Be mindful of this. Work to be consistent in how you interpret and use the rubric from student to student.

> I FOUND IT USEFUL WHEN MY TEACHING PARTNER AND I EVALUATED A FEW PIECES OF STUDENT WORK TOGETHER. THAT HELPED ME MAKE MORE SENSE OF THE RUBRIC AND BECOME MORE CONSISTENT WHEN LOOKING AT OTHER PIECES OF STUDENT WORK.
>
> —FOURTH-GRADE TEACHER

Tip #2 Do the task.

As noted (see Questions, p. 149), take the time to do the task so that you have a sense of what students might do, the misconceptions they might have, and how you would do the task. This will help you to consider evidence or examples of the different levels and to identify your own bias. Be prepared for students who might not complete the task or share their thinking in ways you expect. That is okay! A rubric helps you evaluate the unexpected in clear, consistent ways.

Tip #3 Be aware of bias.

Knowing how you would do the task helps you think about your bias toward what students might do. We may be more likely to favor explanations and justifications that align with our preferences.

Tip #4 Use rubrics with observations.

Rubrics are great for student work. But you can also take notes on a rubric while observing students complete a task, work at a center, or play a game.

Tip #5 Know how a rubric affects grading.

Rubrics can be used for grading and reporting progress. Know that using a single rubric with only three or four levels for a letter grade or percentage is problematic. However, if you use the rubric consistently with multiple data points, the values shouldn't be problematic as points are accumulated over time. For example, using a 3-point rubric 10 times would yield 30 points, so missing a point won't drastically change a student's grade.

Equity and Access

Rubrics help you evaluate student work equitably through clearly defined levels that are communicated with students. But be mindful of biased interpretation of those levels.

ASSESSMENT

Tip #6 · Scrutinize between "Got It" and "Getting There."

It's rather easy to recognize when students don't yet understand. It can be more challenging to discern whether they *fully* understand. Ask yourself if you had to infer any of their reasoning. Ask yourself what's missing and if the reasoning always works or if it is unique to that problem. Ask yourself what else you would want to know, and if needed, ask them follow-up questions. And keep in mind that any one sample isn't enough for determining mastery.

Tip #7 · Make a decision, and get more information.

Using a rubric might seem time-consuming, but that isn't the case, especially when you use the same one routinely. There will be times when a student's work falls squarely between two levels. We encourage you to avoid dwelling on it for too long. Instead, make a decision, and commit to getting more information about that individual. Adjust your evaluation as needed. Know that it is always a good idea to pull a student aside and ask a few more questions to best understand their work.

Tip #8 · Get multiple data points.

Evidence from one task doesn't necessarily tell you the whole story about a student's understanding. You need multiple data points for determining their understanding, which you can collect by varying the types of tasks you use (observation, exit ticket, etc.) and providing different prompts.

Tip #9 · Collaboratively design, customize, and adjust.

Either of the rubrics presented here should serve you well. Customize them as needed. Add examples for a specific task, skill, or concept as you see fit. Create them with other teachers on your team when possible. Solicit student insights about the rubric. Use them and adjust or update your rubrics over the course of the year.

Tip #10 · Communicate with families.

Share your rubric with families so they understand what the levels mean. Communicating what these tools mean and how they are used is especially helpful if you choose to use numbers for the levels (e.g., a "3" instead of "Demonstrates Understanding" or "Got It"). Consider having students share their student-friendly, self-assessment tools (see Self-Assessment, p. 181) with their families. You can even have students explain their work through these tools to their families.

Notes

How Do I Help Students Self-Assess?

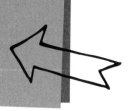

Self-assessment is an important life skill. Consistently engaging your students in self-assessment helps them develop this skill and potentially transfer it to other content areas. Self-assessment shapes students' perceptions of their ability to learn and do math. It creates a sense of agency that they themselves are in charge of their learning and performance on the task. With math instruction, incorporating student self-assessment

- promotes a student-centered approach to teaching and learning by calling for students to think about and evaluate their work;
- improves student engagement, giving them greater ownership of their learning and performance;
- helps students develop reflection skills and metacognition about the quality, clarity, and accuracy of their work; and
- provides you with additional insight and perspective about how well students truly understand math content and how well they exhibit math behaviors.

DEVELOP QUESTIONS FOR STUDENTS TO ASK THEMSELVES

Self-assessment starts with the questions you want students to ask themselves as they complete tasks. You can post these on anchor charts (see Anchor Charts, p. 42). You can print them on small slips of paper and have students complete and attach those forms to their work before submitting it. Some of the questions you might use with students are as follows:

- Does my answer to the problem make sense?
- Did I explain my thinking clearly?
- Could someone else understand my thinking?
    - Did I use math vocabulary?
    - Did I use pictures or drawings? Do they connect to the problem?
- Are my calculations reasonable?
- Are my calculations accurate?

You can also use questions like the following to help students self-assess their mathematical behaviors:

- Did I make sense of the problem, and can I explain it in my own words?
- Did I have a strategy to solve the problem that made sense?
- Did I try something else when I got stuck?
- Did I explain it so someone else will understand my thinking?
- Did I use manipulatives, pictures, numbers, or words to show my thinking?
- Did I use a tool to help?
- Did I make sure my work was accurate?

CONSIDER A STUDENT-FRIENDLY RUBRIC

Another way for students to assess their work is to have them use a student-friendly rubric that is aligned to the rubric you use (see Self-Assessment, p. 181). This rubric builds on the questions students ask themselves before submitting work. The difference here is that they have to think carefully about how well they understand to make a declarative statement about their learning (I Get It, I'm Starting to Get It, I Don't Get It Yet).

I Get It	I'm Starting to Get it	I Don't Get It Yet
❑ I explained my thinking clearly. ❑ I used pictures, numbers, or words to explain my thinking. ❑ My strategy works.	❑ I think I explained my thinking clearly. ❑ I used pictures, numbers, and words to explain my thinking. ❑ I am pretty sure my strategy works but there might be a better one.	❑ I am not sure how to explain my thinking yet. ❑ I am not sure how to use pictures, numbers, or words for this yet. ❑ I think my strategy works ❑ I'm not sure of a strategy for this yet.

Regardless of which approach you use, your most critical action is to help students understand what satisfies these questions/criteria. You teach students how to answer these questions by modeling with teacher think-alouds. You can refer to anchor charts during debriefing discussions having students consider how well a shared idea satisfies any given question from the list.

USE STUDENT-FRIENDLY LEARNING TARGETS

In addition to assessing their work, you want students to assess their progress toward a learning goal or target. Instead of posting a standard or lesson objective on the board, share with students a learning goal or target for the lesson or series of lessons. This helps them focus on *their* learning so that they can self-monitor and ask questions during instruction. These learning targets also help you hone your students' progress relative to a target.

> I WAS SURPRISED TO LEARN THAT I SHOULDN'T WRITE THE LESSON OBJECTIVE ON THE BOARD EXACTLY AS IT WAS WRITTEN IN MY TEACHER'S EDITION. I NOW UNDERSTAND HOW IT IS MORE MEANINGFUL FOR STUDENTS IF I WRITE IT IN A WAY THAT MAKES SENSE TO THEM.
>
> —THIRD-GRADE TEACHER

Identity and Agency

When the learning target is clear, students can take ownership and responsibility for what they are learning.

Good learning targets are

- focused on a specific outcome that is part of a larger topic or standard,
- written in student-friendly language so that they are understood, and
- used during the lesson to check for understanding by you and the student.

"I CAN" LEARNING TARGETS

You can't simply share the standard from your curriculum because a standard generally includes a collection of learning targets and they aren't written for students. You or your curriculum unpacks the standard into learning targets, smaller chunks, that build toward the big idea. Often, these learning targets are written as "I can" statements in order to move toward a practice of self-assessment.

Grade 2 instructional standard	Learning target examples	
Fluently add and subtract within 100 using strategies based on place value, properties of operations, and/or the relationship between addition and subtraction.	• I can add two-digit numbers with base ten blocks.	• I can add two-digit numbers by counting on.
	• I can add two-digit numbers making tens.	• I can add two-digit numbers using partial sums.

Grade 4 instructional standard	Learning target examples	
Compare two fractions with the same numerator or the same denominator by reasoning about their size. Recognize that comparisons are valid only when the two fractions refer to the same whole. Record the results of comparisons with the symbols >, =, or <, and justify the conclusions, e.g., by using a visual fraction model.	• I can use pictures to compare fractions.	• I can compare fractions with the same denominator.
	• I can compare fractions by thinking about how far they are from 0, $\frac{1}{2}$, or 1.	• I can compare fractions with the same numerator by thinking about the size of the pieces.

TIPS FOR LEARNING TARGETS

Your curriculum likely includes learning targets that you might need to put Into student-friendly language or rewrite as "I can" statements. It is possible that you will need to write your own. Here are some tips for doing this:

Tip #1

Start with the standard! One standard may contain several learning targets. Think about the different skills and concepts embedded in it. Write targets for those skills specifically.

Tip #2

Use the targets to help you plan and sequence the lessons within a unit of study.

Tip #3

Use math vocabulary words from the standard and verbs from the math practices (see Math Practices, p. 33) in your learning targets—for example, "I can compare fractions with unlike denominators using pictures and models."

Tip #4

Have students refer to the targets during the lesson or at the end to self-assess their progress.

Notes

Answers to Your Biggest Questions About Teaching Elementary Math

How Do I Give Feedback?

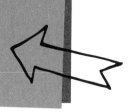

Think about a postobservation conference with your administrator. Scores for different sections will have some value but the scores themselves don't help you grow as a teacher. Instead, you seek feedback about your classroom management, questioning, engagement, or how you supported students. You want someone with experience and expertise to help you think about what you do well, what you might need to adjust, and how you might go about doing so. Your students crave the same thing about learning and doing math. And though good grades are desirable, the grades themselves don't offer much in the way of actionable feedback.

WHAT IS FEEDBACK?

Feedback is an opportunity to deepen understanding about our work by getting insight from someone who has experience and a different perspective. Feedback is information about how one is progressing toward a goal or outcome. It can be oral or written. The goal of feedback is not simply to give students the information you think they need or to tell them that something is correct or incorrect but rather to help them think critically about their ideas and to refine or further develop them.

Feedback has a significant effect on student learning (Hattie & Clarke, 2019). It has been shown to develop student skill in devising diverse strategies, motivation, and ultimately achievement (Vollymeyer & Rehinberg, 2005).

WHAT DOES GOOD FEEDBACK SOUND LIKE?

The truth is many of us were not well trained in how to offer feedback. In math class we often resort to confirming if an answer is correct and, if not, sharing how to do it correctly. From the students' view, feedback becomes a directive from a superior mathematician. To avoid this, you can pose a feedback question or prompt to trigger a thinking response from a student or group. Here are some examples:

Feedback for second-grade students adding 49 + 73

Example 1	Example 2
Student finds a sum of 112. Teacher: *You found a sum of 112. How does that compare with the estimate you made before you added the numbers?* (when an estimate wasn't made)	Student finds a sum of by adding on with jumps of 7 tens and 3 ones. Teacher: *You found the sum by adding on with jumps of tens and ones. That strategy works. How would that strategy work if you started with 73 instead of 49?* Or Teacher: *You found the sum by adding on with jumps of tens and ones. That strategy works. What do you think would happen if your jumps were groups of tens—like adding 50 or five jumps of 10?*

ASSESSMENT

Feedback for fourth-grade students comparing $\frac{5}{6}$ and $\frac{1}{4}$:

Example 3	Example 4
Student draws $\frac{5}{6}$ with a rectangle and $\frac{1}{4}$ with a circle. Teacher: *You drew a rectangle to show $\frac{5}{6}$ and a circle to show $\frac{1}{4}$. The images helped you think about the fractions. How would your thinking change if you drew the same shape for each fraction?* A series of questions with a similar approach to feedback would be *Why did you draw two different shapes? What if you made them both the same shape? How would that change your answer?*	Student compares the numerators, then compares the denominators. Teacher: *You compared 5 and 1. Then you compared 6 and 4. But those are fractions. You have to think about what the 5 and 6 mean together. Try drawing a picture of each fraction to see what they look like.* Other questions you can leverage for feedback for this example might be *Can you tell me why you looked at those numbers separately? What if we looked at them as fractions?*

WHAT TO KNOW AND WHAT TO DO

What to know	What to do
Feedback matters!	Commit to providing it regularly. Know where you are with giving feedback, and make conscious efforts to develop your skill in giving feedback.
Anticipate what students might do.	This helps you think about the feedback you might give. But know you can't anticipate everything.
Feedback can be a question.	Feedback doesn't have to be a statement of action. Instead, it can be a question that causes a student to think more about the task and their reasoning or justification as shown in examples.
Feedback is about the task, not the person.	Give feedback about the evidence in the work. Focus on the purpose of the task, and progress toward it. Avoid judging what might have occurred without getting as much information as possible. Separate behavior from the mathematics by not connecting a student's behavior or attitude to their performance. Statements like "You don't know what to do because you weren't listening" are not a component of effective feedback.
Feedback is clear and user- (student-) friendly.	Offer feedback so the student understands it. Keep vocabulary as basic as possible by avoiding words like *vague* or *abstract*, and try to do the same with sentence structure (see Example 4).
Feedback is actionable.	Provide feedback that students can take action on—e.g., "What would a picture of your thinking look like?" (see Example 4).
Feedback is timely.	The unit test, or even the Friday quiz, can be too late for feedback. Do your best to give it as soon as possible—ideally as students are working on a task or during the debriefing of a task. Each of the examples above was given right after the students finished a task.
Feedback takes many forms.	Feedback can be oral or written. You can use drawings and diagrams in your feedback. You might draw something and ask students to compare your work with theirs. Also, be mindful that nonverbal communication is potential feedback as well. In Example 2 the teacher could have drawn a different way to show the addition and asked the student to think about how the two drawings are similar and different.

What to know	What to do
Feedback isn't advice or evaluation.	Try to avoid "I would . . ." statements. Of course you would—you already know how to do the math!
Feedback isn't a spectator sport.	Feedback in front of an audience compromises (if not damages) confidence and a student's social standing (either perceived or actual), contributing to math anxiety. In short, you wouldn't want your colleagues to join you for a postobservation conference for a lesson that didn't go particularly well.
Students must feel safe.	Establish and maintain a positive, nurturing environment (see Community, p. 19) in which feedback is part of the culture. In that community you give feedback to students, students give feedback to one another, and they give feedback to you as well!
Taking action is collaborative and will be successful.	Affirm that they are not in it alone. They will be supported. They will be successful in time.
Feedback can't overlook what went wrong solely for maintaining positivity.	Don't ignore what went wrong. Student errors are opportunities for learning. They don't happen by chance as there is always some logic behind their approaches. Acknowledge it, and use it to build new, accurate understanding.
Feedback can come from anyone, not just you!	Help students develop skills for giving others feedback. You can model this during your discussions. Encourage students to ask themselves questions as they work on a task and review their work.
Use references in your feedback.	Refer students to resources such as anchor charts, master notes, or worked examples for helping them think about their work. This also helps students give feedback to one another.
Feedback isn't a one-way street.	Solicit feedback from your students. This will help you grow as a teacher and better meet their needs. It also models how to ask for feedback and how to use it. Keep in mind that students might not know the best way to give feedback, so try not to take anything personally.
Be patient, and give yourself grace.	Giving feedback takes time to learn how to do well. Be aware, reflective, and committed to practicing it.

IT WAS HARD FOR ME TO GIVE GOOD FEEDBACK TO MY STUDENTS AT FIRST, OTHER THAN "GOOD JOB!" OR "NICE TRY!" I GOT BETTER AT IT AND SAW THAT IT HELPED TRIGGER THEIR THINKING.

—KINDERGARTEN TEACHER

Notes

ASSESSMENT

How Does Assessment Inform My Next Steps?

Once you've taught a concept, you will have an important decision to make. You will be asking yourself, "Do I move on, or do I spend more time on this concept?" Your next steps will depend on your students' needs—not what is on the next page of the teacher's edition of your curricular program or what comes next on the district's curriculum map. Analyze the evidence of student thinking you have gathered (see Assess Student Thinking, p. 177) to determine how you will proceed.

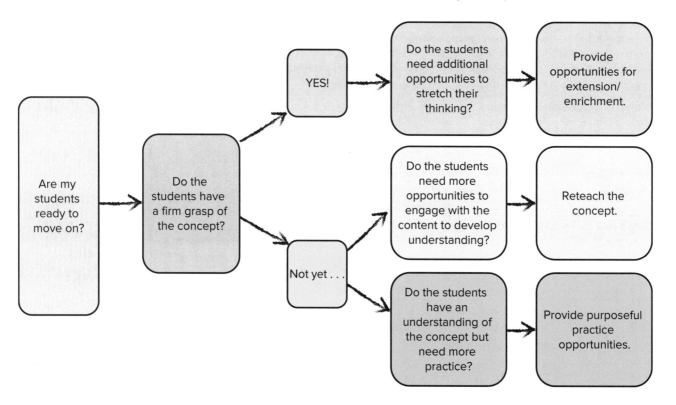

STUDENTS' NEEDS ARE DIFFERENT

Some students will need more time than others on the lessons you allocate for a particular concept. These are the students you describe as "Not Quite There Yet," as they have not yet acquired understanding. It will be important to determine what these students need so you can provide the appropriate targeted instruction.

ACQUISITION (RETEACHING BECAUSE THEY DON'T YET UNDERSTAND)

If a student has not yet developed an understanding of the concept, then reteaching will be necessary. This is when you will engage the student in activities where they can think, talk, and work on constructing their own understanding of the mathematical concept. Students should use manipulatives and representations.

They should talk and have opportunities to connect their own ideas to those of others. Instruction should be student centered (see Student-Centered Math, p. 50). Most likely, this instruction will take place in small groups, as not every child in the room will need reteaching. However, there may be a few instances where reteaching the entire class may be necessary.

REPETITION (MORE TIME FOR MEANINGFUL PRACTICE)

You will have some students who have an understanding of the concept but it may not be fully developed. These are the students who would benefit from more practice, as the repetition will help strengthen their understanding. This doesn't mean that a student should complete 100 practice problems on the concept. Rather, the student should engage in purposeful practice opportunities. This might be through cooperative learning activities with a partner, a game, or an engaging task. The practice should contribute to shoring up the student's knowledge of the mathematical concept they haven't yet mastered.

> I NEVER REALLY THOUGHT ABOUT DIFFERENT REASONS WHY STUDENTS WEREN'T GETTING IT. I JUST RETAUGHT EVERY TIME. I STARTED TO FIGURE OUT THAT SOMETIMES THEY JUST NEEDED MORE EXPOSURES.
>
> —FOURTH-GRADE TEACHER

RETEACHING CAN'T BE MORE OF THE SAME!

When you determine that students need additional opportunities to engage with the content, you then must decide what your instruction will look like. It is important to know that more of the same type of instruction isn't the best approach. If it didn't work well for some students the first time, it probably won't work the second time either! So think about one student who was successful and constructed their own meaning during the initial instruction. What was it that this student had thought about? What type of representation or model did the student use? You might also talk to your peers to see if they used a different strategy that helped their students be successful. These insights will help you think about how you might structure your instruction so your reteaching provides a new, fresh instructional approach for the students who need additional opportunities to engage with the concept.

BE CAREFUL TO NOT STAY ON A CONCEPT FOR TOO LONG (IT'S OKAY TO MOVE ON!)

It may be tempting to stick with a concept or standard until each student reaches mastery. This could become troublesome as, if you do, you might run out of instructional time and never get to other important grade-level standards. Let's think about this using a basketball analogy. You wouldn't want a player to only practice dribbling until they mastered it. Rather, the player needs to also practice shooting, playing defense, and making in-bound plays to be a strong and well-rounded player. The same idea applies to learning mathematics. A third-grade teacher doesn't focus on teaching multiplication facts until each student has mastered all of the basic facts. The teacher should decide when it is appropriate to move on and provide additional opportunities for reteaching and/or practice for those students who need it.

Just because you move on to another concept, it doesn't mean you will completely disregard the one your students still need to work on. Let's say you're working on basic addition strategies with your students. The *make ten* strategy doesn't come as easily for some students as for others. This doesn't mean that you won't ever discuss or apply the make ten strategy again during the year. As students are adding two-digit numbers later on in the year, it is very likely you will highlight the make ten strategy during that time. Even if you shift your focus to another mathematical concept or standard, you will still find ways to revisit those skills and concepts that might be worth the extra attention.

IT'S NOT OKAY TO HOLD BACK THE REST OF THE CLASS

Some students will not require reteaching or extra practice. It wouldn't be fair to these students to keep them from moving on to new topics because there are a handful of students who need more time to engage with the content. Rather, consider all student needs, and continue to structure learning opportunities for each and every student to grow and learn.

Notes

How Do I Celebrate My Students' Progress?

Celebration increases engagement, nurtures student identity, fosters a positive math community, strengthens family partnerships, and, most important, reinforces productive behaviors. When you honor your students' mathematical brilliance and growth, you will notice that they will work to replicate them and begin to thrive because they have a classroom that loves mathematicians and celebrates them!

WHAT DO I CELEBRATE?

Celebration should be saved for strategies and behaviors you want students to continue to perform so they grow as mathematicians. Celebrate when students achieve their learning goals. In other words, don't just celebrate results like correct answers or perfect test scores; celebrate effort and perseverance. Celebrate when they use certain strategies or are engaged in the math practices (see Math Practices, p. 33)—for example, "I loved the way you used an area model to show how you used partial products on this problem!" Praise the growth and effort of students who are not there yet so they are encouraged to keep working at the goal. This may sound something like, "I love your perseverance on this problem!" Both of these examples refer to behaviors we would want to celebrate so students would repeat them. Celebrate when students do the following:

- Demonstrate understanding or growth with a skill or concept
- Use a strategy to get themselves unstuck
- Communicate their thinking
- Take a risk
- Use math vocabulary accurately
- Make connections to mathematics outside of the classroom
- Help classmates (without being too helpful)
- Reach personal learning goals
- Share new strategies

WHAT ARE SOME WAYS TO CELEBRATE?

An easy, effective way to celebrate students is to give vocal praise during a math conference, in the math community during a lesson, or broadcast to the whole school community. Vocal praise should be used often with specific information so that students clearly know what is being praised. Stay away from generic praise like "Good job," "Excellent," or "Awesome" unless you follow it with that specific statement. Generic statements cause students to wonder about what was good or awesome and to guess about what they should do again. They make them feel good but do not necessarily reinforce the behaviors you want. Also, keep in mind that some students are shy and do not want to be celebrated publicly; that is okay, but providing them positive feedback on their work, quietly letting them know that they have done something well, or sending a positive message home goes a long way. Shy students should still be celebrated but in a way that makes them comfortable.

ASSESSMENT

Here are some ways to consider when celebrating students:

 Source: iStock/Anna Pogrebkova.	*Make a positive phone call home:* Make a quick call home to share with families what their child has done well.
 Source: iStock/Valentin Amosenkov.	*Text a picture home:* Snap a picture of a student doing something well in class or of their quality work.
 Source: iStock/Tetiana Lazunova.	*Post exemplary work:* Dedicate wall space in your room to showcase exemplary work, and remember it doesn't necessarily have to showcase correct answers but can also include novel thinking or diverse representations.
 Source: iStock/nickylarson974.	*Post their picture or achievement:* Posting math celebrations on your class walls, in the hallways, or on a website is a way to celebrate for those families and students who feel comfortable having their pictures posted.

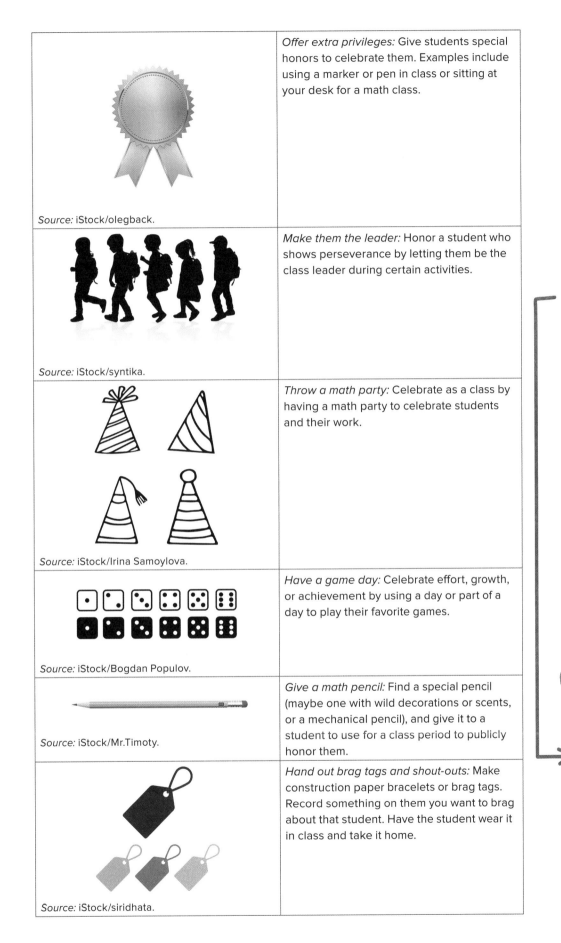 Source: iStock/olegback.	*Offer extra privileges:* Give students special honors to celebrate them. Examples include using a marker or pen in class or sitting at your desk for a math class.
Source: iStock/syntika.	*Make them the leader:* Honor a student who shows perseverance by letting them be the class leader during certain activities.
Source: iStock/Irina Samoylova.	*Throw a math party:* Celebrate as a class by having a math party to celebrate students and their work.
Source: iStock/Bogdan Populov.	*Have a game day:* Celebrate effort, growth, or achievement by using a day or part of a day to play their favorite games.
Source: iStock/Mr.Timoty.	*Give a math pencil:* Find a special pencil (maybe one with wild decorations or scents, or a mechanical pencil), and give it to a student to use for a class period to publicly honor them.
Source: iStock/siridhata.	*Hand out brag tags and shout-outs:* Make construction paper bracelets or brag tags. Record something on them you want to brag about that student. Have the student wear it in class and take it home.

I FOUND THAT MY STUDENTS LOVED GETTING A BRAG TAG TO TAKE HOME. IT WAS A BADGE OF HONOR. IT HELPED THEM TALK ABOUT MATH WITH THEIR FAMILIES.

—FIRST-GRADE TEACHER

How Do I Celebrate My Students' Progress?

 *Source:* iStock/anuwat meereewee.	*Offer math bucks:* Give students math bucks for effort, perseverance, and achievement. They can accumulate math bucks to buy things from your treasure chest of goodies, like special erasers and other fun things.
 *Source:* iStock/Iuliia Kanivets.	*Give stickers:* Stickers are a traditional award that most students love to get. Fun purchased stickers are always a hit. But you can also make them with mailing labels.
 *Source:* iStock/ProVectors.	*Make a morning announcement:* Acknowledge students' work during the school's morning announcements.

HOW DO I ENSURE THAT I CELEBRATE ALL STUDENTS?

Students and families notice who does and does not get celebrated, so be sure you celebrate all your students! Keep track of the students you celebrate by noting the behaviors you are celebrating on a class list. This will help ensure that every student gets celebrated.

	John	Susie	Latrenda	Georgina
Persevering				
Taking a risk				
Using math vocabulary				
Showing growth				
Hitting a math goal				
Engaged in math practices				
Being a great math coach				

You can also have students celebrate others by having them nominate classmates for outstanding work or having a great experience working in a group together. Finally, have students celebrate themselves by having them reflect on their successes in their math journal or by having them write a note to their families sharing what they did well in mathematics. Sharing celebrations will help you develop stronger family connections while helping to build students' math identity.

 Equity and Access

When you ensure that each and every student gets celebrated, it helps to build equitable math classrooms where each student is celebrated for their mathematical skills and talents.

Notes

ASSESSMENT

WHERE DO I GO FROM HERE?

We've learned that we don't know everything yet. We know that what we have shared with you here will change and evolve over time as we learn more as a profession. This book answers the questions that the teachers we support ask us most often. We believe that it will answer some of the most important questions you may have. But there is much to know about teaching and learning mathematics well. With time, you will need to dig more deeply into math content and the strategies for teaching it. This might feel overwhelming, but we urge you to embrace it as an opportunity. You can't know everything about teaching mathematics, but you can commit to learning more and growing your practice.

Great mathematics teaching is a journey, not a destination. Each and every one of us must continue to pursue learning and trying new things in our classrooms. We say this to you because we too have made that commitment and we continue to live it today. We believe that growth begins with personal learning, consistent reflection, and tinkering. We also know it helps to be pointed in the right direction from time to time. Here, we point you toward the activities and resources we have found so helpful.

What Activities Can I Pursue to Learn and Grow?

Great teachers separate themselves from good teachers by their continuous pursuit of learning and growth. They know that there is no perfect lesson. They know there will always be something to do to fine-tune their practice. Great teachers engage with colleagues, coaches, administrators, and district supports. Take advantage of learning from others. Listen to their insights, and ask questions. Share your ideas, and get feedback on them. And as with other endeavors, we encourage you to think critically about what you see and hear during these exchanges. What has worked well for colleagues may not fit well with your skills and attributes.

PARTICIPATE IN COLLABORATIVE PLANNING

When done well, collaborative planning is a powerful tool for designing highly effective lessons and for learning about content and instructional practice. Think about it. To teach a lesson well, you have to select high-quality tasks (see Tasks, p. 91), anticipate what your students will do (see Know the Math, p. 84), think about the questions you will ask (see Questions, p. 149), and know what to look for as they work (see Look for's in Student Work, p. 171). Planning with colleagues gives you insights and perspectives about each. You will learn about strategies and misconceptions that you hadn't considered from teachers with different experiences.

PEER OBSERVATIONS

You can learn a lot from visiting another teacher. Talk with your principal about finding ways to observe teachers from other grades in your school and potentially the same or different grades at other schools in your district. And though visiting teachers in another grade won't frame similar content, it will help you see new approaches to structure, management, and engagement activities. Take note of what the students are doing and how they're responding as much as—or more than—you notice what the teacher does.

WHAT SHOULD I LOOK FOR DURING A CLASS VISIT?

- Where do you see mathematics around the room?
- How do the students engage with one another?
- What is the math community like?
- How is the class structured?
- What does the teacher do to monitor and reinforce expectations?
- What are the procedures of the class? How do the students move from activity to activity?
- How does the class begin, and how do the students react?
- How are math tools and manipulatives housed, accessed, and used?
- How are questions asked and discussions facilitated?
- How are ideas represented and communicated?
- How are the students supported?

CLASSROOM VISIT NOTE-TAKING TOOL

We encourage you to jot down notes and questions about your visit. An easy way to do this is to fold paper in thirds, creating sections for noting what you notice in terms of things you are doing and things you will try, and what you wonder or have questions about. Another option is to look for what the students are doing and connect that to what the teacher is doing or likely has done, creating a list of things you will continue or begin to do.

Visit Recording Tool A		
I *noticed* things I do in my classroom.	I *noticed* things I want to try in my classroom.	I *wondered* about . . .

Visit Recording Tool B		
I noticed students were . . .	Because the teacher . . .	Which reminds me to . . .

Try to find a time to talk with the teacher after the lesson later that day or possibly that evening to share what you saw and to ask your questions.

You may also want to invite a colleague to your classroom to observe what you do and give feedback. You might partner with someone from another grade or work with someone in your team. In fact, collaborating with a teammate teaching the same lesson can be especially helpful. To do this, plan a lesson together, and visit each other as that lesson is taught to see how the implementation is similar and different.

RECORD YOURSELF

Recording yourself is a great way to see what you do and help you think about what you might do differently. In the moment of teaching, your brain is distracted by so many things. It can be hard to reflect on what happened, why it was happening, and what you did in response. Recording a lesson or part of a lesson lets you take another look at what happened. This activity can also help you see details about your questioning, discussion, pacing, and so on.

> ONE OF THE MOST POWERFUL THINGS I DID WAS TO VIDEOTAPE MYSELF TEACHING. AS I WATCHED IT, I NEVER REALIZED I SAID "OKAY" THAT MUCH. IT ALSO HELPED ME SEE HOW FAST I CALLED ON SOME STUDENTS.
>
> —SECOND-GRADE TEACHER

USE YOUR MATH COACH

Math coaches have the content expertise and experience to help you in so many ways. If you are lucky enough to have access to one in your school or district, use them! Ask them to help with planning lessons, finding resources, looking over data, and anything else related to teaching mathematics.

ATTEND PROFESSIONAL CONFERENCES

We would be remiss if we didn't acknowledge the value of attending professional conferences. This activity has served us so well. Virtual, local, state, or even national conferences give you opportunities to learn and connect with other teachers. In fact, our (authors) relationship is a direct outcome of attending conferences and being members of professional organizations. And make no mistake, each of us started attending as classroom teachers looking to learn more about teaching mathematics. You can learn more about math conferences on the NCTM website, or you can find local, state, and virtual options with a quick Google search. Be sure to talk with your principal, district professional learning office, or math office as funding to support you is often available. There are also grants from the organizations and their partners to fund teacher attendance.

Notes

What Resources Should I Use to Learn and Grow?

There is an endless supply of resources beyond your textbook series. First and foremost, you want to rely on the learning resources your school and district put forward. In addition to those, we offer the following.

PROFESSIONAL ORGANIZATIONS

Professional organizations can be a trustworthy source of information, classroom resources, professional learning, and tools for advocacy through their websites, journals, and publications, many of which are noted throughout this book in the Great Resources sidebars and in the reference list at the end of the book.

ONLINE RESOURCES: WEBSITES, WEBINARS, AND BLOGS

There are some truly exceptional tools online, and new ones are being created every day. There are also a large number of poor resources and bad ideas about teaching mathematics. Rather than give you a list of our favorites, because they change all the time, we urge you to be a critical consumer of the sites and resources you access. You can do this by

- comparing what you find with familiar, reliable resources and with what you already know;
- asking colleagues for their thoughts; and
- learning about what professional math education organizations and teacher education departments recommend.

Be on guard for "cutesy" activities and quick, simple fixes. While high-quality materials can look attractive, that doesn't mean all attractive-looking materials are of high quality. Teaching mathematics well, so that learning lasts and students become thinkers and doers, happens with carefully selected materials that leverage the qualities we've described in this book. And also know that those who provide quality content do not have the final say in what is good, proper, or effective.

Webinars and blogs are also good tools for learning about specific content and new instructional practices. Often, webinars connect to a new publication or product, so you can learn even more. Blogs are a good way to gain insights through different experiences, perspectives, opinions, and expertise. As noted, be a critical consumer of these resources as well.

BOOKS

Great resources that connect to the questions in this book have been highlighted throughout. But those are just the start. We offer a list of our greatest hits—professional works and supplemental classroom resources that we have found invaluable over the years. These works are popular across the country, and it's likely that your team, school professional library, and district office have copies they can lend you. It's important to note that this list is not exhaustive and new resources are published every year, so we encourage you to continue seeking new ideas as you continue to grow your practice.

CHAPTER 1: HOW DO I BUILD A POSITIVE MATH COMMUNITY?

Identity, agency, and mindset	
SanGiovanni, J. J., Katt, S., & Dykema, K. (2020). *Productive math struggle: A six-point action plan for fostering perseverance.* Corwin.	Jansen, A. (2020). *Rough draft math: Revising to learn.* Stenhouse Math.
Kobett, B. M., & Karp, K. S. (2020). *Strengths-based teaching and learning in mathematics: Five teaching turnarounds for grades K–6.* Corwin.	Jones, S. M. (2019). *Women who count: Honoring African American women mathematicians.* American Mathematical Society.
Boaler, J. (2015). *Mathematical mindsets: Unleashing students' potential through creative math, inspiring messages and innovative teaching.* Jossey-Bass.	*Marilyn Burns Math and Literature* guides (Hand2Mind).
Monroe, E. E., Young, T. A., Fuentes, D. S., & Dial, O. H. (2018). *Deepening students' mathematical understanding with children's literature.* NCTM.	*Teaching and Learning in the 21st Century* (Math Solutions, 2015).
Horn, I. S. (2017). *Motivated: Designing math classrooms where students want to join in.* Heinemann.	Dance, R., & Kaplan, T. (2018). *Thinking together: 9 beliefs for building a mathematical community.* Heinemann.

Equity in mathematics	
Celedón-Pattichis, S., White, D. Y., & Civil, M. (Eds.). (2017). *Access and equity: Promoting high-quality mathematics in preK–grade 2.* NCTM.	Crespo, S., Celedón-Pattichis, S., & Civil, M. (Eds.). (2018). *Access and equity: Promoting high-quality mathematics in grades 3–5.* NCTM.
Tan, P. (2019). *Humanizing disability in mathematics education: Forging new paths.* NCTM.	Fenner, D. S., & Snyder, S. (2021). *Culturally responsive teaching for multilingual learners: Tools for equity.* Corwin.
Christopher, B. S., & Singh, S. (2019). *Math recess: Playful learning in an age of disruption.* Impress.	Brown, K., & Seda, P. (2021). *Choosing to see: A framework for equity in the math classroom.* David Burgess Consulting.

CHAPTER 2: HOW DO I STRUCTURE, ORGANIZE, AND MANAGE MY MATH CLASS?

Routines	
SanGiovanni, J. (2019). *Daily routines to jump-start math class, elementary school: Engage students, improve number sense, and practice reasoning.* Corwin.	McCoy, A. C., Combs, E., & Barnett, J. (2013). *High-yield routines for grades K–8.* NCTM.
Lucenta, A., Kelemanik, G., & Creighton, S. (2016). *Routines for reasoning: Fostering the mathematical practices in all students.* Heinemann.	Shumway, J. F. (2011). *Number sense routines: Building numerical literacy every day in grades K–3* (Number Sense Routine Edition). Stenhouse.
Humphreys, C., & Parker, R. E. (2015). *Making number talks matter: Developing mathematical practices and deepening understanding, grades 4–10* (Illustrated Edition). Stenhouse.	Parrish, S. (2014). *Number talks: Whole number computation, grades K–5: A multimedia professional learning resource.* Math Solutions.

Instructional practice	
Teaching student-centered mathematics: Developmentally appropriate instruction for grades K–2 (Vol. I) *and 3–5* (Vol. 2) (Student Centered Mathematics Series) (Pearson, 2017).	Monroe, E. E., Young, T. A., Fuentes, D. S., & Dial, O. H. (2018). *Deepening students' mathematical understanding with children's literature.* NCTM.
NCTM. (2014). *Principles to actions: Ensuring mathematical success for all.*	Ray, M. (2013). *Powerful problem solving: Activities for sense making with the mathematical practices.* Heinemann.
Yeh, C., Ellis, M. W., & Hurtado, C. K. (2017). *Reimagining the mathematics classroom: Creating and sustaining productive learning environments.* NCTM.	Hattie, J., Fisher, D., Frey, N., Gojak, L. M., Moore, S. D., & Mellman, W. (2016). *Visible learning for mathematics, grades K–12: What works best to optimize student learning.* Corwin.
The Math Pact series (Corwin, 2021).	Seeley, C. (2014). *Smarter than we think: More messages about math, teaching and learning in the 21st century.* Math Solutions.
Dance, R., & Kaplan, T. (2018). *Thinking together: 9 beliefs for building a mathematical community.* Heinemann.	Thunder, K., Almarode, J., Fisher, D. B., Frey, N., & Hattie, J. (2019). *Teaching mathematics in the visible learning classroom, grades K–2.* Corwin.
Liljedahl, P. (2021). *Building thinking classrooms in mathematics, grades K–12: 14 teaching practices for enhancing learning.* Corwin.	Moore, S. D., Almarode, J., Fisher, D. B., Frey, N., Hattie, J., & Thunder, K. (2019). *Teaching mathematics in the visible learning classroom, grades 3–5.* Corwin.
Wills, T. (2020). *Teaching math at a distance, grades K–12: A practical guide to rich remote instruction* (Corwin Mathematics Series). Corwin.	Nolan, E. C., & Dixon, J. K. (2016). *Making sense of mathematics for teaching grades 3–5.* Solution Tree.
Schuhl, S., Kanold, T. D., Deinhart, J., Larson, M. R., & Toncheff, M. (2020). *Mathematics unit planning in a PLC at Work® K–2 and 3–5.* Solution Tree.	*The Mathematics Lesson-Planning Handbook* series (Corwin, 2018).

Instructional practice	
Moore, S. D., & Rimbey, K. (2021). *Mastering math manipulatives: Hands-on and virtual activities for building and connecting mathematical ideas*. Corwin.	

Differentiation	
Dacey, L., Bamford-Lynch, J., & Eston Salemi, R. (2013). *How to differentiate your math instruction, grades K–5 multimedia resource: Lessons, ideas, and videos with Common Core support, grades K–5*. Math Solutions.	Johnson, S. K., & Sheffield, L. J. (2012). *Using the Common Core State Standards for mathematics with gifted and advanced learners*. NCTM.
Driscoll, M. J., Nikula, J., & DePiper, J. N. (2016). *Mathematical thinking and communication: Access for English learners*. Heinemann.	Chval, K., Smith, E. M., Trigos-Carillo, L., & Pinnow, R. J. (2021). *Teaching math to multilingual students, grades K–8: Positioning English learners for success*. Corwin.

CHAPTER 3: HOW DO I ENGAGE MY STUDENTS IN MATHEMATICS?

Mathematics content	
Dougherty, B., Karp, K., Caldwell, J., & Kobett, B. (2014). *Putting essential understanding of addition and subtraction into practice preK–2*. NCTM.	McNamara, J., & Shaughnessy, M. M. (2020). *Beyond pizzas and pies: 10 Essential strategies for supporting fraction sense, grades 3–5*. Math Solutions.
Chval, K., Lannin, J., & Jones, D. (2013). *Putting essential understanding of fractions into practice in grades 3–5*. NCTM.	Small, M. (2013). *Uncomplicating fractions to meet Common Core Standards in math, K–7*. NCTM.
Gojak, L. M., & Miles, R. H. (2015). *The Common Core mathematics companion: The Standards decoded, grades K–2: What they say, what they mean, how to teach them*. Corwin.	Karp, K., & Dougherty, B. (2019). *Putting essential understanding of number and numeration into practice in preK–2*. NCTM.
Gojak, L. M., & Miles, R. H. (2015). *The Common Core mathematics companion: The Standards decoded, grades 3–5: What they say, what they mean, how to teach them*. Corwin.	

Mathematics practices	
Flynn, M. (2016). *Beyond answers: Exploring mathematical practices with young children*. Stenhouse.	*Taking Action: Implementing Effective Mathematics Teaching Practices* series (NCTM, 2017).
O'Connell, S., & SanGiovanni, J. (2013). *Putting the practices into action: Implementing the Common Core Standards for Mathematical Practice, K–8*. Heinemann.	

Classroom activities and tasks (K–5)	
Britt, B. A. (2014). *Mastering basic math skills: Games for kindergarten through second grade.* NCTM.	*Think Tanks* (Origo).
Franke, M. L., Kazemi, E., & Turrou, A. C. (2018). *Choral counting and counting collections: Transforming the preK–5 math classroom.* Stenhouse.	*Math in Practice* series (Heinemann, 2016).
Kobett, B. M., Fennell, F. M., Karp, K. S., et al. (2021). *Classroom-ready rich math tasks: Engaging students in doing math.* Corwin.	Morrow-Leong, K., Moore, S. D., & Gojak, L. M. (2020). *Mathematize it! [Grades K–2]: Going beyond key words to make sense of word problems, grades K–2* (Corwin Mathematics Series). Corwin.
Petersen, J. (2013). *Math games for number and operations and algebraic thinking: Games to support independent practice in math workshops and more, grades K–5.* Math Solutions.	Moore, S. D., Morrow-Leong, K., & Gojak, L. M. (2019). *Mathematize it! [Grades 3–5]: Going beyond key words to make sense of word problems, grades 3–5* (Corwin Mathematics Series). Corwin.
Hands-On Standards (Hand2Mind).	*Fundamentals* (Origo, 2018).
Petersen, J. (2019). *Math games for geometry and measurement: Games to support independent practice in math workshop and more, grades K–5.* Math Solutions.	

Fact fluency	
O'Connell, S., & SanGiovanni, J. (2011). *Mastering the basic facts in addition and subtraction [or multiplication and division]: Strategies, activities, and interventions to move students beyond memorization.* Heinemann.	Davenport, L. R. (2019). *No more math fact frenzy.* Heinemann.
Bay-Williams, J., & Kling, G. (2019). *Math fact fluency: 60+ games and assessment tools to support learning and retention.* ASCD.	*The Box of Facts* (Origo, 2007).

Computational fluency	
Bay-Williams, J. M., & SanGiovanni, J. S. (2021). *Figuring out fluency in mathematics teaching and learning, grades K–8: Moving beyond basic facts and memorization.* Corwin.	Richardson, K. (1998). *Developing number concepts, book 3: Place value, multiplication, and division.* Dale Seymour.
Richardson, K. (1999). *Developing number concepts, book 2: Addition and subtraction.* Dale Seymour.	

CHAPTER 4: HOW DO I HELP MY STUDENTS TALK ABOUT MATHEMATICS?

Discourse and vocabulary	
Smith, M. S., Bill, V. L., & Sherin, M. G. (2019). *The five practices in practice [elementary]: Successfully orchestrating mathematics discussions in your elementary classroom.* Corwin.	Smith, M. S., & Stein, M. K. (2018). *5 practices for orchestrating productive mathematics discussions.* Corwin; NCTM.
Sztajn, P., Heck, D., & Malzahn, K. (2020). *Activating math talk: 11 purposeful techniques for your elementary students.* Corwin.	Chapin, S. H., O'Connor, C., & Anderson, N. C. (2009). *Classroom discussions: Using math talk to help students learn, grades K–6.* Math Solutions.
Murray, M. (2004). *Teaching mathematics vocabulary in context: Windows, doors, and secret passageways.* Heinemann.	Kazemi, E., & Hintz, A. (2014). *Intentional talk: How to structure and lead productive mathematical discussions.* Stenhouse.
Small, M., & Tomlinson, C. A. (2017). *Good questions: Great ways to differentiate mathematics instruction in the standards-based classroom.* Teachers College Press.	

CHAPTER 5: HOW DO I KNOW WHAT MY STUDENTS KNOW AND MOVE THEM FORWARD?

Formative assessment	
Islas, D. (2011). *How to assess while you teach math: Formative assessment practices and lessons grades K–2: A multimedia professional learning resource.* Math Solutions.	SanGiovanni, J. (2016). *Mine the gap for mathematical understanding, grades K–2 and 3–5.* Corwin.
Keeley, P. D., & Tobey, C. R. (2011). *Mathematics formative assessment: Vol 1: 75 practical strategies for linking assessment, instruction, and learning.* Corwin; NCTM.	Fennell, F. M., Kobett, B. M., & Wray, J. A. (2017). *The formative 5: Everyday assessment techniques for every math classroom.* Corwin.

REFERENCES

Aguirre, J. M., Mayfield-Ingram, K., & Martin, D. B. (2013). *The impact of identity in K–8 mathematics: Rethinking equity-based practices*. National Council of Teachers of Mathematics.

Anderson, R., (2007). Being a mathematics learner: Four faces of identity. *The Mathematics Educator*, *17*(1), 7–14.

Bay-Williams, J., & Fletcher, G. (2017). A bottom-up hundred chart? *Teaching Children Mathematics*, *24*(3), e1. https://doi.org/10.5951/teacchilmath.24.3.00e1

Bay-Wiliams, J., & SanGiovanni, J. (2021). *Figuring out fluency in mathematics teaching and learning, grades K–8: Moving beyond basic facts and memorization*. Corwin.

Boaler, J. (2002). The development of disciplinary relationships: Knowledge, practice and identity in mathematics classrooms. *For the Learning of Mathematics*, *22*(1), 42–47.

Burns, M. (2004). Writing in math. *Educational Leadership*, *62*(2), 30–33.

Chval, K., Smith, E. M., Trigos-Carillo, L., & Pinnow, R. (2021). *Teaching math to multilingual students, grades K–8: Positioning English learners for success*. Corwin.

Fuson, K. C., Kalchman, M., & Bransford, J. D. (2005). Mathematical understanding: An introduction. In M. S. Donovan & J. Bransford (Eds.), *How students learn mathematics in the classroom* (pp. 217–256). National Research Council.

Grootenboer, P., & Zevenbergen, R. (2007). Identity and mathematics: Towards a theory of agency in coming to learn mathematics. In J. Watson & K. Beswick (Eds.), *Mathematics: Essential research, essential practice* (Vol. 1, pp. 335–344). Mathematics Education Research Group of Australasia.

Hattie, J., & Clarke, S. (2019). *Visible learning: Feedback*. Routledge. https://doi.org/10.4324/9781003024477

Herbel-Eisenmann, B. A., & Breyfogle, M. L. (2005). Questioning our patterns of questioning. *Mathematics Teaching in the Middle School*, *10*(9), 484–489. https://doi.org/10.5951/MTMS.10.9.0484

Johnson, S. K., & Sheffield, L. J. (2012). *Using the Common Core State Standards for mathematics with gifted and advanced learners*. National Council of Teachers of Mathematics.

Kobett, B. M., & Karp, K. S. (2020). *Strengths-based teaching and learning in mathematics: Five teaching turnarounds for grades K–6*. Corwin.

Kreisberg, H., & Beyranevand, M. (2021). *Partnering with parents in elementary school math*. Corwin.

Ladson-Billings, G. (1995). Toward a theory of culturally relevant pedagogy. *American Educational Research Journal*, *32*(3), 465–491. https://doi.org/10.3102/00028312032003465

Ladson-Billings. G. (2009). *The dreamkeepers: Successful teachers of African-American children* (2nd ed.). Jossey-Bass.

Lesh, R., Post, T., & Behr, M. (1987). Representations and translations among representations in mathematics learning and problem solving. In C. Janiver (Ed.), *Problems of representation in the teaching and learning of mathematics* (pp. 33–40). Lawrence Erlbaum.

Liljedahl, P. (2021). *Building thinking classrooms in mathematics, grade K–12*. Corwin.

Mathical. (n.d.). *Award winning books archives*. https://www.mathicalbooks.org/portfolio/books/

Melfi, T. (Director). (2016). *Hidden figures* [Film]. Twentieth Century Fox.

Moore, S. D., & Rimbey, K. (2021). *Mastering math manipulatives, grades K–3: Hands-on and virtual activities for building and connecting mathematical ideas*. Corwin.

National Council of Teachers of Mathematics. (2014). *Principles to actions: Ensuring mathematical success for all*.

National Governors Association Center for Best Practices & Council of Chief State School Officers. (2010). *Common Core State Standards for mathematics*. http://www.corestandards.org/Math/

National Research Council. (2001). *Adding it up: Helping children learn mathematics*. National Academies Press.

National Science Teaching Association. (n.d.). *Best STEM books K–12*. https://www.nsta.org/best-stem-books-k-12

Phillips, E. (1987). *Studies in the history of mathematics*. Mathematical Association of America.

Regional Educational Laboratory. (2018, Jan 10–12). *Growth mindset in math* [PowerPoint slides]. Education Northwest. https://ies.ed.gov/ncee/edlabs/regions/northwest/pdf/math-attitudes-training/powerpoint-growth-mindset.pdf

The New Teacher Project. (2018). *The opportunity myth*. https://tntp.org/assets/documents/TNTP_The-Opportunity-Myth_Web.pdf

SanGiovanni, J. J. (2020). *Daily routines to jump-start math class: Elementary school*. Corwin.

SanGiovanni, J., Katt, S., & Dykema, K. (2020). *Productive math struggle: A six-point action plan for fostering perseverance*. Corwin

Seeley, C. (2017). Unleashing problem solvers. *Educational Leadership*, *75*(2), 32–36.

Shanahan, T. (2016). *How many times should students copy the spelling words?* Reading Rockets. www.readingrockets.org

Shepard, L. A. (2008). Formative assessment: Caveat emptor. In C. A. Dwyer (Ed.), *The future of assessment: Shaping teaching and learning* (pp. 279–303). Lawrence Erlbaum. https://doi.org/10.4324/9781315086545-12

Skemp, R. (1978). Relational understanding and instrumental understanding. *Arithmetic Teacher*, *26*(3), 9–15. https://doi.org/10.5951/AT.26.3.0009

Smith, M. S., Bill, V., & Sherin, M. G. (2020). *The 5 practices in practice: Successfully orchestrating mathematics discussions in your elementary classroom*. Corwin.

Smith, M. S., & Stein, M. K. (2011). *5 Practices for orchestrating productive mathematics discussions*. National Council of Teachers of Mathematics.

Sousa, D. A. (2008). *How the brain learns mathematics*. Corwin.

Sztajn, P., Heck, D., & Malzahn, K. (2020). *Activating math talk: 11 Purposeful techniques for your elementary students*. Corwin.

Teaching Channel. (n.d.). *My favorite no: Learning from mistakes* [Video]. https://learn.teachingchannel.com/video/class-warm-up-routine

Van de Walle, J. A., Karp, K. S., & Bay-Williams, J. M. (2019). *Elementary and middle school mathematics methods: Teaching developmentally* (10th ed.). Pearson Education.

Vollymeyer, R., & Rehinberg, F. (2005). A surprising effect of feedback on learning. *Learning and Instruction*, *15*(6), 589–602. https://doi.org/10.1016/j.learninstruc.2005.08.001

Wood, T. (1998). Alternative patterns of communication in mathematics classes: Funneling or focusing? In H. Steinbring, M. G. Bartolini Bussi, & A. Sierpinska (Eds.), *Language and communication in the mathematics classroom* (pp. 167–178). National Council of Teachers of Mathematics.

Young, E., & Marroquin, C. (2006). Posing problems from children's literature. *Teaching Children Mathematics*, *12*(7), 362–366. https://doi.org/10.5951/TCM.12.7.0362

Zwiers, J., Dieckmann, J., Rutherford-Quach, S., Daro, V., Skarin, R., Weiss, S., & Malamut, J. (2017). *Principles for the design of mathematics curricula: Promoting language and content development*. http://ell.stanford.edu/content/mathematics-resources-additional-resources

INDEX

Acceleration program, 73–74

Accuracy
    computational, 135
    operational, 138

Acquisition, 188–189

Activating students curiosity, 50

Activities
    calendar, 60
    doodling, 77
    for estimation, 127–129
    games and centers, 121
    growth mindset, 32
    lesson closure, 75–77
    math meeting, 60
    self reflection, 76
    student discourse, 146–148
    word walls, 162

Adding strategy, 139–140

Advanced learners plan, 72–74
    acceleration program, 73–74
    logic puzzles and strategy games, 72
    problem solving method, 73
    providing choice, 73
    task, 74

Anchor charts
    class-created, 38–39
    community, 43
    concept, 42
    dos and don'ts, 43–44
    interactive, 43
    overview, 42
    process, 42
    types of, 42–43

Anticipating student thinking, 86–87

Application, knowing mathematics, 84

Assessment, students
    acquisition, 188–189
    evidence collection, 170
    exit tickets, 169
    feedback, 185–187
    hand signals, 169
    interviews, 168–169
    learning behavior checklists, 174–176
    methods to, 168–170
    observations, 168
    repetition, 189

samples of students' work, 169
self-assessment, 169–170, 181–184
students' needs and, 188–190
students' progress, 191–195
by students work, 171–173
student thinking, 177–180

Assignments, 78

Assorted counters manipulative, 100

Base-ten blocks manipulative, 101

Basic fact strategies
    accuracy, 133
    commutative property, 132
    inverse operations, 132
    sequence of, 131
    teaching, 130–131
    time settings, 132

Bead strings manipulative, 100

Behaviors, student, 33–34
    checklists, 174–176
    to develop, 36–37

Belief statements about student, 27–28

Books, teachers developmental activity, 200–205

Breakout model, small-group, 57

Calculators, 137

Calendar activities, 60

Catch-and-release teaching method, 68–69

Checklists
    learning behavior, 174–176
    for problem solving, 90

Class observation sheet, 173

Classroom community. *See* Community, math

Classroom walls
    anchor charts, 38–39
    mathematicians, contributions of, 40
    math problems, 40
    overview, 38
    settings of, 41
    showcasing student brilliance, 38
    vocabulary, 39–40

Class visit, teachers developmental activity, 197

Clipboard notes, 173

Coaches and developmental activity, 198

Collaborative planning, teachers developmental activity, 197

Collaborative works, students, 52

Color tiles manipulative, 101

Common Core Standards for Mathematical Practices, 174

Community charts, 43

Community, math
    agreements, 19–20
    anchor charts, 42–44
    classroom walls, 38–41
    culturally relevant pedagogy, 22–26
    establishing and maintaining, 19–21
    family involvement and communicating tips, 45–47
    formation, 19
    identifying students ability, 12–14
    mathematical practices, 33–37
    nurturing math identity, 15–18
    overview, 19
    strengths-based instruction and, 27–29

Computational strategies, 134–137
    algorithm, 135
    calculators and, 137
    family involvement in, 137
    fluency and, 135
    methods of, 135
    number line, 136
    questions about teaching, 134–137
    representations, 136

Conceptual charts, 42

Conceptual understanding of mathematics, 84

Connecting cubes manipulative, 101

Cuisenaire rods manipulative, 102

Culturally relevant pedagogy
    instructional practices and, 26
    knowing student, 23–24
    open tasks, 25
    overview, 22
    personalize learning tasks, 25

social justice issues, 24
tasks and, 24
Curriculum and math practices, 35

Debriefing discussion
overview of, 153
student learning and, 153
tips for, 153–155
Debriefing task, 67
Developmental activities, teachers, 197–199
books, 200–205
class visit, 197
coaches and, 198
collaborative planning, 197
note-taking tool, 198
online resources, 200
peer observations, 197
professional conferences, 199
professional organizations, 200
recording yourself, 198
resources, 200–205
Discussions, students
anticipating, 147
in classroom activities, 146–148
debriefing, 153–155
journals in, 163–165
language and vocabulary, 160–162
monitoring, 147
planning, 146–148
questioning and, 149–152
representations in, 156–159
sequence, 147
solutions, 148
students' work, 147
supporting tools, 148
Diverse learners, 70–74
advanced learners plan, 72–74
graphic organizers and, 71
overview, 70
representations, 71
revoicing, 72
students' interests, incorporating, 70
talk time and, 71
task modification and, 71
vocabulary, 71, 72
Division strategy, 142–143
Dominos manipulative, 100
Doodling closure activity, 77

Effective teaching, 88
checklists for problem solving, 90
precise mathematical vocabulary, 89–90
rhymes and catchy sayings, 88–89
rules, 89
shortcuts, 88

Efficiency
computational, 135
operational, 138
Engaging in mathematics
computational strategies, 134–137
effective practice, 123–126
effective teaching, 88–90
estimating activities, 127–129
games and centers, 119–122
high-quality tasks, 91–94
knowing mathematics, 84–88
learning basic facts, 130–133
manipulatives and, 95–102
operational fluency, 138–143
problem solving methods, 109–112
strategies to solve difficult problem, 116–118
student thinking and reasoning, 113–115
using literature, 106–108
visual tools, 103–105
Equitable mathematics, 6–7
Equity and growth mindset, 31
Estimating activities, 127
computational problems and, 129
with containers, 127
with counting, 128
with pictures, 128
solving problems and, 128
Exit tickets, 169

Family involvement
communicating tips, 45–47
in computational strategy, 137
homework policies, 46–47
manipulatives and, 98
rubric evaluation tool and, 180
school-wide math events, 46
students' progress, 46
surveys, 45
teaching content, 45
Feedback, 185–187
5 Practices for Orchestrating Productive Mathematics Discussions (Smith and Stein), 146–148, 151
Flexibility
computational, 135
operational, 138
Fluency
computational strategies and, 135
routines, 63–64
Focusing pattern of questioning, 150
Fraction tiles manipulative, 102
Funneling pattern of questioning, 150

Game night events, 46
Games and centers activity

assigning, 121
introduction of, 120–121
organizing materials, 120
overview, 119
preparations for, 120
questions on, 119
recording sheet, 121–122
rotational system, 121
selection of, 119
self-selected system, 121
Gaming, student identification, 13–14
Google Forms, 172
Go-to/must-have manipulatives, 99–102
Grading
homework, 79
rubric evaluation tool and, 179
Gradual-release teaching model, 66
Graphic organizers, 71
Growth mindset, 30–32
activities, 32
equity and, 31
models, 30
phrases, 31
success of, 31–32

Hand signals, 169
High-quality tasks
context of, 91–92
in high-quality curriculum materials, 93–94
importance of, 91
multiple entry points, 92
multiple solution pathways, 92–93
Homework
assignments, 78
in classroom, 79–80
grading, 79
policies and family involvement, 46–47, 80
student achievement and, 78
Honor student thinking, 28–29, 51

Identifying student ability
games/open math activities, 13–14
journals and, 13
math inventory, 12–13
overview, 12
problem solving method, 12
Index cards, observation, 172
Instructional routines
cultural and community, 26
fluency routines, 63–64
number, 63
overview, 63
for problem solving and reasoning, 64
See also Routines

Instructions, 3–6
Interactive charts, 43
Interviews, 168–169
Inventory, student identification, 12–13
Is This the End number routine, 63

Journaling
    in discussions, 163–165
    lesson closure and, 77
    student identification and, 13
    types of, 164–165

Keywords, shortcut strategy, 88
Knowing mathematics
    anticipating student thinking, 86–87
    application, 84
    conceptual understanding, 84
    description, 84–85
    growth of, 85
    to learning targets, 85
    procedural fluency, 84

Language in math discussions, 160–162
Language routines, 64
Launch-engage-debrief (L-E-D)
        teaching method, 66–67
Learning behavior checklists, 174–176
Learning capability, students, 27
Learning precise vocabulary, 89–90
Learning targets, 85
    self-assessment, 182–184
Lesson closure activity
    doodling, 77
    journal prompts and, 77
    one word summary, 76
    overview, 75
    routine activities for, 75–77
    self reflection activity, 76
    "That's what!" activity, 76
Lesson openings, 60–62
Listening skill, 16

Manipulatives
    choices, 97
    classroom norms, 97
    go-to/must-have, 99–102
    list of, 95–98
    overview, 95
    selection of, 99–102
    supplies of, 97
    virtual, 96, 99
Math and muffins, 46
Mathematical community. See
        Community, math
Mathematical identity
    nurture, 15
    overview, 15

performance of student and, 18
    representation, 17
    student's math stories, 16–17
    student's relationships, 16–17
Mathematical practices, 33–37
    behaviors of student and, 33–34
    importance about, 35
Mathematical processes. See
        Mathematical practices
Math inventory, 12–13
Math meeting activity, 60
Math olympiads, 46
Math problems, 40
Math stories and student identity, 16–17
Monitoring student progress, 18
Multiplication strategy, 141–142
Myths and facts, 5

Note-taking tool, 198
Number line strategy, 136
Number routines, 63
Number sense/fluency routine activity,
        59–60
Nurture mathematical creativity, 15

Observing student work, 168
    class observation sheet, 173
    clipboard notes, 173
    index cards, 172
    photo snaps, 172
    questions related to, 173
    recording information during, 171
    sticky notes, 172
One word summary, 76
Online resources, 200
Opening activity, 13–14, 59
    calendar activities, 60
    homeworks and, 61
    lesson openings, 60–62
    math meeting, 60
    number sense/fluency routine,
        59–60
    warm-ups/bell ringers, 61
Open tasks, 25
Operational fluency, 138–143
    adding strategy, 139–140
    dividing strategy, 142–143
    dos and don'ts, 138–139
    multiplication strategy, 141–142
    subtracting strategy, 140–141
The Opportunity Myth, 22

Pattern blocks manipulative, 101
Peer observations, teachers
        developmental activity, 197
Personalized learning tasks, 25
Photo snaps for observation, 172

Place-value disc manipulative, 101
Planning math discussions, 146–148
Practices for effective learning,
        123–126
    maximizing tips for, 124–126
    methods of, 123
    steps to follow, 123–124
Problem solving, 50–52
    checklists for, 90
    estimating activities and, 128
    routines and, 64
    strategies for, 116–118
Procedural fluency, 84
Process charts, 42
Productive learning environment, 26
Professional conferences, 199
Professional organizations, 200
Progress celebration, 191
    methods of, 191–194
    students list for, 194–165

Questioning discourse tool, 149
    focusing, 150
    funneling, 150
    gathering information, 150
    observation and, 173
    planning for, 151–152
    probing thinking, 150
    purpose of, 149
    samples, 152
    types of, 149–150
Questions, self-assessments, 181
Question stems discourse tool, 148

Recording yourself, teachers
        developmental activity, 198
Rekenrek manipulative, 100
Repetition, students' needs, 189
Representations
    benefits of, 156
    computational, 136
    forms of, 156
    in math discussions, 156–159
    math lessons and, 156–159
    word walls, 161–162
Revoicing, 72
Rhymes and catchy sayings, 88–89
Rotational gaming system, 121
Rotation model, small-group, 56
Routines
    language, 64
    working process, 65
Rubric evaluation tool, 177–178
    bias awareness, 179
    communicating families, 180
    consistency, 179
    grading and, 179

multiple data points, 180
with observations, 179
self-assessments and, 182
task and time taken, 179
working tips, 179–180
Rules in effective teaching, 89

School-wide family math events, 46
Self-assessments, students, 169–170
importance of, 181–184
learning targets, 182–184
questions and, 181
student-friendly rubric, 182
Self reflection activity, 76
Self-selected gaming system, 121
Sentence starters discourse tool, 148
Shortcut strategy, 88
Showcasing student brilliance, 38
Small-group instructional model
breakout model, 57
importance of, 57
overview, 56
rotation model, 56
steps to follow, 57–58
working process, 56
Smith, M. S., 146–148, 151
Social justice issues, 24
Standards for Mathematical Practice
that are part of the Common Core
State Standards, 33
Stations. See Games and centers
Stein, M. K., 146–148, 151
STEM events, 46
Sticky notes, observation, 172
Storytime events, 46
Strategies to solve difficult problem,
116–118
Strengths-based instruction, 27–29
belief statements about student,
27–28

honor student thinking, 28–29
learning capability, students, 27
suggestions/support, 28
Structure and management, classroom
diverse learners, 70–74
homework, 78–80
lesson closure, 75–77
opening activity, 59–62
routines, 63–65
small-group instructional model,
56–58
student-centered classroom, 50–52
teaching methods, 66–69
whole-group instructional model,
53–55
Student-centered classroom, 38, 48
activating curiosity, 50
collaborative working, 52
instructional tips, 50–52
overview, 50
problem solving methods, 50–52
student ownership, 52
Student-friendly rubric, 182
Students' agency and mathematical
processes, 33
Students' progress
assessment and, 191–195
celebration, 191–195
families and, 46
identity and, 18
Student's relationships and
mathematical identity, 16–17
Student talk time, 71
Student thinking assessment, 177
rubrics, 177–178
Subtracting strategy, 140–141
Suggestions/supporting student, 28
Surveys, 45

Tasks
cultural relevance and, 24
high-quality, 91–94
launch-engage-debrief (L-E-D)
structure and, 66–67
modification of, 71
selection of, 91–92
See also High-quality tasks
Teacher-centered approach, 50–51
Teaching content and family
involvement, 45
Teaching mathematics today, 3
Teaching methods
catch-and-release, 68–69
gradual-release model of, 66
launch-engage-debrief (L-E-D)
structure, 66–67
lesson, 66
Ten-sided dice manipulative, 102
"That's what!" activity, 76
Trust, 16
Turn and talk discourse tool, 148

Virtual manipulatives, 96, 99
Vocabulary, 39–40, 71, 72
dos and don'ts of, 160
learning words, 160–161
in math discussions, 160–162
precise/correct usage, 89–90
writing, 161

Whole-group instructional model
importance of, 54
overview, 53–54
steps to follow, 55
working process, 54
Word walls, 161–162
Writing vocabulary, 161

Supporting TEACHERS | Empowering STUDENTS

PETER LILJEDAHL

14 optimal practices for thinking that create an ideal setting for deep mathematics learning to occur
Grades K–12

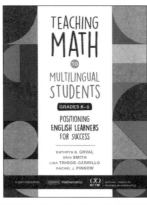

KATHRYN B. CHVAL, ERIN SMITH, LINA TRIGOS-CARRILLO, RACHEL J. PINNOW

Strengths-based approaches to support multilingual students' development in mathematics
Grades K–8

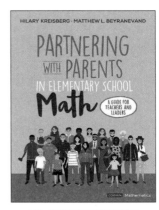

HILARY KREISBERG, MATTHEW L. BEYRANEVAND

Guidance on building productive relationships with families about math education
Grades K–5

BETH MCCORD KOBETT, FRANCIS (SKIP) FENNELL, KAREN S. KARP, DELISE ANDREWS, TRENDA KNIGHTEN, JEFF SHIH, DESIREE HARRISON, BARBARA ANN SWARTZ, SORSHA-MARIA T. MULROE

Detailed plans for helping elementary students experience deep mathematical learning
Grades K–1, 2–3, 4–5

BETH MCCORD KOBETT, KAREN S. KARP

Your game plan for unlocking mathematics by focusing on students' strengths
Grades K–6

JOHN J. SANGIOVANNI, SUSIE KATT, KEVIN J. DYKEMA

Empowering students to embrace productive struggle to build essential skills for learning and living—both inside and outside the classroom
Grades K–12

To order, visit corwin.com/math

JENNIFER M. BAY-WILLIAMS, JOHN J. SANGIOVANNI

Because fluency is so much more than basic facts and algorithms

Grades K–8

KAREN S. KARP, BARBARA J. DOUGHERTY, SARAH B. BUSH

A schoolwide solution for students' mathematics success

Elementary, Middle School, High School

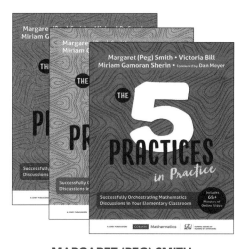

MARGARET (PEG) SMITH, VICTORIA BILL, MIRIAM GAMORAN SHERIN, MICHAEL D. STEELE

Take a deeper dive into understanding the five practices—anticipating, monitoring, selecting, sequencing, and connecting—for facilitating productive mathematical conversations in your classrooms

Elementary, Middle School, High School

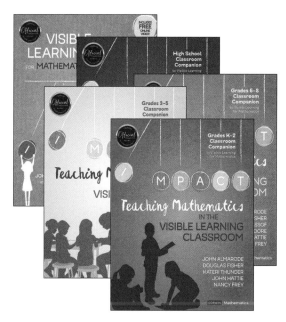

JOHN HATTIE, DOUGLAS FISHER, NANCY FREY, JOHN ALMARODE, LINDA M. GOJAK, SARA DELANO MOORE, WILLIAM MELLMAN, JOSEPH ASSOF, KATERI THUNDER

Powerful, precision teaching through intentionally designed, guided, collaborative, and independent learning

Grades K–2, 3–5, 6–8, 9–12

CORWIN

A SAGE Publishing Company

CORWIN HAS ONE MISSION: to enhance education through intentional professional learning.

We build long-term relationships with our authors, educators, clients, and associations who partner with us to develop and continuously improve the best evidence-based practices that establish and support lifelong learning.